# SUN TZU

## AND THE

# ART OF

# BUSINESS

# SUN TZU

## AND THE

# ART OF

# BUSINESS

## SIX STRATEGIC

## PRINCIPLES

## FOR MANAGERS

# MARK McNEILLY

OXFORD
UNIVERSITY PRESS

To my parents, James and Esperanza, for their love,
To my wife Sandy, for her help and support in all things,
To my children, Alex, Logan and Kenzie, for being themselves,
And to God, who makes all things possible.

# OXFORD
UNIVERSITY PRESS

Oxford   New York
Auckland   Bangkok   Buenos Aires   Cape Town
Chennai   Dar es Salaam   Delhi   Hong Kong   Istanbul   Karachi
Kolkata   Kuala Lumpur   Melbourne   Mexico City   Mumbai   Nairobi
São Paulo   Singapore   Taipei   Tokyo   Toronto

Copyright © 1996 by Oxford University Press, Inc.

Published by Oxford University Press, Inc.
198 Madison Avenue, New York, New York 10016

www.oup.com

Oxford is a registered trademark of Oxford University Press

Library of Congress Cataloging-in-Publication Data
McNeilly, Mark.
Sun Tzu and the art of business :
six strategic principles for managers / Mark McNeilly.
p. cm.   Includes bibliographical references and index.

ISBN 13 978-0-19-513789-7 (Pbk.)

1. Strategic planning.   2. Sun-tzu, 6th cent. B.C.—
Views on management.   I. Title.
HD30.28.M3857   1996   658.4'012—dc20      96-26080

The Art of War by Sun Tzu, translated by Samuel B. Griffith.
Copyright © 1963 by Oxford University Press;
renewed 1991 by Belle Nelson Griffith.
Used by arrangement with Oxford University Press, Inc.

20 19 18 17 16 15 14 13 12 11

Printed in the United States of America

# PREFACE

Sun Tzu's *The Art of War* has proved to be a classic work on strategy, applicable to both military and business situations. While it has been relatively easy to apply the military concepts to wars, both past and current, it has proved much more difficult to translate Sun Tzu's strategic concepts into successful business strategies. The purpose of this book is to crystalize the concepts and ideas put forth in *The Art of War* into six strategic principles that can be more easily understood and applied in the world of business. These principles are then illustrated by business examples, which explicitly describe how the principles can have a direct impact on the strategies of real companies around the world.

My interest in writing this book resulted from the combination of insights I gained working as a business strategist for a major global corporation, the thoughts I'd compiled from my readings as an amateur military historian, and my interest in Sun Tzu's strategic philosophy. These three forces led me to begin work on *Sun Tzu and the Art of Business* five years ago.

It should be of comfort to the reader that, in the process of researching this book, I found more and more evidence of the soundness of its principles. For example, when I started writing, I began by using business examples that were still in the process of sorting themselves out. Many of the companies I followed were involved in situations that only came to closure as the book neared its final draft. It was very reassuring that the examples I had chosen of good and bad implementation of strategy turned out as the principles of Sun Tzu had predicted. The problems of Kmart, AT&T Global Information Systems, and Philip

Morris as well as the effectiveness of Southwest Airlines, to name a few, proved that the principles are extremely useful in predicting business success or failure and implementing strategy. I believe that if you understand and use the principles of *Sun Tzu and the Art of Business* appropriately, you too will see their effectiveness.

*Zumbrota, Minnesota*                                                                   M.R.M.
*May 1996*

# ACKNOWLEDGMENTS

This book has been several years in the making, and through that time I've had the opportunity to have my strategic thinking influenced by a number of people. Their insights and actions have made a significant impact on me and have made this book better.

Joe Pine, author of *Mass Customization: The New Frontier in Business Competition*, has been a great friend and advisor. Julie and Tom Furey, Bill Zeitler, Vic Tang, Emilio Collar, Roy Bauer, and Larry Osterwise were all instrumental in introducing me to business strategy and sharing their wisdom. Jack Scheetz, Bruce Jawer, Bill Meinhardt, Don Mitchell, Pete Hanson, Michael Cheng, Niall Coughlin, Nelson Martel, Steve Gessner, and Bill Leskee were great sounding boards for ideas and each in their own unique way helped me develop my thinking further. All my good friends and co-workers throughout IBM, especially those in the AS/400 Division, have helped me personally and professionally. The faculty of the Carlson Business School, University of Minnesota, gave me an excellent academic base on which to build, and my classmates from the Carlson MBA program broadened my horizons.

I am also very grateful to my editor Herb Addison for his excellent insights on improving this book and the reviewers, James Blandin, Dean of Management and Security Studies at the U. S. Naval Postgraduate School, Ming-Jer Chen, Associate Professor of Strategic Management at the Columbia Business School, and Weijian Shan, the Chinese Business Representative for J. P. Morgan in Hong Kong whose ideas added value to this work. I would also like to thank the heirs of Samuel B. Griffith, who graciously allowed Griffith's translation to be a major part of this book. Thanks are due as well to Terry McManus, Deb Benson and Deb Garry for cheering me on to finish.

Lastly, I want to thank my wife, Sandy. She read and reread each chapter, gave honest and insightful feedback, and provided me the time and support necessary for completing the book. Most important, she shared the dream.

Although I have written this during my employment at IBM and some of the examples are from the computer industry, I have taken great care to be objective and factual in my analysis in those instances. Furthermore, IBM has neither supported nor hindered my writing of this book and all comments, interpretations, and errors of fact are my own.

# CONTENTS

# SUN TZU

## AND THE

# ART OF

# BUSINESS

# Introduction

Some time around 400 B.C., during a period in China known as the Age of the Warring States, there arose a general from the state of Ch'i known as Sun Tzu. His ability to win victories for his warlord gained him fame and power.

To hand down the wisdom he had gained from his years of battles, Sun Tzu wrote a book, *The Art of War*, that became the classic work on strategy in China. His book, which details a complete philosophy on how to decisively defeat one's opponent, has given guidance to military theorists and generals throughout the ages, both in the East and the West. *The Art of War* not only contains Sun Tzu's insights but also provides additional elucidation by military commentators who came after him, such as Li Ch'üan, Tu Mu, and others. In *The Art of War*, military readers found an holistic approach to strategy that was powerful yet succinctly communicated—it is truly a masterpiece on strategy.[1]

## Uses of The Art of War

In China, the first Emperor Qin Shihuang studied *The Art of War*. Adhering to its principles, he united China for the first time around 200 B.C.[2] Twenty-one centuries later, Mao Zedong used Sun Tzu's writings to defeat Chiang Kai-shek and the Nationalists in 1949, again reuniting China. Sun Tzu also influenced Mao's writings on guerilla warfare, which in turn provided the strategy for communist insurgencies from Southeast Asia to Africa to the Americas.

Japan was introduced to Sun Tzu's writings around 760 A.D. and her generals quickly absorbed its lessons. The three most well-known of her samurai—Oda Nobunaga, Toyotomi Hideyoshi, and Tokugawa Ieyasu—all mastered *The Art of War*. This mastery enabled them to transform Japan from a collection of feudal states into a single nation.

In the West, *The Art of War* first made its appearance in 1772 in Europe after being translated into French by a Jesuit missionary. It is possible that Napoleon read and was influenced by Sun Tzu's work, given both his interest in all things military and his culture's interest in Chinese literature.[3]

B. H. Liddell Hart, the British military historian whose theories on armored warfare led to the development of the German blitzkrieg, was amazed at the depth of Sun Tzu's military philosophy and instruction. He was impressed by how closely Sun Tzu's ideas mirrored his own theories of warfare and thought that, had *The Art of War* been more widely read and accepted by World War I generals, much of the terrible slaughter of trench warfare could have been avoided.[4]

The principles discussed in *The Art of War* have been used successfully in countless battles throughout time. Speed was an essential factor in the victories of Genghis Khan and his Mongolian horde. Shaping their enemies by the skillful use of alliances allowed the Romans to expand and maintain their empire. Secrecy and deception were used in major World War II battles, both by the Japanese in their attack on Pearl Harbor and by the Allies to mislead the Germans about the exact location of their invasion of France. The use of intelligence was critical to American success in the Cuban missile crisis. The Viet Cong lived by the rule of avoiding strength and attacking weakness, while the Red Army used this principle to deal Germany's Sixth Army a devastating defeat at Stalingrad.

Most recently, Sun Tzu's principles were put to the test in Desert Storm. By controlling the air both to follow Iraqi movements and mask his own troops' movements, General H. Norman Schwartzkopf fooled Saddam Hussein as to the location of his attack. Threatening an amphibious assault in the east, Schwartzkopf did an end-run on the Iraqi army in the west, thus winning a stunning victory with extremely low casualties. Deception, speed, and attacking the enemy's weakness—all part of Sun Tzu's philosophy—added up to amazing success.[5]

## The Art of War *in Business*

Today, Sun Tzu's appeal has extended beyond the military realm into the world of business. Because business by definition deals with competition, Sun Tzu's principles are ideally suited to competitive business situations. In the United States and Europe, *The Art of War* has been quoted in numerous books on strategy, organization and competition. Many of its more striking verses have been the lead-in for countless business articles. The popular movie *Wall Street*, a tale of corporate mergers and hostile takeovers, utilized Sun Tzu's wisdom in the battle of wits between Gordon Gekko, the film's villain, and the young hero Bud Fox. In the booming world of Asian business, Sun Tzu's strategic principles are revered, and have been used by numerous CEOs to lead their companies to prosperity.[6] Because business, like warfare, is a contest of wills, dynamic and fast-paced, based both on morale and machines, dealing with the effective and efficient use of scarce resources, and is both timeless and ever-changing, many businesspeople across the globe have found value in Sun Tzu's teachings.

Unfortunately, for the many who would like to gain insight into Sun Tzu's strategic philosophy, there is no recourse but to read *The Art of War* and attempt to directly apply Sun Tzu's phrases about military operations to today's business problems. That is no simple task. *The Art of War* is arranged according to military topics and jumping the chasm between the realm of ancient warfare to today's business world is not easy. Many have tried but found the task too daunting. Therefore, to offer a more straightforward bridge between today's business world and Sun Tzu's ancient wisdom, I have written *Sun Tzu and the Art of Business*.

This book takes the writings of Sun Tzu, organizes them to better reveal his holistic perspective on competitive strategy, and then applies them to the world of business in a way that is readable, useful, and practical. My hope is that people will use the principles in this book to create strategies that make their own company much more competitive. This is important to me for two reasons:

First, more creative competition will lead to greater prosperity for the stakeholders in the company as well as better products and services at lower prices for consumers. Further, improvement in competitive strategy will not necessarily mean that one company will take away a piece of the pie from another. Creative use of strategy will more likely lead to a larger pie. When Burger King overhauled itself in late 1993, it stimulated its competition to improve their products and services. McDonalds offered more choices, put them together in "value-meals," and spiffed up service. Wendy's launched a marketing blitz that revolved around its founder David Thomas.[7] When Aleve, a new painkiller from Procter & Gamble, was released into the market, its advertising campaign and those of its rivals actually boosted overall pain-reliever sales.[8]

Indeed, on a global level, it has been shown that when competition in an industry or country is most demanding and creative, companies in that market go on to greater successes in other markets. The smarter the competition in a marketplace, the better the chance for company survival and prosperity. In essence, creative competition means an improved standard of living.[9]

Second, by using the principles of Sun Tzu and competing more creatively, business leaders will be able to avoid the huge casualties of corporate downsizing caused by dull strategic thinking. Just as the lives of millions of soldiers in World War I were sacrificed because of lack of strategic insight on the part of their generals, a similar tragedy has occurred in corporations during the first world war of global competition. While some of it was necessary, too much of the corporate downsizing that has negatively impacted millions of people's lives is the result of the mistakes of business leaders who lacked strategic vision. I believe that the widespread use of the principles in this book by executives and managers will help avoid more corporate casualties in the future.

### Business and the Military Model

In this era of "flat" organizations, teams, and empowerment, some may question how a treatise on warfare could possibly apply to business today. Quite a number of articles have postured that the military model is out of date.

In fact, business strategy first evolved from military strategy. As you read on, you will see how closely ancient and current military organizations and strategies have successfully implemented what many companies today are only beginning to understand. Ever since the first Chinese warlord deployed cavalry and infantry in battle together, armies have been successfully dealing with the problem of cross-functional coordination and teams. Since the time of Xenephon's Persian expedition, military leaders have intelligently dealt with balancing discipline and control with empowerment and delegation. Since Napoleon's era, when coordinating the movement of huge armies led to their arrival at the exact time and precise place of decision in battle, generals have been successfully handling large numbers of people working at great geographic distances from each other. Since the American Civil War, military officers have worked diligently to implement new technological advances brought on by the Industrial Revolution for competitive advantage.

Articles and books written by marketing gurus Philip Kotler, Al Ries, and Jack Trout have explained the applicability of military strategy to business.[10] More recent articles such as "New Ideas from the Army (Really)," bear this out.[11] The success of the book *Moving Mountains—Lessons In Leadership and Logistics from the Gulf War* by Lt. General William Pagonis, written after his masterful handling of logistics for the Persian Gulf War, is another indicator of the robustness of the true military model.

### The Six Principles and the Plan of This Book

To make the transition from Sun Tzu's *The Art of War* to *Sun Tzu and the Art of Business*, I have extracted what I believe are the most important and pertinent strategic principles from Sun Tzu and devoted a chapter to each.[12] These principles are:

1. Win All Without Fighting
   Capturing Your Market Without Destroying It

2. Avoid Strength, Attack Weakness
   Striking Where They Least Expect It

3. Deception and Foreknowledge
   Maximizing the Power of Market Information

4. Speed and Preparation
   Moving Swiftly To Overcome Your Competitors

5. Shape Your Opponent
   Employing Strategy To Master The Competition

6. Character-based Leadership
   Providing Effective Leadership In Turbulent Times

Each chapter discusses how these principles apply in the real world of business, giving examples of companies that have used them effectively.

The final chapter describes how to go about putting the principles into practice. It provides a systematic way of creating winning strategies based on the timeless ideas of Sun Tzu. The book is made complete by the inclusion of the original translation of *The Art of War* by Samuel B. Griffith. Throughout, quotations are referenced in parentheses to that translation.

## Ethics *and* The Art of War

While there is much that businesses can learn from military strategy and examples, businesspeople should not follow the philosophy of the destruction created by total war. Business must be performed ethically. Almost four hundred years have passed since the British East India Company used its own army and navy to capture the markets and resources of India and Asia, then ruled them with its own civil service.[13] The days of imperialist companies setting forth to conquer and exploit less developed parts of the world are over; the era of the infamous American robber barons in railroads, steel, and timber is gone. The proper rules of business conduct and ethics must be followed for business and society to function effectively and prosperously. Therefore, ethical use of the principles put forth here is required.

## The Journey

When you come to understand the principles of *Sun Tzu and the Art of Business*, how they relate to one another and how to implement them, you will be well on your way to becoming a master strategist. Let us now begin the journey by discussing the first principle: how to win your competitive battles without actually having to fight a war.

# 1 ■ Win All Without Fighting
*Capturing Your Market Without Destroying It*

■ War is a matter of vital importance to the State; the province of life or death; the road to survival or ruin. It is mandatory that it be thoroughly studied. (I.1)

In Sun Tzu's time, warfare and statecraft, not commerce, were the means by which states grew rich and powerful. Battles and campaigns were fought, cities were captured, and booty was taken. Alliances were created and thrown away as circumstances dictated. Warfare and diplomacy were constant as states struggled to survive and vied with each other for territory, growth, and prosperity. War was most definitely "a matter of vital importance to the State."

However, as we learned and relearned during the twentieth century, warfare can bring with it not booty but burden, not riches but waste. The two world wars cost millions of dead all over the world, devastated all of Europe and much of Asia, and left even many victors weaker and poorer than when the fighting began. Later, during the four decades of the Cold War, the United States was forced to spend much of its treasury to stop communism from dominating the world. In the process, billions of dollars went for armaments all over the globe, especially by developing countries that could ill afford them. Finally, in the late 1980s, communism and planned markets were finally uncovered as dead ends, the Cold War ended, and a relaxation in military tensions between the superpowers ensued.

In contrast to decreased military competition, the end of the Cold War brought economic competition between countries and between companies to a new and higher pitch. Global competition has become more fierce, and leaders of nations and leaders of corporations both understand that now business "is a matter of vital importance to the State . . . the road to survival or ruin."

Like Sun Tzu's Age of the Warring States, today's business world is one of continual conflict between companies as they strive for survival and success across the globe. Faced with scarce and expensive resources and an ever-changing environment, competitors seek even the slightest advantage. Meanwhile, executives and managers attempt to cope with the overwhelming flood of information coming at them from their market research and the mass media. Add to that consultants clamoring for contracts, trying to sell either true strategic insight or the latest management fad. The result is often not clarity, but confusion; not calm but consternation. It becomes difficult, if not impossible, to build a coherent, cohesive strategy.

To overcome this problem, it is essential to gain understanding of a philosophy that is geared toward competition, survival, and success. One that is both integrated and holistic—one that has stood the test of time. *The Art of War*'s principles of strategy are that philosophy.

This chapter discusses the first principle of Sun Tzu's philosophy and outlines the others, showing how they are interrelated.

### The Goal of Strategy: Win All Without Fighting

Many city-states, countries, and empires have been built by leveraging their unique history, geography, and assets to control their environment. Thus, they were able to survive, achieve stability, expand, dominate their neighbors, and ultimately prosper for hundreds of years.

The Roman Empire grew from a small area surrounding Rome to extend from Britain to the Black Sea to Egypt to Gibralter. It lasted over five hundred years. The Mongol Empire began with a single nomadic tribe in central Asia but grew to rule lands from China to India to Europe. And, of course, the sun never set on the British Empire for several centuries.

Businesses, like countries, have a unique history and a set of assets. But how does one judge whether a business has been successful? The Western view is that a business exists primarily to provide a return on investment for stockholders. In contrast, the Asian view is that a business exists primarily to provide jobs for its employees. Although both views differ, there is one constant between them: to meet either goal, a business must survive and prosper. Therefore, successful businesses, like successful countries, are those that may have started small but ended up surviving and prospering over a long period .

If the goal of a business is to survive and prosper, then what is the goal of its strategy? Sun Tzu offers this advice:

■ **Your aim must be to take All-under-Heaven intact. Thus your troops are not worn out and your gains will be complete. This is the art of offensive strategy. (III.11)**

The goal of business strategy must be "to take All-Under-Heaven intact"—to capture your marketplace. You must define the markets you are going after and commit to achieving relative market dominance in those markets. By doing so, your company will ensure its survival and prosperity.

There are many examples of companies that have done this. They began as seedlings, but used creative strategy to bring value to the marketplace, grow quickly, and continue doing business successfully for a number of years. They had to be able to gain a position in their industry or niche that enabled them to protect themselves and shape the forces in their industry in their favor. They achieved relative market dominance.

Market dominance can appear in many forms; technology leadership, brand recognition, or cost leadership are some signs of it. Market dominance can also be thought of in terms of market share. Companies with dominant market share in an industry segment or an entire industry are more able to influence the industry, direct its evolution, and establish an excellent competitive position. Their powerful position allows them to set the industry's standards and define the playing field. Firms that have achieved dominant market share most likely also enjoy the advantages of higher customer loyalty, larger volumes, better economies of scale, and strong distribution capabilities. In addition, substantial data and research have shown that market share and profitability go hand-in-hand in a number of industry environments. Those same advantages tend to increase revenues and lower unit costs, thus increasing profitability. If a company can achieve relative market dominance properly, prosperity will eventually come.[1]

In the 1970s and 1980s, Japanese companies, with their long-term view of strategy, emphasis on competition and survival, and belief that business is war, supported this thinking. Japanese companies were very successful at capturing market share and achieving a dominant position in many industries. Whether the industry involved automobiles, consumer electronics, or office equipment, the inroads they made in U.S., European, and Asian markets were significant. This provided these Japanese companies with the ability to influence their respective industries and ensure their survival, even when American and European firms began to successfully respond to their attacks.

In the United States, GE's John Welch charged his business units to be number one or number two in their industry or face being sold off. Microsoft's dominance of the software market for personal computer operating systems has enabled it to call the tune that other computer system companies, application software companies, and PC hardware firms have danced to for the last decade. Microsoft's CEO and chief strategist, William H. Gates III, has been able to influence the industry so effectively that it is difficult for any firm to make a move without considering how Microsoft will react. Both Microsoft and GE have experienced prosperity utilizing this strategy; GE, a $60-billion-dollar company, became America's most profitable company in 1994 with earnings of $6 billion. Microsoft has also done well; between 1990 and 1994, its sales grew 47% and its profits increased 53% per year.[2]

One may argue that relative market dominance is not necessary for survival and prosperity, pointing to small "corporate Switzerlands" as examples. The country of Switzerland has survived hundreds of years and prospered; it has done this not by seeking expansion and domination but by creating a strong defensive position. Switzerland combines a well-trained citizen army with its forbidding terrain, thus making the costs of attacking it outweigh the benefits of conquering it. The Swiss also use their neutrality to serve the warring nations of the globe, playing a key role as a site for negotiations and a go-between for antagonists. Switzerland utilizes the assets it has been given and a unique strategy to find a defensible position in the world.

Likewise, companies do exist with low market share that have found defensible positions in their industry along with sustained profitability. They too have done so by understanding their strengths and weaknesses and using strategy to create a place in which they can survive and prosper.[3]

However, these businesses, like Switzerland, exist at the whim of the dominant players. Like major world powers, at any time market leaders may decide that these little "Switzerlands" have served their purpose in the industry and choose to eliminate them. Although a small company might cause a lot of problems for a dominant player before going away, in the end it would be eliminated. Thus, the only true way to control your firm's destiny is to drive for relative market dominance. This must be your purpose.

■ The Grand Duke said: "One who is confused in purpose cannot respond to his enemy." (III.23 Meng)

### Capturing Your Market Intact

While market share and industry dominance are your end goal, they should not be pursued blindly.

■ Generally in war the best policy is to take a state intact; to ruin it is inferior to this.

To capture the enemy's army is better than to destroy it; to take intact a battalion, a company or a five-man squad is better than to destroy them. (III.1 and III.2)

The best policy is to take All-under-Heaven "intact" for victory to be complete. In a business context, this means your battles for market dominance should not destroy the profitability of your industry in the process.

There are several examples of executives who, thinking that they are defeating their enemies, end up destroying themselves as well.

Before April 1993, Philip Morris Companies was the owner of what was arguably the world's most profitable brand, Marlboro. In 1992, over 124 billion Marlboros had been sold just in the United States and Marlboro revenues were bigger than the total revenues of large, well-known brand companies such as Campbell's Soup. Profits from the brand totaled in the billions—big enough so that had Marlboro been its own company it would have ranked in the top tier of the Fortune 100.

However, Marlboro was slowly losing market share to discount cigarette brands. So, in an effort to hit competitors hard and regain market share, the CEO of Philip Morris agreed to cut the price of Marlboros by 40 cents per pack, or 20%. This strategy was based on a single market test in Oregon, in which Marlboro was able to get back four points of share from the discount brands. However, the test was not carried out long enough to track the responses of competitors, nor had the Marlboro marketing team thought through how competitors might react to Philip Morris' move.

What competitors decided to do became clear soon enough. As the other major industry players cut prices drastically, soon no one was making money. Philip Morris itself lost $1 billion in profits and Wall Street responded by chopping $13.4 billion off the market value from the company in the days following the price cut. This 23% drop in stock price was the largest one-day decline of a stock in six years and, for the first time in twenty-five years, Philip Morris was unable to increase its dividend. In an effort to return to profitability Philip Morris announced it would eliminate 14,000 employees (8% of its workforce) and close forty plants. Finally, faced with no support by the board for his future plans, the Philip Morris CEO resigned. As you can see, a strategy based solely on cutting prices to attack competitors is seldom beneficial.[4]

The airline industry is another example of rampant price-cutting to gain market share. Prior to deregulation, airlines found means of competing other than price. However, after deregulation and the entrance of such competitors as PeopleExpress (who focused on no-frills flying with cheap tickets), the nature of the competition changed. The 1980s saw mergers, takeovers, bankruptcies, and restructurings. The early 1990s saw continued price wars between the major airlines. Even when American Airlines CEO Robert Crandall attempted to restore sanity to the industry's pricing by wiping out discounts and simplifying fare structures, the other airlines chose to ignore his lead. Instead, they reacted by cutting their fares even deeper.

Since deregulation, 120 airlines have gone bankrupt, the industry lost $12 billion between 1989 and 1993, and it laid off 100,000 employees between 1989 and 1995 while forcing pay cuts on those who remained. In fact, only one airline was consistently profitable between 1989 and 1993—Southwest Airlines.

Problems in the airline industry caused by price wars hit the airline manufacturing industry as well. Companies like Boeing took it on the chin as orders for new aircraft from U.S. carriers dropped from 1,800 in 1989 to 350 in 1993, forcing Boeing to cut thousands of jobs. In fact, by 1996 the aircraft and parts manufacturing industry had lost over 250,000 jobs, mostly because of problems in the airline industry.

Even customers suffered; although ticket prices fell and many more people were able to fly than before, most flyers weren't satisfied with the industry. The cutbacks in personnel and pay lowered customer service and raised tempers of both airline employees and customers. New, narrower planes introduced to reduce costs featured half the cabin space of their ancestors, crowding passengers. And the number of older planes that airlines kept flying far past the time their designers had planned increased passenger concern about safety.[5]

Judging by their results, companies in the airline industry in the 1989–1995 timeframe could not claim to meet the standards of either Western or Eastern measures of success: profits or jobs. As you can see, it does you no good to "take All-under-Heaven" if there is nothing left of it when you are done. In strategy, as in life, you make your decisions, then they make you.

*The Art of War* states:

- **War is a grave matter; one is apprehensive lest men embark upon it without due reflection."   (I.1 Li Ch'üan)**

The ancient Chinese military sages were cautiously respectful of war's awesome power and its ability to lead one to unforeseen circumstances. Thus, one should not begin a business "war" lightly. One does so only after carefully weighing the potential responses of competitors, forecasting possible outcomes, and understanding the risks and benefits of acting.

Sun Tzu has more to say on this subject:

- **To triumph in battle and be universally acclaimed 'Expert' is not the acme of skill, for to lift an autumn down [hare] requires no strength; to distinguish between the sun and moon is no test of vision; to hear the thunderclap is no indication of acute hearing.**

   **For to win one hundred victories in one hundred battles is not the acme of skill. To subdue the enemy without fighting is the acme of skill.   (IV.9; III.3)**

Thus, the goal of strategy is not only to achieve market dominance in a manner that leaves the industry intact, but to do so "without fighting."

### Winning Without Fighting

You may think that this is a ridiculous proposition. With a book titled *The Art of War*, why would Sun Tzu say that the epitome of skill is to win without fighting? Similarly, isn't it the role of companies to fight over market share, and, if so, how can one win the industry without fighting your competitors? Sun Tzu provides additional insight:

■ Do not put a premium on killing.

He who struggles for victory with naked blades is not a good general.

Battles are dangerous affairs.

Thus, those skilled in war subdue the enemy's army without battle. They capture his cities without assaulting them and overthrow his state without protracted operations.

They conquer by strategy.   (III.1 Li Ch'üan; 6 Chia Lin and Wang Hsi; 10 Sun Tzu and Li Ch'üan)

This point can be illustrated by showing the difference between two popular games: Go, an Asian favorite, and chess, a Western one.

In chess, the object is to destroy the opponent's pieces in an effort to "take" his King. In fact, the saying "checkmate" is derived from the original Persian *shah mat,* meaning "the king is dead." In the beginning of the game, the board is full of pieces. However, by the end, chess resembles a medieval battlefield, with several "dead" pieces strewn about, one king taken, and the board empty except for the few men left standing (see Figure 1.1).

Contrast this to the ancient game of Go, which was invented in China over 4,000 years ago. One wins in Go by capturing and holding the greatest amount of territory with the smallest investment in pieces (either black or white stones). While each of the two players can surround an opponent's stones and capture them, in Go the destruction of an opponent's stones is secondary to the object of capturing territory. In games between masters, very few stones are taken.

Unlike chess, Go begins with the game board empty; the players then take turns placing their stones to control territory. Players can put their stones anywhere on the board, balancing the need to acquire territory against the possibility of overextension and capture. The best strategy is to claim the open areas of the board, then, as the board fills, to attack an opponent's unsupported pieces. One cannot win by being satisfied with merely defending a small piece of territory; one must

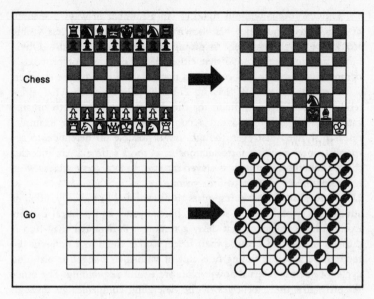

FIGURE 1.1   Chess and Go.

defend by attacking, keeping one's opponent always on the defensive. Played by masters, the game will end with just enough pieces on the board to control the greatest amount of territory.[6]

In business, you should follow the philosophy of Go rather than chess. You should seek to control the most market territory with the smallest investment, not to destroy your competitor and your company in endless fighting. You will win not by wiping out your competition but by avoiding fighting and moving strategically to achieve relative market dominance, survival, and prosperity. This approach leaves your industry intact, allowing your firm to dominate a healthy industry rather than a sick one.

- Replace the enemy's flags and banners with your own, mix the captured chariots with yours, and mount them.

  Treat the captives well and care for them.

  This is called "winning a battle and becoming stronger." (II.18–20)

One can "win without fighting" in a number of ways. Research of competitive industries has shown that subtle, indirect, less visible attacks are much less likely to prompt a competitive response. Obviously, any successful move that either delays or does not provoke a competitive response will result in a market share gain by the attacker.

Furthermore, attacks that are radically different from what a defender expects or are difficult for the defender to respond to organizationally will delay or avoid a competitive response. For example, research showed that even though it was possible for defenders to respond to new-product introductions in as short a time as six months, the typical response time was eleven months. In fact, some attacks were not responded to for up to four years!

The reasons for slow responses to unexpected or radically different attacks are twofold. First, strategic, bureaucratic, and political barriers exist within companies that delay a response. A defender may find it difficult to respond because their strategy takes them in a different direction, because the timing does not fit with their budget or planning cycle, or because internal power blocs are against responding. The other reason is that the executives of the defending companies go through denial that the attack will be successful, and spend time finding evidence to support their view instead of building an effective response.

In contrast, high-profile attacks, attacks perceived as significant threats (such as one directed at a defender's most important markets), and attacks that the defender believes can be responded to successfully for gain are almost certain to elicit an aggressive competitive response. In addition, it was found that price actions were especially provocative, with defenders more likely to respond to a price attack than any other type. Price attacks tended to be countered more quickly and directly than any other type.[7]

Clearly, if you hope to win all without fighting, you must utilize strategy and tactics that enable you to gain share prosperously, without destroying your industry.

In sum, remember that market dominance is the means, but survival and prosperity are the end, that the essence of fighting is not fighting. Fighting takes resources, which are limited and, if used up, leave one defenseless. Outright price confrontation, as witnessed in the tobacco and airline industries, should be avoided, for intense and prolonged fighting will destroy an industry. To attack indirectly and win without fighting means your company will use less resources and your industry will remain intact. It is then possible to dominate and prosper in a

---

**1. WIN ALL WITHOUT FIGHTING**

Capturing Your Market Without Destroying It

---

**2. AVOID STRENGTH/ATTACK WEAKNESS**

Striking Where They Least Expect It

---

**3. DECEPTION AND FOREKNOWLEDGE**

Maximizing the Power of Market Information

---

**4. SPEED AND PREPARATION**

Moving Swiftly To Overcome Your Competitors

---

**5. SHAPE YOUR OPPONENT**

Employing Strategy To Master the Competition

---

**6. CHARACTER-BASED LEADERSHIP**

Providing Effective Leadership in Turbulent Times

---

FIGURE 1.2    Principles of *Sun Tzu and the Art of Business.*

healthy industry instead of just surviving in a sick one. How to do so but still capture your market is explained in Sun Tzu's other principles.

### Sun Tzu's Remaining Principles

The remainder of this book explains the other five principles of *The Art Of Business*, with a chapter devoted to each one. As you will see, each principle builds on and is supported by the others.

The second principle is an important tenet of this philosophy: avoid strength, attack weakness (see Figure 1.2).

■ Now an army may be likened to water, for just as flowing water avoids the heights and hastens to the lowlands, so an army avoids strength and strikes weakness.   (VI.27)

Although many companies prefer to attack each other head-on, this approach is very costly. Battles of attrition can last for months and even years, leaving both sides in a weakened state. Instead, using the method of avoiding strength and attacking weakness maximizes your gains while minimizing the use of your resources. This, by definition, increases profits. This principle is discussed in detail in Chapter 2, Avoid Strength, Attack Weakness: Striking Where They Least Expect It.

To find and exploit your competitor's weakness requires a deep understanding of their executives' strategy, capabilities, thoughts, and desires and a similar depth of knowledge of your own strengths and weaknesses. It is critical that you study the mind of your competition's managers and understand how they will react to your moves. It is also important to understand the overall competitive and industry trends in order to have a feel for the "terrain" on which you will do battle.

- Therefore I say, "Know the enemy and know yourself; in a hundred battles you will never be in peril."   (III.31)

It also demands a corresponding masking of your plans.

- All warfare is based on deception.   (I.17)

Chapter 3, Deception and Foreknowledge: Maximizing the Power of Market Information, sheds light on these topics.

To fully utilize deception and foreknowledge effectively, you must be able to act with blinding speed.

- Speed is the essence of war. Take advantage of the enemy's unpreparedness; travel by unexpected routes and strike him where he has taken no precautions.   (XI.29)

To move with such speed does not mean you do things hastily. In reality, speed requires much preparation. Reducing the time it takes your company to make decisions, develop products, manufacture them, or service customers is crucial. To think through and understand possible competitive reaction to your moves also is essential.

- To rely on rustics and not prepare is the greatest of crimes; to be prepared beforehand for any contingency is the greatest of virtues.   (III.28 Ho Yen-hsi)

Chapter 4, Speed and Preparation: Moving Swiftly To Overcome Your Competitors, expands on these topics.

Putting all these factors into play successfully does not occur naturally. You must be able to "shape" your competition.

- Therefore those skilled in war bring the enemy to the field of battle and are not brought there by him.   (VI.2)

Shaping your competitor means changing the rules of the contest and making the competition conform to your desires and your actions. It means taking control of the situation away from your competition and putting it into your own hands. One way of shaping the competition is by the skillful use of alliances. By building a strong web of alliances, the moves of your competitor can be limited. Also, by eliminating its alliances, you can weaken your competition.

- Look into the matter of his alliances and cause them to be severed and dissolved. If an enemy has alliances, the problem is grave and the enemy's position strong; if he has no alliances the problem is minor and the enemy's position weak."   (III.5 Wang Hsi)

By keeping your plans and strategy closely held and using tactics to deceive your competitors about your true intentions, you can continue to shape the competition by employing direct and indirect approaches.

- He who knows the art of the direct [Cheng] and the indirect [Ch'i] approach will be victorious.   (VII.16)

A direct attack is one that occurs in an expected place at an expected time. An indirect assault is one that comes as a surprise, both in location and timing. By combining direct attacks on your competitor to fix their executives' attention and deceive them, you can then use indirect attacks to win complete victory.

By utilizing the indirect and direct approaches and skillfully crafting alliances you can put your competitor on the defensive and make it more vulnerable to your attacks. Chapter 5, Shape Your Opponent: Employing Strategy To Master the Competition, will tell you more about this subject.

To achieve everything we have discussed takes a special kind of leader—one who can see the correct course of action and take it immediately, who can relate to all stakeholders and gain commitment, who can empower employees to carry out the company's strategic intent, and who can use all personnel wisely. The attributes of this type of leader are discussed in detail in Chapter 6, Character-based Leadership: Providing Effective Leadership in Turbulent Times.

One more point must be made before we continue. Successful strategies are ones that are integrated and synergistic. An excellent definition of strategy is a set of "integrated actions in pursuit of competitive advantage."[8] Sun Tzu's approach is exactly that. Holistic, integrated, and synergistic, with each principle interlocked with the others to form a sum greater than its parts. Think of them as the cords in a very strong rope; separate from one another they may be strong, but woven together they become unbreakable.

### Summary

Your goal is relative market dominance, which is necessary for long-term survival and prosperity. One must achieve this dominance not by destroying your industry but in a manner that leaves the industry intact. To do so requires you to seek and strike your competitor's weaknesses by shaping the mindsets of its executives and making them conform to your wishes. To shape effectively, you must use your knowledge of the industry, your competition, and your own company. This allows you to launch direct attacks to fix your competitor's attention and then use deception and the indirect approach to close the battle. Speed and preparation, combined with excellent leadership, make this possible.

- Anciently, those called skilled in war conquered an enemy easily conquered.

  For he wins his victories without erring. "Without erring" means that whatever he does insures his victory; he conquers an enemy already defeated.

  Therefore the skillful commander takes up a position in which he cannot be defeated and misses no opportunity to master his enemy.

  Thus a victorious army wins its victories before seeking battle; an army destined to defeat fights in the hope of winning. (IV.10, 12–14)

You have now taken the first step toward becoming a master strategist. Let us continue the journey by discussing the second principle: Avoid Strength and Attack Weakness.

# 2 ▪ Avoid Strength, Attack Weakness

## Striking Where They Least Expect It

▪ Now an army may be likened to water, for just as flowing water
avoids the heights and hastens to the lowlands, so an army avoids
strength and strikes weakness. (VI.27)

On February 24, 1991, the 1st and 2nd Divisions of the U.S. Marine
Corps launched their assault headlong into the Iraqi units blocking their
way to Kuwait City. The attack landed exactly where Saddam Hussein
expected it; along the most direct route the Americans could take to
liberate Kuwait. It was there that the Iraqi dictator had positioned the
majority of his million-man army.

But it was two hundred miles to the west that the real strike force
of Desert Storm was located. One day after the Marines had fixed the
attention of the Iraqis, a tempest of artillery fire announced the attack
of the Coalition Army's Eighteenth Airborne Corps and Seventh Corps.
Making easy work of the defenses in front of them, these two units
performed an end run around the strongest part of Hussein's line (see
Figure 2.1). Although outnumbered, by concentrating its strength
against its opponent's weakness, the Coalition Army bagged thousands
of prisoners, tons of military hardware, and brought Iraq to the peace
table—all in one hundred hours.[1]

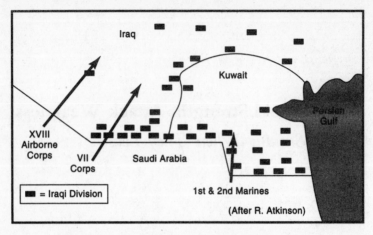

FIGURE 2.1 Operation Desert Storm—ground war attacks.

## *Avoid Strength*

Avoid strength, strike weakness. This idea is central to Sun Tzu's philosophy and the remaining principles flow from it. This principle enabled General Schwartzkopf's forces in the Gulf War to defeat the Iraqis in four days while suffering almost no casualties.

In the business world, if "win all without fighting" is the goal of your strategy, then "avoid strength/attack weakness" is the key to achieving that goal. By focusing your company's resources against your competitor's critical weak point, you achieve success.

The reasoning behind this principle is simple; attacking your competitor's weak points is a much more effective and efficient use of your resources than attacking its strength. Attacking weakness leverages your company's limited resources; attacking strength wastes resources. Attacking weakness shortens the road to victory; attacking strength makes it longer. Attacking weakness increases the value of your victory; attacking strength throws it away. In sum, avoiding strength and attacking weakness achieves the maximum return for the least expenditure of resources in the shortest possible time, thereby maximizing profits.

Unfortunately, pitting strength against strength is often the preferred method of competition among many Western companies. This is because the direct approach is strongly embedded in the Western mind. It makes its appearance in our legends, our sports, and, at times, our military adventures. It's two knights alone in armed combat, riding their chargers toward each other at high speed with the sole purpose of driving a lance through the opponent's heart. It's the stand-up shoot-out at OK Corral, the "hand-off-to-the-fullback, run-it-up-the-middle" mentality, the "fight-fire-with-fire" approach. It's the frontal attack philosophy; impatient, unsubtle, and heads-down.

Let me give you a business example. Starting in 1990, Kmart spent three years constructing 153 new discount stores and revamping 800 existing ones in a $3 billion strategy to take on up-and-coming Wal-Mart. At the time, Wal-Mart was expanding beyond its rural locations into Kmart's urban territory. In response, Kmart's CEO launched a direct assault against Wal-Mart, lowering prices on thousands of products to be more competitive. To offset the lower prices on other items, Kmart began pushing more apparel, which carries higher margins. Five years later, the expensive direct attack strategy was proven unsuccessful. In the first three years of implementation, Kmart's new store sales per square foot fell from $167 to $141. The apparel inventory Kmart bought for the most part either went unsold or was let go at clearance prices. Meanwhile, Kmart was not able to draw customers away with lower prices since Wal-Mart dropped prices to match them. A Wal-Mart manager was quoted as saying, "It's very simple. We are not going to be undersold."

In early 1995, the board of Kmart forced the resignation of its CEO. The cost of the CEO's direct attack on Wal-Mart's strength included a drop in Kmart's market share from 35% to 23%, falling or negative profits, and flat stock performance. Meanwhile, Wal-Mart's market share doubled to 40%, profits soared, and its stock quadrupled.[2]

The principle of avoiding strength and attacking weakness makes what occurred plain. Kmart took on Wal-Mart at its strongest point—its cost structure—and failed. It was unable to get below Wal-Mart's five-point advantage in operating costs. As a Wal-Mart manager was quoted as saying, "What that means is that in an all-out price war they'll go broke 5% before we will."

- If the general is unable to control his impatience and orders his troops to swarm up the wall like ants, one-third of them will be killed without taking the city. Such is the calamity of these attacks. (III.9)

Because strength-on-strength attacks are so direct, they can often become personal. Although he denies making the comment, Kmart's former CEO is said to have referred to Wal-Mart executives as "those snake oil salesmen." As wills and egos become involved, these debilitating battles last even longer than they should have.[3]

> ■ The Emperor T'ai Wu led one hundred thousand troops to attack the Sung general Tsang Chih at Yu T'ai. The Emperor first asked Tsang Chih for some wine [as was customary before battle]. Tsang Chih sealed up a pot full of urine and sent it to him. T'ai Wu was transported with rage and immediately attacked the city, ordering his troops to scale the walls and engage in close combat. Corpses piled up to the top of the walls and after thirty days of this the dead exceeded half his force.   (III.9 Tu Mu)

This tendency toward direct, head-to-head competition results not only from our culture. It also comes from a line of reasoning that is misguided yet dangerously appealing. The thought process is this: If our competitor has been successful by being the lowest-cost provider or by increasing spending on research and development or marketing, than we could be too. We only need to imitate the best practices of our competitors and we can become the market leader. A variation on this theme is: If they can produce a good candy bar (camera, car, etc.), then we can too. This strategy of competitive imitation leads many executives to attack strong competitors at their strongest point.

A company that followed this logic was AT&T, with its foray into the computer market. In the 1980s, as the communications and computer industries became more entwined, AT&T grew enamored with attacking IBM, DEC, Hewlett-Packard, and others with its own computer line. With a large treasury, the technology jewel of Bell Labs, and ownership of the UNIX operating system, AT&T executives must have felt assured of success. Eight years, thousands of layoffs, and $2 billion in losses later, AT&T executives realized that the attempt had failed. So, in 1991, AT&T executed a $7.5 billion hostile takeover of NCR, paying 20% over NCR's market value for another crack at this market. It still was not successful. In 1994, AT&T dropped the NCR brand name and replaced it with AT&T Global Information Systems (GIS), hoping a third shot would finally be rewarded. In late 1995, AT&T finally gave up. After losing $3 billion since the merger, AT&T took a $1.5-billion write-off, laid off 8,500 more employees, and spun off GIS (which again became NCR). Clearly, AT&T's mistake of relying on competitive imitation and sheer size to directly attack major competitors head-on is the epitome of an unsuccessful frontal attack.[4]

■ In war, numbers alone confer no advantage. Do not advance relying on sheer military power.

Although. . . . the troops of Yueh [are] many, of what benefit is this superiority in respect to the outcome?   (IX.45; VI.18)

The AT&T fiasco illustrates the problem with the strength-against-strength approach; since it is not very creative nor based on attacking the competition's weakness, it dooms a company to a battle of attrition. The basic philosophy behind an attrition strategy is that your resources will outlast those of your competitor. In practice, this means that your company must not only have resources sufficient to overcome the competitor but also the will to expend them until your competitor capitulates. Often, an opponent stubbornly refuses to do so.

From an historical perspective, the most obvious and searing example of an attrition strategy not working was the United States' involvement in Viet Nam. The plan was to outlast the enemy and defeat him by expending whatever resources were required. It was thought to be an unbeatable strategy since the United States had several times the resources of North Viet Nam. However, U.S. leaders drastically underestimated the ability of the communists to leverage their limited resources so effectively. They also dramatically misunderstood that the communists' strength was their ability to prolong the fighting by utilizing guerilla warfare. As time went on, the American effort in Viet Nam became a bottomless pit that consumed its resources at an ever-increasing rate and distracted the United States from dealing with dramatic changes at home and abroad. Finally, elections brought new leadership to run the U.S. government, which then changed the strategy to end American involvement. In the end, it was the United States that was outlasted.

■ Now when an army of one hundred thousand is raised and dispatched on a distant campaign the expenses borne by the people together with the disbursements of the treasury will amount to a thousand pieces of gold daily. There will be continuous commotion both at home and abroad, people will be exhausted by the requirements of transport, and the affairs of seven hundred thousand households will be disrupted.   (XIII.1)

Regardless of whether the arena is business or war, the end result of an attrition strategy, of matching strength against strength, is failure.

Precious resources are expended for little or no gain. In business, established products end up being withdrawn or left to languish, customers who bought from you are unsatisfied, new products that could have created new markets are without funding, and the company's coffers are drained. While in the short term each failure may appear as only a small setback, repeated instances of attempting this strategy debilitate a company and allow competitors to grab market share.

That is what happened to Xerox several years ago as they expended resources trying to beat established competitors in the computer, office duplicator, and word processor markets. With its famous Palo Alto Research Center (PARC) providing promising potential products and a treasure chest filled with revenues from its very profitable high-end copier business, Xerox attempted to expand into other businesses by attacking companies like IBM at their strongest point.

They were stymied at every turn. In the process, they missed an opportunity to move into the low-end copier business. Meanwhile, Canon Co. viewed the marketplace and saw Xerox's vulnerability in the low-end segment. Moving swiftly, Canon created products to serve that segment, thus taking away huge market share from Xerox and making inroads into Xerox accounts at the department level. Many of the researchers from PARC left Xerox to enjoy huge personal success in the budding personal computer market, including several who helped Apple Computer create that industry. Imagine where Xerox would be now if they had created the personal computer market in addition to owning the high- and low-end copier business!

Although Xerox has since made a comeback, because it chose to attack strength instead of weakness, it lost both the opportunity for higher revenues in its original market segment and potential opportunities for growth in new segments or markets.[5]

Even if you have several times the resources of your competitor and a very strong will, your probability of winning the battle is still low if you attack your competitor's strength. Thus, the end result is not creative competition but destructive competition, for even if you do "win," what does winning mean in this type of situation? You may have "defeated" your competitor, but paid a high cost in resources. You may have lost sight of other opportunities by being distracted by this all-consuming contest. Even if you are now aware of other opportunities, the resources may no longer exist to pursue them. Perhaps this is why one of the names for the frontal attack concept is the heads-down approach. When your head is down, it really is impossible to see what is happening around you.

- Victory is the main object in war. If this is long delayed, weapons are blunted and morale depressed.

  For there has never been a protracted war from which a country has benefited.   (II.3, 7)

### Attack Weakness

So how can you as a strategist be successful? How can you master this principle?

- The nature of water is that it avoids heights and hastens to the lowlands. When a dam is broken, the water cascades with irresistible force. Now the shape of an army resembles water. Take advantage of the enemy's unpreparedness; attack him when he does not expect it; avoid his strength and strike his emptiness, and like water, none can oppose you.   (IV.20 Chang Yü)

Do not be misled into thinking that using this principle is unfair or somehow unsporting. You do not need to prove yourself by taking competitors head-on. Recall that even a lion doesn't go after the fastest antelope in the herd; instead he runs down the slowest.

- Create an invincible army and await the enemy's moment of vulnerability.   (III.28 Ch'ên Hao)

In business, there are several ways you as a strategist can replicate this approach and create a situation where your company's strengths are applied against your competitor's weaknesses.

One way is to attack the weakest part of your competitor's value chain. If they are strong in manufacturing but have a weak tie to their distributors, attack them there. Reinforce your distribution channels to take their customers away. Better yet, woo away their distributors and make them your own. Without them, their manufacturing prowess will prove worthless. Japanese companies employed the technique of attacking the weak point in their competitor's value chain when they leveraged their strengths in quality manufacturing to beat American competitors, who were weak in that link.

If your company is a major player in a market with a few large companies and many small ones, another method may prove successful. Do not attack the other large companies to try and take market share from them. Instead, attack the weaker players one at a time. You then surround the major players with new customers and gain greater market share without confronting them directly.

This is what Wal-Mart did against Sears, Kmart and other large retailers. Wal-Mart's success is the result of several factors, many of them operational. However, a major strategic reason for Wal-Mart's success is that it chose as competitors little Mom & Pop stores in small towns instead of taking on the big retailers head to head in large markets. Using their huge buying power and lean distribution methods to drive costs down, they defeated the small stores and "attacked the enemy where he did not expect it" in small towns. Wal-Mart gobbled up market share and surrounded its main competitors.

There are other ways to apply your strengths against a competitor's weakness.

- That you may march a thousand *li* without wearying yourself is because you travel where there is no enemy.

  Go into emptiness, strike voids, bypass what he defends, hit him where he does not expect you.   (VI.6 Sun Tzu and Ts'ao Ts'ao)

Your company too can "go into emptiness, strike voids, and bypass what he defends" by creating new products, attacking niches in the market, or entering new geographic markets.

CNN, ESPN, and MTV chose the first two strategies by using the latest technology to create new products targeted at specific niches. While the major networks fought to gain a few points of market share from each other with similar sitcoms and soap operas, the new competitors avoided the strengths of these major players and struck their "emptiness." With CNN targeting the unfulfilled needs of TV-news addicts, ESPN supplying sports around the clock to fanatic fans, and MTV routing rock and roll into the homes of teens, and all three leveraging cable TV as a means of entry, they helped change the face of the entertainment industry forever. Going "into emptiness," CNN, ESPN, and MTV avoided their larger competitors, marching around them to hit them where they "least expected it."

- Troops thrown against the enemy as a grindstone against eggs is an example of a solid acting upon a void.

  Use the most solid to attack the most empty.   (V.4 Sun Tzu and Ts'ao Ts'ao)

GE has chosen a similar approach by investing heavily in emerging geographic markets. The end of the Cold War and the shift to capitalism around the world opened up new opportunities for companies in developing or redeveloping countries. Billions of dollars of capital are flowing there daily as smart players move to entrench themselves in these markets before their competition. GE has made it a priority to deploy resources to China, India, and Mexico. They want to be well positioned in the appliance, jet engine, plastics, and medical and power systems markets early on.

- To be certain to take what you attack is to attack a place the enemy does not protect. To be certain to hold what you defend is to defend a place the enemy does not attack. (VI.7)

GE's CEO John Welch believes that investments in these growing but yet untapped markets could very well decide the company's fate. Therefore, it is important to him that GE be well established in those markets before the competition arrives. Assuming GE executes its strategy correctly, when their competitors finally decide to move to these emerging markets they will find GE already dug in and ready to fight.[6]

- Close to the field of battle, they await an enemy coming from afar; at rest, an exhausted enemy; with well-fed troops, hungry ones. (VII.24)

Additionally, this preemptive move can be done without much risk on GE's part. Welch explains that if the plan "is wrong, it's a billion dollars, a couple of billion dollars. If it's right, it's the future of the next century for this company."

- Thus one need use but little strength to achieve much. (V.25 Tu Mu)

As these examples show, there is an advantage to being the "first mover" to launch a preemptive attack to gain competitive advantage.

Interestingly, in the Asian game of Go, the advantage of first mover is acknowledged and accounted for. The game can be made even either by allowing the weaker player to move first or awarding the player who moves second additional points.

As mentioned earlier, your company could launch a preemptive attack at many places along the value chain: getting new customers via

- **Supply Systems**
    - Secure access to raw materials or components
    - Preempt production equipment
    - Dominate supply logistics
- **Product**
    - Introduce new product lines
    - Develop the dominant design
    - Positioning
    - Secure accelerated approval from agencies
    - Secure product development and delivery skills
    - Expand the scope of the product
- **Production Systems**
    - Proprietary processes
    - Aggressive capacity expansion
    - Vertical integration with key suppliers
    - Secure scarce and critical production skills
- **Customers**
    - Segmentation
    - Build early brand awareness
    - Train customers in usage skills
    - Capture key accounts
- **Distribution and Service Systems**
    - Occupation of prime locations
    - Preferential access to key distributors
    - Dominance of distribution logistics
    - Access to superior service capabilities
    - Development of distributor skills

FIGURE 2.2   Sources of preemptive opportunities.

a unique segmentation (à la CNN, MTV and ESPN), occupying prime retail locations, introducing proprietary production processes, wrapping your product in value-added services, or securing sole access to raw materials or components. Figure 2.2 contains a more complete list of areas in the value chain that are sources of preemptive opportunities.[7]

Apple was successful in launching a preemptive move by moving quickly into primary, secondary, and college classrooms before any of the other personal computer vendors could get there. In the process, they created a very loyal customer base.

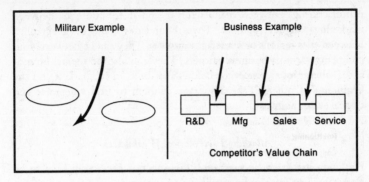

FIGURE 2.3   Attacking boundary points.

Hewlett-Packard's philosophy to remain ahead of the competition in printers is to carry out preemptive moves to make its own products obsolete. Offering improved products with new features that replace still-successful products allows Hewlett-Packard to continually seize the high ground even as the technology terrain causes it to shift. Hewlett-Packard CEO Lewis Platt states, "We've developed a philosophy of killing off our own products with new technology. Better that we do it than somebody else." It is much better to have a "growing out of business" strategy than a "going out of business" one.[8]

### Attacking Weaknesses at Boundary Points

Another place weaknesses occur is at the boundaries between organizations. In war, these boundaries occur where two unit's areas of responsibility meet (see Figure 2.3).

In these boundary areas, responsibility for coverage may be unclear, coordination is difficult, gaps may appear, and weaknesses develop. It is often possible for a good commander to find these boundary areas and launch an attack that forces the two units to separate in an effort to protect themselves. This just makes the gap even wider, and allows the wily attacker to defeat each unit separately.

Just as two allied units may have trouble coordinating their efforts at a boundary point, allied companies or functions within companies may have difficulty as well. It is to your advantage to find the boundaries of your competitor. These boundaries could occur in your competitor's value chain, such as the boundary between development and manufacturing, between manufacturing and distribution, or between marketing and development. These boundaries could be geographic, between sales regions or manufacturing sites. They can be between your competitor and its business partners. They can also be mental boundaries, where your competitor defines the limits of its markets and the beginning of others. Take advantage of them to find vulnerable and critical weak points.

### Attacking Psychological Weaknesses

For your attacks to be successful, they do not necessarily have to be physical. They can also be psychological, directed at and focused on the mind of your competitor.

- **The supreme excellence in war is to attack the enemy's plans.**

  **Next best is to disrupt his alliances.**

  **The next best is to attack his army.**

  **The worst policy is to attack cities.**

  **Anger his general and confuse him.**

  **Keep him under strain and wear him down.** (III.4 Li Ch'üan, III.5–7; I.22, 24)

The tactic of attacking your competitor's strategy and plans is perhaps best exemplified in such high-technology industries as computers. Customers of computer companies have huge investments in installed hardware and software. With technology changing so rapidly, computer companies try to keep customers loyal by announcing their future product strategy. They attempt to show how their products will continue to be advanced and stay vital over the coming years. To gain an advantage, one competitor will attack another's strategy by casting doubts on its technical viability, thus worrying the other's customers and causing them to desert. These verbal attacks are carried out at industry trade shows, in magazine interviews, or press releases. The trade press then picks up the story, industry consultants trumpet it, and soon the creators of the strategy are forced into spending time trying to reassure customers instead of promoting their product to new prospects.

If you think about it, this is the least resource-intensive means of attacking a competitor. It requires little investment, yet it can be a very effective technique if properly executed. That is why Sun Tzu is adamant that "the supreme excellence in war is to attack an enemy's plans."

### Selecting and Concentrating Your Attack: The Schwerpunkt

As you can see, it does not take great resources to apply the principle of "avoid strength, attack weakness." As pointed out earlier, great resources may even be a hindrance to creative strategy. What is critical, especially if you have limited resources, is that you apply the right amount of resources at just the right spot. Then, with a little push, the avalanche is released.

- Therefore when using troops, one must take advantage of the situation exactly as if he were setting a ball in motion on a steep slope. The force applied is minute, but the results are enormous. (V.25 Chang Yü)

The German Army of World War II called this point of attack the schwerpunkt. It means "the center of gravity" and is the place where one concentrates one's resources to achieve the most impact. You must determine this point of weakness in your competitor and mass your power accordingly. For example, in the Gulf War the F-117A "Stealth" bomber constituted less than 3% of U.S. air power. However, the United States leveraged this secret weapon's tremendous strength of radar invisibility to carry out 31% of all air attacks on the first day of the air campaign.[9]

I have pointed out many potential places of attack; you must decide which weakness would be the most effective to attack. This is done by balancing the vulnerability of a weakness to your attack against the damage that would occur to your competitor by attacking that weakness. Obviously, the best weakness to attack would be one that not only is extremely vulnerable but, if attacked successfully, would be especially damaging to your competition.

This weak point is precisely where your schwerpunkt must be. You must concentrate your efforts physically in time and space here; all other efforts must be secondary. Again, the Gulf War provides an excellent example. The main strike force of Desert Storm was the Seventh Corps, which had the mission of sweeping around the Iraqi right flank and destroying the Republican Guard divisions. This Corps contained 1,300 high-tech Abrams and Challenger tanks, the largest amount of armor ever assembled in a corps in the history of warfare. This powerful force was concentrated at the most vulnerable point of the Iraqi line, and it proved also to be the point where the Coalition Army could inflict the most damage.[10]

Southwest Airlines, the unconventional, low-cost airline, serves as an excellent business example of concentrating resources at the point of attack. When opening a route at a new airport, Southwest does not start out tentatively. Instead, before the route is open, they pepper the new locale with publicity stunts, targeted advertising, and special promotions—all building demand. When the route opens, waves of Southwest flights are made available to satisfy this pent-up demand, thus achieving concentrated mass at the critical time and place. These methods allow Southwest to set records for advance bookings and flights per gate, driving its revenue and profits up and its competitors out.[11]

At this point, you may be thinking that Sun Tzu's philosophy means that one should not make the effort to improve those parts of your own organization that are weak or failing. This is not the case. Competition is a relative concept. Therefore, if your manufacturing plants are obsolete, they must be upgraded. If your service employees lack training, ensure that they get it; resources should be expended to bring them up to par. However, the majority of your resources must be concentrated to build strength that can be used against your competitor's weak point. Only in that fashion can they be used most effectively. To parcel out resources in an attempt to make every function in your organization "world class" is wasteful. No company in the world has the resources to do that. Remember, to be strong everywhere is to be strong nowhere.

### Going on the Defensive To Prepare To Attack

You may need to bide your time before concentrating your forces and launching an attack on your competitor. You may need time to prepare, to solidify your position in your current market segments, to build up your reserves. This is as it should be. However, remember that your company cannot grow merely by defending its customers. It must move to the attack to gain market share and profits.

■ Invincibility lies in the defense; the possibility of victory in the attack.

One defends when his strength is inadequate: he attacks when it is abundant.  (IV.5–6)

## Final Considerations

As a strategist, it is critical not only that you determine where weakness exists and attack there, but also that you have the personal fortitude to avoid attacking when the situation has changed.

For example, a new opportunity may seem promising. A new market appears to be emerging and several people in your company are saying that it is important for your firm to be a player. They maintain that it is a "strategic imperative" or that "it is fundamental to survival" to be in that marketplace. The pressure to take action is immense.

However, after studying the situation, you find that the positions of the existing players are too strong to attack at the moment. You as a strategist must be able to stand firm and refrain from ordering an immediate assault that is destined to fail.

- They do not engage an enemy advancing with well-ordered banners nor one whose formations are in impressive array. . . . Therefore, the art of employing troops is that when the enemy occupies high ground, do not confront him; with his back resting on hills, do not oppose him.  (VII.25–26)

You must wait until you can find a weakness and attack then.

- If your troops do not equal his, temporarily avoid his initial onrush. Probably later you can take advantage of a soft spot. Then rouse yourself and seek victory with determined spirit.  (III.16 Tu Mu)

You must recognize that not only might this not be the appropriate time to attack, it may not even be the appropriate place.

- A road, although it may be the shortest, is not to be followed if one knows it is dangerous and there is the contingency of ambush.

  An army, although it may be attacked, is not to be attacked if it is in desperate circumstances and there is the possibility that the enemy will fight to the death.

> A city, although isolated and susceptible to attack, is not to be attacked if there is the probability that it is well stocked with provisions, defended by crack troops under command of a wise general, that its ministers are loyal and their plans unfathomable.

> Ground, although it may be contested, is not to be fought for if one knows that after getting it, it will be difficult to defend, or that he gains no advantage by obtaining it, but will probably be counter-attacked and suffer casualties. (VIII.11 Chia Lin)

Given the great risks of entering battle, you must carefully weigh the potential gains against the chance of loss. Do so without emotion but with deep thought. Remember, the wise strategist will not attack unless victory is ensured.

- Thus a victorious army is as a hundredweight balanced against a grain; a defeated army as a grain balanced against a hundredweight. (IV.19)

### Summary

A crucial tenet of Sun Tzu's philosophy that will enable you to "Win All-under-Heaven" is to avoid strength and strike weakness.

Unfortunately, too often managers get locked into doing the "safe" strategy. They "solve" strategic problems by imitating their competitors and attacking them at their strongest points, as Kmart and AT&T did. By using the obvious solution (what the competition is doing), no one can blame them if it goes wrong.

However, the reality is that for complex problems, such as those found in competitive strategy, the most obvious answer may not be the right one. Although competitive imitation may be the highest form of flattery, it is the lowest form of strategy. To be successful, you must not follow strategies that your top competitor is pursuing; if you try to be someone else, the best you can be is second best. Instead, you must find your own differentiated strategy.

The situation you as a strategist must create is the application of your strength against the competitor's weak point. This principle maximizes the return on your investment, conserves resources, and avoids long and costly wars of attrition. It forces one to constantly look for new openings to exploit and demands creativity. It is perhaps a more

Eastern and certainly more subtle approach than the frontal attack, but it is both more efficient and effective.

It can be accomplished in several ways. You can attack weak links in your competitor's value chain. You can choose to attack the weaker competitors in your marketplace rather than the strong ones. Or you can avoid your competitors all together by creating new markets or being an early entrant into emerging geographic ones. The key to your success will be knowing where the weaknesses are and when to release the attack. Attacking only when you have found the right weakness will dramatically improve your chances for victory.

■ When he concentrates, prepare against him: where he is strong, avoid him.   (I.21)

To find those weaknesses and keep your competitor from discovering yours is the subject of the next chapter.

# 3 ▪ Deception and Foreknowledge

*Maximizing the Power of
Market Information*

▪ Now the reason the enlightened prince and the wise general
conquer the enemy whenever they move and their achievements
surpass those of ordinary men is foreknowledge.   (XIII.3)

As Sun Tzu states, to defeat the competition and achieve your goals,
you must have "foreknowledge." Sun Tzu then explains exactly what
foreknowledge is.

▪ What is called "foreknowledge" cannot be elicited from spirits,
nor from gods, nor by analogy with past events, nor from calculations. It must be obtained from men who know the enemy
situation.   (XIII.4)

Foreknowledge is not projecting the future based on the past; it is
not simple trend analysis. Foreknowledge is firsthand insight and a deep
understanding of what your competitor is about: its strengths, its weaknesses, its plans, its people.

▪ Generally in the case of armies you wish to strike, cities you wish
to attack, and people you wish to assassinate, you must know
the names of the garrison commander, the staff officers, the ush-

ers, the gatekeepers, and the bodyguards. You must instruct your
agents to inquire into these matters in minute detail.   (XIII.16)

Obviously, no matter how much you would like to defeat your
competitors, you are not going to assassinate their executives! However,
Sun Tzu's point is still well taken. To understand and defeat your competition, you must do a very deep level of research and analysis. It must
not lack for detail. Unfortunately, most of what passes for competitive
analysis these days is very shallow.

Because of lack of funding, lack of interest or lack of skills, the
competitive analysis arm of a company will often do only a skin-deep
review of the competition. Another reason some firms may not perform
a good job of competitive analysis is that they feel it is somehow unfair
or unethical. They concur with Henry L. Stimson, the Secretary of
State who closed down his codebreaking department, that "gentlemen
do not read other gentlemen's mail." Indeed, corporate espionage has
occurred on a large scale. In the 1970s and 1980s, the government of
France recruited "moles" inside high-tech U.S. companies such as IBM
and Texas Instruments. These employees would steal leading-edge technology secrets and pass them to French agents. The latter, it has been
suggested, passed them on to French companies.[1] However, as you will
see, all the competitor data you require can be obtained from public
sources. No intrigue is required.

Whatever the reason for the lack of good competitive data, it is
essential to have it. One might be able to satisfy management by showing them a few facts about the competition, allowing your executives
to pretend to fashion effective strategies and predict the responses of
your competitors. However, in reality, your executive team would be
operating in the dark. To be satisfied with such a simplistic level of
analysis is to invite disaster.

■ One ignorant of the plans of neighboring states cannot prepare
alliances in good time; if ignorant of the conditions of mountains,
forests, dangerous defiles, swamps and marshes he cannot conduct the march of an army; if he fails to make use of native guides
he cannot gain the advantages of the ground. A general ignorant
of even one of these three matters is unfit to command the armies
of a Hegemonic King.   (XI.51)

On November 21, 1970, American special forces troops attacked a
POW camp in North Viet Nam with the mission of freeing U.S. pris-

oners. After weeks of preparation, the raid on Sontay went like clock-work; total time on the ground was only twenty-six minutes. The guards were quickly dispatched and the only casualty in the strike force was a badly sprained ankle. Quite a success. However, there was just one problem—the prisoners had been moved out of the camp weeks before. A lack of intelligence preempted what could have been a major coup for the American forces in Viet Nam and instead led to failure.[2]

Companies make the same mistake. They attack markets they know little about. They take on new competitors without learning their strengths, weaknesses, and capabilities. They engage old competitors they think they know, but in truth do not. And instead of seeking and probing for weaknesses and attacking them, these companies blunder and thrash about, bumping into one competitor after another, occasionally hitting a weakness but more often running head-on into strengths.

To beat the competition, you must know your competition, know your own company, and know your marketplace.

### Know Your Competition

To be successful, to find weaknesses, you must do as Sun Tzu states: you must elicit knowledge "from men (and women) who know the enemy situation." You must "inquire into these matters in the most minute detail."

As a starting point, you must begin with the basics, the facts. What are your competitor's financial results, how many employees does it have, what products does it have, and in which markets? Determine your competitor's manufacturing costs by buying and dissecting its products. These are the facts—they provide the basis for your analysis. However, realize that, by themselves, even they are insufficient.

You must go deeper. You must build on the facts with information that tells you what your competitor's strategy is. This information can be obtained from the company itself, such as its annual and quarterly reports, its advertising, and announcements. Trade journals and business press are another means for gathering information. Executives love to tell the press how brilliant their strategies are and how they will be executed; you can use this information to discern their plans. Also, look closely at your competitor's past behavior; how has it responded to attacks in the past? How has it launched and executed its attacks? What signs have its executives given before taking an action? Did they schedule an announcement? Did they make certain investments? Did they hire new talent? Look for these signs.

- When the trees are seen to move the enemy is advancing.

  Birds rising in flight is a sign that the enemy is lying in ambush; when wild animals are startled and flee he is trying to take you unaware.

  Dust spurting upward in high, straight columns indicates the approach of chariots. When it hangs low and is widespread infantry is approaching.

  When light chariots first go out and take position on the flanks the enemy is forming for battle.   (IX. 20, 22, 23, 29)

Now you know two things: what your competitor is capable of and what its current plan of attack is. However, even this is still insufficient. You must also know what your competitor's executives will do in response to your actions.

- When the enemy's envoys speak in humble terms but he continues his preparations, he will advance. When their language is deceptive but the enemy pretentiously advances, he will retreat. When the envoys speak in apologetic terms, he wishes a respite. When without a previous understanding the enemy asks for a a truce, he is plotting.   (IX.25–28)

To know these things you must go beneath the facts and surface information and delve even deeper—right into the minds of your competitor's executives. It is not enough to know what your competitor *can do*; you must know what your competitor *will do*. You must learn as much as possible about the culture of your competitor and the mindset and assumptions of those who run it.

- If you wish to conduct offensive war you must know the men employed by the enemy. Are they wise or stupid, clever or clumsy? Having assessed their qualities, you prepare appropriate measures.   (XIII.16 Tu Mu)

You must find out not only the names of the executives running the company but where they graduated from, what experiences have molded them, where they get their information, how they view the industry, the degree of risk they are willing to take, how important different business goals are to them, and what their ambitions are. You should also know if there are any disagreements on strategy within the corporation that could be exploited.

■ When the King of Han sent Han Hsin, Ts'ao Ts'an, and Kuan Ying to attack Wei Pao he asked: "Who is the commander-in-chief of Wei?" The reply was: "Po Chih." The King said: "His mouth still smells of his mother's milk. He cannot equal Han Hsin. Who is their cavalry commander?" The reply was: "Feng Ching." The King said: "He is the son of General Feng Wu-che of Ch'in. Although worthy, he is not the equal of Kuan Ying. And who is the infantry commander?" The reply was: "Hsiang T'o." The King said: "He is no match for Ts'ao Ts'an. I have nothing to worry about." (XIII.16 Tu Mu)

Find out more about your opponent's people. Do the executives move fast or are they slow to take action? How will they respond to your attacks? You must know this before attacking.

As mentioned in Chapter 2, Hewlett-Packard is an excellent company that has achieved top-notch financial results. However, even good companies make mistakes.

In late September 1994, Hewlett-Packard announced "AS/sault," a marketing campaign that directly targeted IBM's successful AS/400 midrange computer. Its goal was to entice IBM customers with price discounts to move to Hewlett-Packard's 9000 series product line. The campaign opened with publicity in the *Wall Street Journal* describing Hewlett-Packard's forthcoming ad, that showed a fortune-teller looking at an AS/400 and saying "But I see no clear future here." The attempt to portray the AS/400 as a dying product was a straightforward attack on a very important and profitable product for IBM.

Had this attack occurred earlier, when IBM was being run by another management team and the AS/400 wasn't having a good year, Hewlett-Packard may have gotten away with it. However, the executive team at Hewlett-Packard failed to take the time to understand IBM's new management team led by Louis Gerstner. One of Gerstner's top priorities since joining IBM in 1993 was to make the company more proactive in dealing with the competition. Hewlett-Packard also failed to take into account the new capabilities IBM had recently announced for the AS/400, making it a much more attractive product.

When the Hewlett-Packard direct attack came, publicly trumpeted in the *Wall Street Journal*, IBM's response was fast and hardhitting. IBM ran an ad in the *Journal* the next week, positioning Hewlett-Packard as simply a number two player in the market who was making a last-ditch shot at taking on the leader, AS/400. The ad headline read, "Nice Try, HP." The ad also gave IBM the opportunity to compare the benefits of owning an AS/400 versus an HP 9000.

What were the results? Many industry observers saw limited, if any, success by Hewlett- Packard at taking away IBM customers. One said, "Eventually somebody's going to compete with IBM. But if HP is IBM's strongest competitor, and strong in only a couple of industries, IBM is going to laugh all the way to the bank." A trade magazine noted,"After reviewing HP's campaign, I conclude that HP has misconceptions about the AS/400, resulting in an unjustified self-confidence in the HP 9000's superiority." James Yu, the executive in charge of HP's AS/sault campaign admits that Hewlett-Packard didn't expect to wipe out the AS/400. He agreed that "The AS/400 is the biggest, most popular midrange machine out there."

In this instance, Hewlett-Packard made a strategic error: they took their biggest competitor head-on and did so very publicly. The reason they made this mistake is that they did not take the time to understand the strength of their opponent's product, the minds of their opponent's executive team, nor project what their response might be. Instead, Hewlett-Packard made IBM even more aware of the threat Hewlett-Packard posed and increased the urgency and priority IBM placed on that threat.

What could Hewlett-Packard have done instead? In the years prior to the direct attack, Hewlett-Packard was wooing the AS/400's top business partners. These were companies providing the critical application software that runs on AS/400 and makes customers want to buy it instead of other computers. Hewlett-Packard had been able to forge working relationships with eleven of the AS/400's top fifteen business partners. Instead of taking on IBM head-on, HP should have quietly continued this subtle, indirect approach.[3]

■ **Therefore, determine the enemy's plans and you will know which strategy will be successful and which will not.** (VI.20)

This does not mean that you never use a direct attack; you just don't use one to achieve a major objective or goal. As the next quote from *The Art of War* states, you may want to launch small, direct assaults in minor product categories to see how your competitor responds. When you find a pattern, you can use it to predict how that firm will react at a later time. You can then take advantage of your new knowledge by creating a strategy for an assault in a more major product category.

- Agitate him and ascertain the pattern of his movement.

  Determine his dispositions and so ascertain the field of battle.

  Probe him and learn where his strength is abundant and where deficient. (VI.21–23)

Some types of companies are better at understanding their competition's capabilities and mindset than others. Companies that are in the hostile takeover business must be able to do it well on a continuing basis because their business depends on it. When you see a merger or acquisition go sour, in many cases it is because the company doing the takeover did not do detailed research and wound up misjudging the situation.

For example, Hanson PLC is a British-based company that in 1989 was one of the ten biggest companies in the United Kingdom. It is a conglomerate that grows primarily via acquisitions; over time it has compiled an excellent record of successful takeovers and profits. From 1974 to 1989, the company's stock multiplied eighty times while the London Stock Exchange average was only fifteen, and its 1992 revenues were $15.6 billion. Sir Gordon White, the head of Hanson PLC's U.S. affiliate, was reputed to have been the real-life model for Gordon Gekko's British opponent in the movie *Wall Street*.

One key trait of acquisitions that Hanson PLC has undertaken is to target companies from which major parts can be sold off to reduce debt. Hanson PLC was so good at finding juicy targets that in some instances they are able to sell off some of the parts of the acquired company for more than they paid for the entire firm. One of their most successful coups was their hostile takeover of Smith-Corona for $930 million in 1986, followed by the subsequent sale of its real estate and other divisions for $964 million. Hanson PLC then kept the typewriter and chemical divisions, which they had gotten virtually for nothing.

- Therefore in the enemy's country, the mountains, rivers, highlands, lowlands, and hills which he can defend as strategic points; the forests, reeds, rushes and luxuriant grasses in which he can conceal himself; the distances over the roads and paths, the size of cities and towns, the extent of the villages, the fertility or barrenness of the fields, the depth of irrigation works, the amounts of stores, the size of the opposing army, the keenness of weapons—all must be fully known. Then we have the enemy in our sights and he can be easily taken.   (VII.11 Ho Yen-hsi)

Critical to Hanson's success in these volatile and dynamic takeover situations, where the stock price changes by the minute and nerves of steel are essential, is a deep understanding of the mind of their opponent. Although Sir Gordon says he can learn everything he needs to know about a takeover candidate from one page of information, he has an excellent staff that does in-depth research on the takeover target and condenses it down into a consumable document. He also has key contacts in the investment banking community who can provide him with insights into a company's current management. This combination of rigorous analysis and firsthand intelligence is competitive research at its best.[4]

- We select men who are clever, talented, wise, and able to gain access to those of the enemy who are intimate with the sovereign and members of the nobility. Thus they are able to observe the enemy's movements and to learn of his doings and his plans. Having learned the true state of affairs they return and tell us. (XIII.11 Tu Yu)

### Know Yourself

Foreknowledge does not stop at knowing your competition. You must also know your own company's strengths and weaknesses;

- Therefore I say, "Know the enemy and know yourself; in a hundred battles you will never be in peril.

  When you are ignorant of the enemy but know yourself, your chances of winning or losing are equal.

  If ignorant both of your enemy and yourself, you are certain in every battle to be in peril."   (III.31–33)

So, to pit your strengths against your competitor's weakness and avoid getting surprised by their attacks, it is critical to realize both where you are strong and where you are weak. You need to understand a broad array of things about your company: who your customers are and why they buy your product, what your costs are, which offerings are the most profitable and which the least, what your critical processes are, the length of your cycle times, and who your essential managers and employees are. You must know this information in detail and have access to it on a real-time basis.

> ■ If I know that the enemy is vulnerable to attack, but do not know that my troops are incapable of striking him, my chance of victory is but half.   (X.23)

As a strategist, for you to understand your company's capabilities, your knowledge must be firsthand. You can glean this information from talking to your managers and employees on a daily basis—management by walking around. For a deeper and more long-range understanding of what the strengths and weaknesses are in your company, you might do well to perform a structured self-assessment using a framework that covers the whole range of your business.

In *The Art of War*, Sun Tzu often talks of military frameworks such as "the five fundamental factors" and the "nine varieties of ground." As a parallel, despite the controversy over the effectiveness and usefulness of the Malcolm Baldrige Award, the Baldrige framework itself is a good way to get an all-encompassing, yet detailed view of your firm's operations. The seven Baldrige categories cover a cross-functional view of leadership, information and analysis, strategic planning, human resources, process quality, operational results and customer satisfaction. Thus, they provide an excellent means of organizing an investigation to elicit your strengths and weaknesses in a more structured manner (regardless of whether you're going for the award). By forcing you to answer such questions as "Are there three years of data showing gains in the number of customers" and then requiring proof, you can take a really close look at your company and expose its strengths and weaknesses.[5]

### Utilizing Information Technology

Information technology is essential for gaining real-time control and understanding of how your company is operating since it can be used to gather large amounts of information and assist in analyzing it. The speed and pervasiveness of computer technology are factors Sun Tzu, living in a time where beating drums and waving flags were used to signal commands, may not have comprehended. However, if he were familiar with their capabilities, he would easily see ways of deploying them for competitive advantage.

For example, there's a company called S-K-I Limited, in Killington, Vermont. As its name implies, S-K-I Ltd. operates ski resorts. However, it is not your typical ski resort company. It employs information systems not only for mundane things like payroll but to gain real-time operational control for competitive advantage.

S-K-I Ltd. has weather monitoring equipment placed on key slopes to determine the optimal mixture of air and water for their snow-making machines and then monitors the machines from a central control room. They use bar-code scanners to keep track of customers as they move between different slopes and various resort bars and restaurants, and then deploy employees to where the action is. They have a database to track 2.5 million skiers, slice and dice the information to understand where their skiers live, the kinds of slopes they like to ski, and the amenities they seek at a resort, and then go after them with direct mail to attract them to S-K-I Ltd. facilities. Lastly, they can generate reports that tell them on a weekly and even daily basis which resorts and departments are making money and which aren't. They can then take appropriate action.

S-K-I Ltd. has used this information system to achieve excellent financial results. S-K-I Ltd. had thirty consecutive years of profit growth between 1959 and 1989 and hit a record revenue high in 1994 of $99 million.

Lest you think that S-K-I Ltd. only uses computers to get a handle on its business, I should mention that it's a requirement for managers to hit the slopes early and often. As CEO Preston Smith says, "It's a way of sharing the customer's experience."[6]

## Knowing Your Market

In addition to knowing the strengths and weaknesses of yourself and your competitor, you must also know the "terrain" on which you will be fighting, the business environment in which you will operate.

- When employing troops it is essential to know beforehand the conditions of the terrain. Knowing the distances, one can make use of an indirect or a direct plan. If he knows the degree of ease or difficulty of traversing the ground he can estimate the advan-

> tages of using infantry or cavalry. If one knows where the ground
> is constricted and where open he can calculate the size of force
> appropriate. If he knows where he will give battle he knows
> when to concentrate or divide his forces.   (I.6 Mei Yao-ch'en)

To know the business terrain, you need to perform in-depth market research and analysis. You must know the size of the markets you wish to battle over, how fast they are growing, and the industry forces in each market. You will then be able to project "the ease or difficulty of traversing the ground" and whether to "concentrate or divide" your forces.

To discover basic market information, you can rely on industry trade journals and market estimates or conduct primary research on your own. You can also rely on your sales force and those employees who are constantly coming into contact with customers. However, an infrastructure must be in place to ensure that market information is getting back to you, the strategist. Without this infrastructure, much of the information you need to know to understand the market terrain will be lost.

It is amazing the number of instances in companies where vital data on the marketplace or on competitors exist but the infrastructure does not allow it to get back to the decision-makers. By infrastructure, I mean formal processes that exist to link up the sources of competitor and market information with the analysts who can interpret the data, and who then bring that new information forward to executives for action on a timely basis.

For instance, much of the reason Borden, Inc was one of the food industry's worst performers in 1993 was the result of a lack of fore-knowledge. Sales fell from $7.1 billion in 1992 to $5.5 billion in 1993, while common-share earnings were −40 cents per share. The Borden CEO at the time stated that poor internal controls were a major factor contributing to lackluster results in Borden's dairy division. In trying to deal with price-fixing allegations, the CEO wiped out forty regional managers who could change prices independently based on local market conditions. Losing these regional sources of information destroyed Borden's ability to understand those local market forces. On top of that problem, Borden's computer systems were incompatible. Efforts to fix them, combined with the centralizing of pricing and corresponding loss of local market intelligence sources, resulted in disaster. "If we had sat there and done nothing to dairy, our bottom line would be better," said the CEO. As a result of these failures, Borden's board forced its CEO and other top officers to resign, then put the company up for sale.[7]

Market information has become so critical to companies that business gurus talk of "information wars" in which different companies in the same value chain battle to get customer information. Whoever has the customer information has the competitive advantage because they can use that information to create closer ties to their customers, reduce the number of middlemen, and make faster decisions. In the information age, the old adage that knowledge is power is more true than ever.[8]

Military organizations understand the need for intelligence. In well-run military organizations, data-gathering infrastructures include processes that train individual soldiers to look for key enemy information and bring it back to teams of intelligence analysts who visit the frontline units on a regular basis. The infrastructure also provides for the collection of data from satellites and listening posts that pick up signs and signals of larger enemy movements. These two types of data are then pieced together to form a complete, holistic picture of the situation.

For example, during Desert Storm, the American intelligence team in Riyadh, Saudi Arabia, developed a unique approach for assessing the damage Allied aircraft were inflicting on the Iraqi army. Combining interviews with pilots and gun-camera footage with satellite and aerial photos, they were able to fashion a sophisticated and accurate method of understanding the fast-moving battlefield dynamics. To communicate this intelligence to General Schwartzkopf, they created a simple color-coded scheme that could tell him at a glance the state of the forces that opposed him. The ground-attack portion of Desert Storm proved that this information system provided excellent and accurate data, while that compiled by the CIA solely by satellite back in Washington, D.C., was off by a factor of two to three times.[9]

As master strategist, you should establish a similar infrastructure. Train salespeople to find out what your competition is doing and what your customers are asking for and then set up a means (standard reports, E-mail) to get that information quickly back to headquarters. Send your market and competitive analysts out to meet with groups of customers and salespeople regularly to find out what is happening "on the ground." Have monthly or quarterly meetings with your analysts that provide a forum for discussion of this information and the overall "big picture."

One specialty chemical company was able to do this without huge resources. Its CEO built an intelligence-gathering system that extended throughout the company. He had employees group themselves into seven-person cross-functional teams. These teams were then assigned to scan ten newspapers or magazines a month; these periodicals were to be ones that the group would not normally look at. This approach got the group finding out about things that were happening outside their industry and their functional specialty.

By cutting out interesting articles, putting them into files that circulated among the seven team members, and then meeting quarterly to discuss their findings, these teams were able to inform themselves of important trends. This process was assisted by having these groups review the articles with three thoughts in mind:

1. What is the future event that will have the greatest impact on our business?

2. What will happen when that event occurs?

3. What can we do now to prepare for that event?

These key events were then sent to top management so that executives could make strategic plans with a much better grasp of the environment. It also made every employee his or her own futurist, expanding their views beyond their original job scopes.[10]

As this example shows, while it is certainly possible to have too much data coming at you, an intelligence-processing infrastructure allows you to turn that data into knowledge about yourself, your competitors, and the business terrain. Without it, "you are certain in every battle to be in peril."

### Deception

It is not enough to know yourself, the business terrain, and your competitor. The other side of the equation is ensuring that your competition is unable to know you. This is where deception comes in.

■ All warfare is based on deception.  (I.17)

By leaving the Trojan horse abandoned outside the walls of Troy and supposedly sailing away, the Greeks deceived the Trojans into bringing the horse within their city. After night fell, the Greeks emerged from the horse and sacked Troy. By using his cavalry to screen his quick movements and deny his enemy knowledge of his intentions,

Robert E. Lee kept the Union's numerically stronger Army of the Potomac on the defensive for most of the Civil War. By setting up a fake Army Group under General George Patton with bogus camps and radio traffic, the Allies deceived the Germans about the location of their invasion of Europe. Success in conflict is indeed based on deception and companies can find the selected use of deception effective.

- The ultimate in disposing one's troops is to be without ascertainable shape. Then the most penetrating spies cannot pry in nor can the wise lay plans against you. (VI.24)

The logic is straightforward. To beat your competitor, you must first deceive its executives about the true nature of your plans. If they do not know where you will attack next, they will be confused and unable to respond effectively.

- The enemy must not know where I intend to give battle. For if he does not know where I intend to give battle he must prepare in a great many places. And when he prepares in a great many places, those I have to fight in any one place will be few. (VI.14)

Deception not only allows you to force your competitor to waste resources by allocating them incorrectly, it also creates weak spots to attack by making its management unsure of your intentions.

- For if he prepares to the front his rear will be weak, and if to the rear, his front will be fragile. If he prepares to the left, his right will be vulnerable and if to the right, there will be few on his left. And when he prepares everywhere he will be weak everywhere. (VI.15)

A study in the use of deception takes us back to Hanson PLC's hostile takeover of Smith-Corona, also known as the SCM Corporation.

Sir Gordon White first moved to acquire SCM with a formal tender offer of $60 per share. SCM's management, interested in buying the firm itself, offered a bid of $70 per share to stockholders. In response, Hanson PLC increased its bid to $72 per share. In an effort to shake Sir Gordon loose, SCM management gave Merrill Lynch the option to buy two of its best divisions at a large discount if Hanson PLC gained control of the company.

White promptly withdrew his tender offer, which on Wall Street meant that he was giving up. Like the Greeks, he appeared to have boarded his ships and sailed away. SCM management thought the battle was over so they let down their guard. However, it was far from over. Contrary to Wall Street custom, White instead purchased 25% of SCM's shares at $73.50 per share on the open market, thereby increasing Hanson PLC's stake to 27% of the total shares outstanding. SCM management was furious and launched a lawsuit. Hanson PLC countersued and won on appeal. White then purchased even more stock and now held almost 33% of the outstanding shares, thus stopping SCM management's leveraged-buyout plan, which required approval by two-thirds of SCM's shareholders.

After more moves, countermoves, and lawsuits, Hanson PLC ultimately took over SCM and made out handsomely by selling off pieces as mentioned earlier. However, the key to Hanson PLC's success was that Sir Gordon knew that he could not let his competition know where and how he intended to give battle.[11]

> ■ Lay on many deceptive operations. Be seen in the west and march out of the east; lure him in the north and strike in the south. Drive him crazy and bewilder him so that he disperses his forces in confusion.   (XI.26 Meng)

Hanson PLC's takeover of SCM is only one example of ethical and lawful misdirection in business. Indeed, there are many ways to deceive the competition.

> ■ Therefore, when capable, feign incapacity: when active, inactivity.
>
> When near, make it appear that you are far away; when far away, that you are near.
>
> Offer the enemy a bait to lure him; feign disorder and strike him.   (I.18–20)

For instance, if you are planning to come out with a new product whose capabilities will surprise your competitors and you are asked by the press if these are your plans, do not feel constrained to disclose everything. That is proprietary information. Instead, give answers that leave open many possibilities or conclusions.

On the other hand, if competitors expect you to come out with an offering in a certain market but you are not planning to, it may be to your advantage to encourage their belief. They will then waste resources preparing for an attack that will never come.

When asked about the strengths of your company, do not list them all or tell everyone how you do things. You may as well give away your products or services for free! Instead, be opaque about the workings of your firm and hide the secrets of your success.

> ■ I make the enemy see my strengths as weaknesses and my weaknesses as strengths while I cause his strengths to become weaknesses and discover where he is not strong. . . . I conceal my tracks so that none can discern them; I keep silence so that none can hear me.   (VI.9 Ho Yen-hsi)

At times it may be better to let your competitors think you are not as strong as you really are. Let them underestimate your potential. Then when you attack they will be unprepared. Thus, deception provides surprise, which in turn produces victory.

> ■ Therefore, against those skilled in attack, an enemy does not know where to defend; against the experts in defence, the enemy does not know where to attack.
>
> They make it impossible for an enemy to know where to prepare. They release the attack like a lightning bolt from above the nine-layered heavens.   (VI.8; IV.7 Tu Yu)

To deceive requires discipline, to mislead requires control, to ensure secrecy requires security. A company poorly led cannot deceive convincingly.

> ■ Apparent confusion is a product of good order: apparent cowardice, of courage, apparent weakness, of strength.   (V.18)

In the 1970s and early 1980s IBM was a very security-conscious company. In its research and development labs, badge-readers stopped people at the door, security personnel ensured that all desks were locked at night, and only a limited number of employees were allowed to talk to the press or even to customers. In the late 1980s, in an effort to become more open with its customers, IBM allowed much more liberty to employees and greater access to its labs. Although increased openness was beneficial, at times the liberty to talk to the press was abused. Employees from different divisions publicly attacked each others' products. Too many employees were allowed to give their view of IBM strategy. The result was confusion for customers and employees. Furthermore, IBM's competitors were able to pick up on and exploit the weaknesses that had been brought out into the open by employees. The openness had gone too far.

After taking over IBM in 1993, Louis Gerstner observed that at times IBM had been its own worst enemy. Using a more disciplined approach to communications, Gerstner worked to put his house in order by stopping the public infighting, emphasizing teamwork, and ensuring that only approved messages go out. Although for reasons we'll discuss next, large companies such as IBM cannot intentionally mislead people about their strategy, the use of simple methods shows that a company can deliver a clear and consistent story to its customers while stopping leaks about its weak points to competitors.[12]

## Constraints on Deception

Obviously, there are constraints on deception. Small firms and private firms have more leeway when it comes to practicing deception, since private firms are not accountable to public stockholders and smaller firms' actions are less noticed. Conversely, it is not as easy for large, public multinational firms to practice all facets of a deception strategy. The need for reporting to the board and shareholders limits what one can do in this arena. Also, firms that have customers with high switching costs, such as computer firms, must be very careful what they say, since their customers have so much riding on future products.

It is also more difficult to keep secrets in the open culture of the United States. Countries with more secretive cultures may have an advantage here as well. In 1993, I visited a auto manufacturing plant in Hungary that was run by Suzuki. In the entire plant population of 500 people, there were only two Japanese employees. Talking to Suzuki's Hungarian spokeswoman, I got the impression that, while there were Hungarians in management, the two Japanese managers were the ones who really ran the place. And, interestingly, the official languages of the plant were not Hungarian and Japanese, but Hungarian and English. The spokesperson told our tour group that learning Japanese was discouraged. My feeling was that this allowed top management to keep their strategy and plans to themselves and communicate only what they felt was necessary for their employees to do their jobs. While I think that this perhaps goes beyond the positive use of deception, it does serve as an example of how secrecy is much more revered and utilized in some corporate cultures than others.

So, there are limits to deception depending on whether your firm is public or private, small or large, American or global. However, there is still room for taking advantage of this secret. You can have good security and curtail leaks by disciplining people via dismissals and legal action. You can set aside small groups to come out with new products and sequester them from the rest of the organization. Finally, you can avoid giving out responses to the press, for silence can be as effective as misdirection. When it was rumored that Procter & Gamble was considering a new pricing scheme to cut distribution costs, a P&G spokeswoman said that the company didn't have "a specific plan to change pricing in place, and we simply are not going to comment on what we may or may not do in the future."[3]

### Summary

To conquer, you must combine foreknowledge and deception. Learn everything you can about your competition—not just the facts about your competitor but also its capabilities, culture, and mindset. Know what your competitor will do in response to your attacks.

Learn the details of the workings of your own firm. Know its products, its processes, and its people. Understand its strengths and weaknesses. Determine what it is capable of doing and, just as important, what it is incapable of doing.

Know the business terrain on which you will meet your competition. Determine which markets are fertile and which are fallow, which can support your company on its march toward victory and which are wastelands that should not be entered. Build an intelligence infrastructure to provide this knowledge.

Lastly, practice deception where prudent to mask your intentions from your competitor. Keep their executives in the dark and ignorant about your movements. Do not let them know the time and the place of your attack.

■ If I am able to determine the enemy's dispositions while at the same time I conceal my own then I can concentrate and he must

> divide. And if I concentrate while he divides, I can use my entire
> strength to attack a fraction of his. There, I will be numerically
> superior. Then, if I am able to use many to strike few at the
> selected point, those I deal with will be in dire straits.   (VI.13)

Foreknowledge and deception give you the advantage. As you will
learn in the next chapter, speed and preparation allow you to capitalize
on it.

# 4 ■ Speed and Preparation
## *Moving Swiftly To Overcome Your Competitors*

■ Speed is the essence of war. Take advantage of the enemy's unpreparedness; travel by unexpected routes and strike him where
he has taken no precautions.   (XI.29)

In business, as in war, speed is essential. The very nature of business
competition is change, and its pace continues to accelerate; to be slow
is to become extinct. To survive and prosper in the dynamic and chaotic world that is today and tomorrow's business environment, a company must move with rapid relentlessness. And to execute Sun Tzu's
principles successfully, your company must be able to seize the opportunities it has created.

■ Therefore at first be shy as a maiden. When the enemy gives
you an opening be swift as a hare and he will be unable to withstand you.   (XI.61)

Speed in execution is essential for a number of reasons; speed is a
substitute for resources, it shocks and surprises your competitors, it is
critical to exploiting weaknesses and opportunities, and it allows you
to build momentum (see Figure 4.1).Let's look at each aspect of speed
in detail.

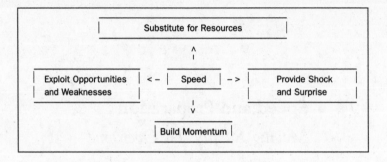

FIGURE 4.1   The uses of speed.

## Speed Is a Substitute for Resources

Speed is a substitute for resources. For example, in warfare a smaller, more mobile army can defeat a much larger one by rapid movement. Moving quickly to attack parts of the larger one before it can react and coordinate its forces, the smaller army defeats the enemy "in detail." By this I mean it destroys each piece of the opposing army before others can come to its aid.

> ■ If I am able to determine the enemy's dispositions while at the same time I conceal my own then I can concentrate and he must divide. And if I concentrate while he divides, I can use my entire strength to attack a fraction of his. There, I will be numerically superior. Then, if I am able to use many to strike few at the selected point, those I deal with will be in dire straits.   (VI.13)

Although General Stonewall Jackson earned his name by having his troops stand "like a stone wall" at the first battle of Bull Run, his true genius was his ability to plan and execute quick-hitting, highly mobile operations. Those campaigns exemplify the substitution of speed for resources.

One of those operations was Jackson's seven-week campaign in the Shenandoah Valley in 1862. In that short timeframe Jackson traveled the length of the valley twice, defeated three Union armies in five battles, threatened Washington, D.C., with capture and achieved his strategic objective of splitting the Union forces in two. With only

17,000 men, Jackson tied up 50,000 of the enemy, thus epitomizing the use of speed to overcome a lack of resources.[1]

- **In attacking a great state, if you can divide your enemy's forces your strength will be more than sufficient.   (XI.52 Mei Yao-ch'en)**

The same strategy can be applied in business. By moving faster than the competition, one can make up for scarce resources. For instance, if your salespeople can perform a sales call in a half hour while your competition takes two hours, you may need only one-quarter of their sales personnel to match them. If your company can produce a product in half the time of the competition, you need but half of their assets and personnel. Greater speed equals fewer resources, which in turn equals better return on investment.

In 1993, IBM's personal computer plant in Greenock, Scotland, cut its manufacturing time for each unit from five days down to eight hours by splitting its single, monolithic production line into six mini-lines. This action contributed to an increase in output of 50% even as the number of workers dropped 30%. In addition, quality improved and unit costs dropped significantly. By becoming faster, IBM's European PC operations improved profitability, shortened delivery times, and regained market share.[2]

Baxter Health Care Corporation, the largest distributor of health care products in the United States, reduced their order-processing time by 78%, their order-receiving time by 85%, and the number of steps in one key process from 103 to 41. This enabled them to reduce inventories by 66% and cut the number of warehouses required from 34 to 24, all while sales were increasing.[3]

These are not unique instances. It is well documented that companies significantly faster than others in their industry have returns on investment anywhere from two to five times those of their competitors. They also grow at a much faster rate. For instance, Wal-Mart was clocked at being 80% quicker than its competitors, enabling it to grow three times faster. Thomasville Furniture Company was estimated to be 70% speedier than others in its industry, allowing it to achieve a return on assets ratio double that of its competition.[4]

- **Come like the wind, go like lightning.   (VI.10 Chang Yu)**

## Speed Exploits Fleeting Opportunities

Speed is also tightly linked to attacking weakness and exploiting opportunity. You must be bold and aggressive.

- He whose advance is irresistible plunges into his enemy's weak positions; he who in withdrawal cannot be pursued moves so swiftly that he cannot be overtaken. (VI.10)

If an attack on your competitor's weak point develops slowly, your competitor has more time to counter it. This was the case in World War I with the Allies. Although they were able to achieve a breakthrough in the German trench system several times, because of their lack of mobility they never were capable of moving quickly enough to exploit the opening. German generals were consistently able to close the breach by quickly moving reserves by train to the threatened area and then counterattacking to regain the lost ground. The result was years of bloody trench warfare in which the Allies focused on wearing Germany down through a costly war of attrition.

- Experts in war depend especially on opportunity and expediency. They do not place the burden of accomplishment on their men alone. (V.21 Ch'ên Hao)

On the other hand, if your attack proceeds with speed, the battle may be over before your opponent can respond. In 1940, Germany was again at war with the Allies. The large, well-equipped French army sat entrenched behind the Maginot Line and most people expected a replay of the trench warfare of World War I. However, a new element of speed had been brought to the battlefield in the form of the tank. Able to use firepower to break through enemy defenses and then move rapidly into vulnerable rear areas to create chaos and confusion, the tank became the signature weapon of the German Army in WW II. This new paradigm of warfare was called blitzkrieg. Germany's skillful use of it to go around the Maginot Line and hit the weakest part of the French defenses was the key to forcing France to surrender after only a few weeks of fighting.

A little known fact about the battle for France was that the French Army not only had better tanks than the German Army but also had more of them. Yet the French still lost the campaign. Why? The reason involved the French method of deploying the tank. French Army doctrine called for tanks to be scattered about in small numbers and tied to slow-moving infantry divisions. These divisions could move only as fast as their feet could carry them.

In contrast, German Army strategy called for motorizing their infantry (putting them in trucks) so that they could keep up with the fast-moving tanks and exploit their breakthroughs. Furthermore, German doctrine dictated that these tanks be concentrated in large units to apply maximum shock and firepower against the enemy's weaknesses. These units, panzer divisions, were then massed at the point of attack to achieve the breakthrough. Thus, in France, a smaller army based on speed, shock, and concentrated firepower won the day over a larger one composed of widely dispersed tanks tied to slow-moving infantry.

As this example shows, you need not worry if your competitor has more and better equipment. Speed can overcome those impediments and allow you to exploit your opportunities before your slower-moving competitor can respond.

- Strike the enemy as swiftly as a falcon strikes its target. It surely breaks the back of its prey for the reason that it awaits the right moment to strike.

  Its movement is regulated. Thus the momentum of one skilled in war is overwhelming, and his attack precisely regulated. (V.14 Tu Yu; 15 Sun Tzu)

For example, five days after Southwest Airlines decided to provide service to Little Rock, Arkansas, they were up and running with two gates. Within weeks they had captured 25% of the market. When airline giant USAir retreated from their Sacramento, California, services in 1991, Southwest rapidly advanced. Within weeks of taking over USAir's gates, Southwest had captured 39% of the Sacramento to Burbank business.[5]

- What is of the greatest importance in war is extraordinary speed; one cannot afford to neglect opportunity. (I.26 Ho Yen-hsi)

### Speed Surprises and Shocks the Competition

Speed is essential in surprising your competition. By combining deception with quick movement, you can keep their management from dis-

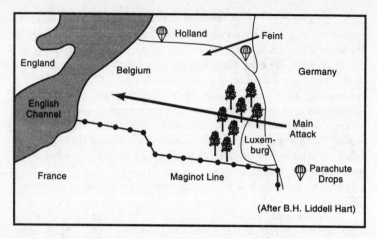

FIGURE 4.2   The German Strategy in France: 1940.

cerning your intentions until it is too late. The initial surprise throws them off balance. Then, as one of your attacks quickly follows another, they become even more bewildered and unbalanced. Finally shocked into submission, your competitor's executive team ends up paralyzed and unable to respond.

- When campaigning, be swift as the wind . . . in raiding and plundering, like fire. As unfathomable as the clouds, move like a thunderbolt.   (VII.13)

The German campaign in France was successful largely because of surprise and shock. First was Allied surprise at the place of the German attack; second was the Allied shock at the speed with which the attack was carried out.

The Germans launched their attack in the north, with two dazzling airborne assaults; one in Holland and one in Belgium. These lightning-quick paratrooper landings captured important river crossings, knocked out supposedly impregnable fortifications, and cut critical communications. More important, they drew Allied attention to the north, where the French and British expected the German attack to develop. It was there that the Allies began to move their best, most mobile forces (see Figure 4.2)

However, the real German attack came further south, through the heavily wooded Ardennes. The Allies did not believe the Wehrmacht could mass any sizeable force there, especially tanks, given the rough and forested terrain. However, it was here that Germany packed fifty of their 135 divisions, including seven deadly panzer divisions.

Blasting through the weak French divisions holding the line in the Ardennes (French units in the Ardennes were composed mostly of old men with poor equipment), the Wehrmacht's panzers drove deep into Allied lines.

Covering several miles per day, they moved faster than the Allies ever imagined, and in a week the German panzers reached the English Channel. As the battle for France developed, French and British leaders and soldiers could not comprehend the fast pace of the blitzkrieg. They were still on the World War I time clock, where attacks lasted months, not hours, and progress was measured in yards, not miles. The speed with which the initial assault came created surprise; the speed with which it continued created shock; the result was a disorientation from which the Allies could not recover.[6]

In the Hanson PLC takeover of SCM discussed in Chapter 3, one of the factors responsible for Sir Gordon White's success was his ability to execute his strategy quickly. In August 1985, White decided to make the acquisition. When SCM management attempted to stymie it on August 30, White responded by upping his offer. After SCM made a second attempt to forestall Hanson PLC, White moved into the stock market in September. SCM management, surprised at Sir Gordon's unorthodox move and the speed with which he made it, went to court on September 30 to slow him down. White responded with his own lawsuit on October 10 and on November 26 the court ruled in his favor. On January 6, 1986, Sir Gordon White and Hanson PLC were awarded control of SCM. From conception of strategy to victory in battle took only about 100 working days, including the time spent in court.

Sir Gordon's combination of surprise and speed ensured that, by the time SCM executives figured out his plans, there was little they could do except try to stop White in court. There they also met with failure.[7]

■ **When the thunderclap comes, there is no time to cover the ears.**
(I.26 Ho Yen-hsi)

## Speed Builds Momentum

The final reason speed is critical to success is that speed provides the ability to sustain and exploit market momentum once a breakthrough has been achieved. German military philosophy in both world wars was to launch simultaneous attacks within the schwerpunkt and determine which ones were stalling and which succeeding. Instead of sending reinforcements to attacks that had stalled, the German command sent reinforcements to those that were succeeding. This allowed them to push deeper into enemy territory, cut off areas of resistance, and continue the attack's tempo and momentum. Later, after the enemy had been soundly defeated, the Germans would take the time to mop up the remaining enemy strongholds.

The same strategy applies to business. For instance, suppose your company has introduced two new products to the marketplace; one is doing well and the other is performing poorly. What should you do? Which one should get more resources?

Managers often respond by giving more support to the product that is doing poorly. They figure that since the other is already doing well, additional resources should be deployed to fix the one that isn't successful. Time after time, products that are failing get attention and resources while products that are starting to take off get starved just as they are about to break loose.

This is exactly the wrong thing to do; instead of reinforcing failure, you must reinforce success and starve failure. When you have a breakthrough, exploit it. When you have found a weak point in your opponent's product line with a hit product of your own, pour resources behind it. Keep the momentum going and turn your enemy's retreat into a rout.

Further, you should never launch an attack unless you are ready to reinforce in case it is successful. If you are not prepared but launch an attack anyway, you have forfeited surprise, lost an opportunity for taking market share, wasted resources, and given your competitor a chance to learn your strategy and tactics. Why start something you cannot finish?

For instance, given the prior discussion on the German Army's proficiency with the tank, you might think they had invented it. In fact, it was the World War I brainchild of a British war correspondent and Winston Churchill. Churchill, at that time First Lord of the Admiralty, saw Lt. Colonel Ernest Swinton's idea for tracked fighting vehicles as "landships" that could break the trench warfare stalemate and return the war to one of maneuver. Although it was very difficult to convince shortsighted Allied generals that they needed one, the first tank was finally produced in 1916.[8]

To keep the new weapon a secret, it was christened the "tank," whose purported purpose was to carry water to the front lines. After being used haphazardly in minor battles, the tank's first major test came at the battle of Cambrai.

In the early morning mist of November 20, 1917, 374 tanks poured from British lines, supported by 1,000 artillery pieces and fourteen squadrons of British aircraft. The goal was to punch a hole in Germany's Hindenburg line and reach the "green fields beyond," where cavalry could exploit the breach and attack the enemy rear areas.

Surprise was complete, as German soldiers fled at the sight of the mechanical monsters. German lines were penetrated to a depth of five miles and a gap six miles wide. Unfortunately, the British generals were as surprised as the Germans. They had no tank reserves to push through the gap and the cavalry reserve was incapable of exploiting this breakthrough. The attack withered, and with it went the one chance the Allies would have to change the course of the war from stalemate to strategic breakthrough. That opportunity would not come again until many lives later.[9]

The same problem occurs in business. A product or marketing campaign is launched, but, at the critical moment, reserves are unavailable to exploit a breakthrough. For example, GM's Saturn Corporation couldn't keep its dealers supplied with enough cars in 1993. Saturn's catchy advertising program and well-engineered cars had allowed it to achieve a good deal of success in the first years of its life. Saturn's customer satisfaction ratings in 1993 were above those of Acura, Mercedes-Benz, and Toyota and Saturn headquarters was receiving 350 letters a week from ecstatic Saturn owners. Meanwhile, Saturn was beating the Japanese automakers in California, essentially Honda and Toyota's home turf.

However, early 1994 found Saturn with a ballooning inventory of cars, dropping sales, no advertising, limited capacity, and a stalled dealer expansion program. In addition, Saturn's plan to bring out larger and more profitable models was on hold. The reason: GM had put on the brakes for capital just when Saturn had started to go into orbit.

Despite Saturn's successes and the fact that Saturn had made a profit in 1993 (not bad for a start-up company in an industry that requires huge capital investments), a top GM Executive Vice-President was quoted as saying, "Saturn has got to fight for capital like any other business. It's causing them some trouble."

The GM Vice-President was right. The "trouble" caused by choked-off capital flows from GM meant that Saturn had to delay plans to upgrade the interiors of the new models, improve their styling, install a more modern engine and chassis, and add plant capacity to be able to ship 500,000 cars per year. Instead, just as Saturn was starting to take off and beat the Japanese automakers, GM decided to move their investments toward larger and more profitable cars made by the other GM divisions.[10]

■ Now to win battles and take your objectives, but to fail to exploit these achievements is ominous and may be described as "wasteful delay."   (XII.15)

The amazing thing about cutting off the capital flows in 1994 was that, when Saturn was originally conceived, GM knew it had to produce 500,000 cars per year and offer larger models to be economically viable. Yet after all the development, manufacturing, and marketing investment necessary to create a new business, funds were stopped, plant capacity was stuck at roughly 300,000, and larger models were pushed out to later years. This could certainly be described as "wasteful delay."[11]

Remember, to be successful at the strategic level, reinforce your successes at the tactical level. Exploit your breakthroughs and create market momentum.

■ When torrential water tosses boulders, it is because of its momentum.   (V.13)

The corollary of reinforcing a successful product is: when a product is failing, drop it like a live grenade. Believing that throwing resources at the problem will fix it is like thinking that throwing more soldiers against a well-entrenched defensive line will allow you to capture it. The costs will pile up and you still may not obtain your objective.

Take Crystal Pepsi. When it was launched in 1993, this "non-cola" was targeted to gain at least 2% of the U.S. soft drink market within a year. Unfortunately, it gained only half that. "I'm more than a little disappointed. We were not able to satisfy people's taste," said the chief executive of Pepsi-Cola North America.

So, in March 1994, the product was relaunched—repositioned as a citrus cola, totally reflavored, and renamed "Crystal" instead of "Crystal Pepsi."

The results? In addition to spending the increased investment the relaunch required, Crystal distracted the company from supporting its top brands, Pepsi and Diet Pepsi. "Our people can only execute so many things. If they're building extra Crystal displays, they can't build as many Pepsi displays," said the same Pepsi executive. Partly as a result of the Crystal failure and subsequent focus, Pepsi and Diet Pepsi lost market share in 1993.[12]

What should Pepsi-Cola Company have done? Dropped Crystal Pepsi in a heartbeat when they saw it wasn't the right product for the market. All the marketing hype in the world is not going to save a soft drink that people don't like to drink. Remember, reinforce success, starve failure.

- ■ Hence what is essential in war is victory, not prolonged operations. (II.21)

### Achieving Speed

Now that we know why speed is crucial, the question becomes, "how does my company become faster?" The answer is cycle-time reduction. Most often executives think of cycle-time reduction in terms of manufacturing, materials logistics, distribution, and product development cycles. These cycle times are crucial; however, two other cycle times are at least as important. These are a company's decision-making cycle time and customer responsiveness cycle time (see Figure 4.3).

Making timely decisions is essential to moving quickly . You must look at your company and think about how information is gathered and analyzed, how decisions are made, and how they are turned into action.

For example, how long does it take for information from the field to get to your headquarters? How long does it take for recommendations from subordinates to reach your executives?

Once the information is there, how quickly are decisions made? Once a decision is made, how quickly is it carried out and turned into action? Is there a means or a process to ensure that information gets to decision-makers, that decision-makers meet and come to a decision, and that decisions are followed through? Or is this all left to chance?

Think of all the companies you know with faster decision-making

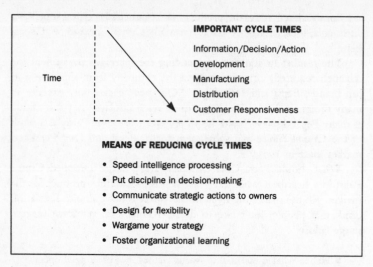

**IMPORTANT CYCLE TIMES**

Information/Decision/Action
Development
Time                    Manufacturing
Distribution
Customer Responsiveness

**MEANS OF REDUCING CYCLE TIMES**

- Speed intelligence processing
- Put discipline in decision-making
- Communicate strategic actions to owners
- Design for flexibility
- Wargame your strategy
- Foster organizational learning

FIGURE 4.3    Increasing your company's speed.

ability that found potential markets, built products, and then claimed those markets—all while their competitors are still debating whether a market exists in the first place. The Japanese automakers decided there was a profitable small-car market before Detroit did. Several small, nimble competitors found niches in the computer market before IBM identified them as opportunities. The same has happened in many other industries, and those companies that made and executed their decisions faster than their competitors are now the market leaders in their segments. Those that didn't found the market much harder to break into once a leader was established.

■ Generally, he who occupies the field of battle first and awaits his enemy is at ease; he who comes later to the scene and rushes into the fight is weary.   (VI.1)

If you wish to act with speed, you must focus on improving your information/decision/action cycle time. You can cut all the other execution cycle times—product development, manufacturing, and distribution—in half, but if you do not shorten the time it takes for your company to make and execute decisions, your company will be a strategic sloth. Your competitors will beat you every time.[13]

Let's go back to the Saturn example discussed earlier. In 1981, GM realized they could not go ahead with a proposal for a new small car when they found out the Japanese could make one for thousands less. However, in June 1982, discussion of a new small car was revived, with the knowledge that GM would have to do things radically different to compete with the Japanese. At this point, the new project was code-named "Saturn," after the NASA rocket that bolted the United States ahead of the USSR in the space race.

As you may know, the space race began when the Soviets launched Sputnik in 1957 and it shook American complacency of technological superiority. The fact that the USSR was the first to put a satellite in space and that this satellite was six times heavier than anything the United States was planning to put in orbit was frightening. In response, the United States redoubled its efforts and, by October 1961, a huge Saturn rocket was lifting off the launch pad. By January 1964, a Saturn rocket put a 10-ton payload into space—at the time, the largest payload ever placed in orbit. Eventually, a Saturn rocket, taller than the Statue of Liberty, would power the Apollo moon mission.

It took four short years from the time that America realized it had a problem until it was putting Saturn rockets into space. One might expect that work on GM's Saturn namesake would progress just as quickly. However, from the time GM realized they had a problem in 1981 to the time the Saturn Corporation was established in January 1985 was three and a half years. From there it was almost another six years before the first Saturn cars came off the line at the Spring Hill, Tennessee, plant in late 1990. Nine and a half years is certainly not record time for recognizing a problem, making a strategic decision, and implementing it. Given that GM knew what needed to be done in the small-car arena but took that long to actually get a car out is mind boggling. And, you must admit, building a small car is not exactly "rocket science."

Partially as a result of their failure to act quickly, GM's share of the U.S. passenger-car market fell from the mid-forties in 1980 down to the low-thirties in 1990, most of it coming from the small car segment. The late 1980s and early 1990s found GM's North American operations consistently losing money. One can see the effects of slow decision-making and why it must be avoided.[14]

By shortening your decision-making time, you increase the speed and tempo of your attacks. This in turn throws your competitor off balance, reduces its ability to respond effectively, and increases the possibility of having new opportunities surface. This is your aim! You must not only be able to deal with a fast-changing business environment, you must desire it, thrive on it and nourish it!

■ A general prizes opportune changes in circumstances.

The general must rely on his ability to control the situation to his advantage as opportunity dictates.   (VIII.10, 9 Chia Lin)

Listen to this quote from Southwest Airlines CEO Herbert D. Kelleher: "We tell our people all the time, 'You have to be ready for change.' In fact, sometimes only in change is there security."[15] Therefore, to shorten the time it takes your company to implement decisions, focus on each stage of the information/decision/action cycle.

As mentioned in Chapter 3, put a process in place to facilitate intelligence making it from the field to headquarters. Set up the infrastructure, using such tools as E-mail, to enable the quick sharing of competitive and market information. Reduce the barriers that prevent subordinates from coming forward with information and recommendations—too many layers of management, overly formal reviews, and hierarchically driven egos.

To increase the timeliness of decision-making, put rigor into this part of the cycle. Get the decision-makers together regularly to close on important issues. It is critical that they meet often as a group to share ideas, solve long-range problems, and create strategy. This is the only way to create synergy within an executive team. The goal is to have them know each other so well that they can anticipate each others' thinking and act in concert. They should be like a championship team, with each player knowing their part, how it contributes to winning, and how to work with the other team members for victory. If you can get your executives working at this level, you are well on your way to success.

■ He whose ranks are united in purpose will be victorious. (III.27)

In these executive strategy sessions, there must be discipline as well. Too often strategy meetings flounder because of a lack of structure or focus. There is no agenda, there is lack of agreement on which issues are strategic, there is no method for coming to a decision. At these times, it is very easy for the group to go off on tangents and accomplish nothing. Meetings like these leave everyone frustrated and give executives an unfavorable perception of strategy.

Fortunately, this is an easily solved problem. It can usually be remedied simply by implementing meeting discipline and having a staff person responsible for ensuring that the key strategic items are covered and that they come to closure. The list of strategic items to be covered should be as short as possible; it should contain only those items that must be decided immediately. Also, presentations at these meetings should be limited to those that have a direct bearing on the issues to be decided. Finally, those presentations should include no extraneous information; only data that is necessary for making the few key decisions should be permitted.

To help you avoid getting bogged down by gathering data and studying a problem until it's too late to do something about it, consider a rule that General Colin Powell followed. Using zero to represent having no information and 100% as having all the information you would ever need to make your decision, make your decision when you have about 60% of the information available. Making a decision any later than 60% risks delaying so long that the opportunity vanishes.[16]

As this book is being written, new technologies like electronic meeting systems are emerging that facilitate the decision-making process. These tools allow brainstorming, voting, and prioritization of strategic issues in a way that both facilitates discussion yet ensures closure. Typically, simpler systems include a personal computer, handheld keypads for voting, and a device that displays results. They are fairly simple to use and have several benefits, such as allowing the group to create numerous alternatives, providing the framework in which to hold the strategy discussion, keeping participants from going off on tangents, and facilitating clear and fast resolution of issues (voting tends to have that effect). In addition, documentation of the ideas created and the voting records are available in the computer for printing or electronic distribution once the meeting is over. You may want to consider these devices as a means of supporting your decision-making process.[17]

In the final stage of the information/decision/action cycle, you must ensure that the agreed-to strategy is actually implemented. Therefore, put down in writing (prose form, not an outline) all the strategic decisions that were made, and tie each required action to the name of the responsible executive. Also, list a date by each action so everyone knows when it must be completed. Be as clear and unambiguous as possible. Send the letter out to all participants, along with the date for the next strategy session. At this session, the first agenda item must be a review of the last meeting's action items. When people are making their commitments, applaud them. If people are not making their commitments and there are no good reasons why, they must be removed from their position. While this may seem harsh, you must realize that if the leaders of the business are not up to the task, many will suffer, including customers, employees, managers, and stockholders.

> ■ A sovereign of high character and intelligence must be able to know the right man, should place the responsibility on him, and expect results.
>
> The Grand Duke said: "A sovereign who obtains the right person prospers. One who fails to do so will be ruined." (III.29 Wang Hsi; III.18 Chang Yu)

Therefore, the key to shortening your information/decision/action cycle is to understand which issues must be decided immediately, to limit the information to only those pieces that have a direct bearing on those issues, to discuss strategy frequently as a group, and to use written communications and regular follow-up meetings to track results. With this discipline and Sun Tzu's other principles you can beat your competitors to the market.

> ■ When the general lays on unnecessary projects, everyone is fatigued.
>
> When administration and orders are inconsistent, the men's spirits are low, and the officers exceedingly angry.
>
> To manage a host one must first assign responsibilities to the generals and their assistants.
>
> Order or disorder depend on organization. (IX.39 Ch'ên Hao, Chang Yü; V.1 Chang Yü; 19)

### Reducing Other Cycle Times

Having just gone through the officer's course for field artillery at Fort Sill, Oklahoma, I was somewhat surprised when I joined the corporate world in 1981 to find that manufacturing functions had focused so little on set-up time. Because the modern role of artillery in battle is to quickly provide devastating firepower at the request of the forward troops and then move rapidly to another position to avoid detection, its emphasis is heavily focused on speed and fast set-up time. A properly trained artillery battery can quickly move its huge guns into a new position and be firing rounds twenty miles down-range in as short a time as six minutes. The key is that this is the way artillery is designed to function, and artillery personnel are trained and measured on it. In contrast, since American manufacturing process engineers in the early 1980s felt that speed was not important, they had not designed in a means for quickly changing their large machines from producing one product to another. Consequently, they were not able to keep up with the Japanese when they shortened manufacturing cycle times via faster set-up. The lesson to be learned here is that if you want to act with speed, you must design your processes and equipment for speed at the outset.

Since the Japanese first showed the way to reduce set-up and other cycle times, several American and European companies have successfully followed suit. The Consumer Electronics Division of the Dutch Philips Corporation cut their manufacturing and distribution cycle times by creating closer links to customers, Motorola slashed their manufacturing cycle time for pagers from three weeks to two hours, and several eye-care companies offer glasses done while you wait. There are even California hospitals that offer drive-through flu shots; you drive up, stick out your arm, get the shot and drive out.[18]

A major focus of Southwest Airlines is speed and cycle-time reduction. In 1991, its turnaround time for an airplane once it landed was fifteen minutes, versus a one-hour average for the industry. This kept Southwest's planes in the air (and making money) eleven hours per day versus only eight for the rest of the industry. It was also responsible for Southwest's cost being anywhere from 29% to 39% lower than the big airlines.[19]

All these organizations have proven that if you focus on speed in execution and cycle time, the payoff will be a reduced need for assets, lower costs, and quicker response to the marketplace. They have demonstrated how to win victories by reducing product development, manufacturing, and distribution cycle times. Because implementing these concepts has been well documented in so many other books, I will not go into detail on the "how to's," but will just mention a few. You can reduce product development time by building tighter links between your R&D function and manufacturing and ensuring that products are designed for manufacturability. You can reduce your manufacturing cycle times by shortening parts lead times and reducing capital equipment set-up times. You can reduce your distribution time by improving your order process and designing the process for fast customer fulfillment. All will lead to increased efficiency and profits.

### Improving Customer Satisfaction Cycle Time

Although time may be money, money can't buy time. Throwing money at a process complexity problem will more likely make it worse, not better. Often the answer is not automation but simplification. This requires a deep understanding of the current process as well as the desired process, and a willingness to get one's hands dirty in the detail. Process improvement is not for the faint of heart. And while the time it takes to implement these changes is significant, the payoff is the ability to respond quickly to a fast-changing environment and reduce the amount of resources necessary to provide the same amount of revenue.

Another area that must be leveraged is improving the speed with which your company fixes customer satisfaction problems. There is a lot of mileage to be gained in this arena. By responding quickly to customer satisfaction issues, your company can show it stands behind its product and is ready to remedy any problems that may have occurred. Research has shown that when a customer has a problem with a company's product but the company fixes it to the customer's satisfaction, that customer will buy again from the company 92% of the time. They will also recommend the company's product 94% of the time to others and tell an average of three people about how the company made things right. However, if they have a problem but do not get satisfaction, that customer will only repurchase 46% of the time and recommend the product to others only 48% of the time. Worse, they will tell *seven* people about the problems they had.[20] Therefore, when a customer has a problem, it pays to fix that problem and quickly!

There are several ways to do that. One is to seek out quality problems with your product or service as early as possible. You should continually survey customers who have recently used your offering, determine their level of satisfaction, and find out about any problems they may be having. In this way, you learn about potential problems and can then take appropriate action before they get out of control.

Another means is to have a closed-loop customer satisfaction process in place ensuring that people who call in with problems are guaranteed that their problem will be addressed. By closed loop, I mean that a customer complaint is tracked from the time it comes in until the customer is satisfied. Furthermore, the root of the problem is determined by understanding the underlying cause was that created the problem in the first place. Then the cause, not the symptom, is fixed.

Lastly, having a corporate culture and measurement system that ensures that management and employees focus on customer satisfaction (perhaps by tying it to compensation) is critical.

An example of finding potential problems early is Otis Elevator. The OtisLine call-in center tackles calls from customers who are experiencing problems with their elevators, including having people trapped in them. When a call comes in to the Otis representative, the rep is able to bring up information on the customer's building and have the history of its elevators at that site readily available. The representative is then able to elicit additional information prompted by the computer. The rep will then send the information quickly to an Otis repairperson, who goes out to fix the problem.

However, Otis does not stop there. Otis employees dig deeper to understand the root cause of the incident once the immediate problem is fixed at the customer location. The problem description is sent back to the plant and a team of engineers reviews it to see if it's similar to other problems they have encountered. If so, they find a means to fix the root problem once and for all. With this method, Otis has made significant improvement in reducing the number of repeat problems, thus improving customer satisfaction.[21]

### Preparation

At this point you, may be thinking that, for a company to be fast, everyone in it must run around in a frenzy trying to execute strategy. This is not the case. To act with great speed requires not frenzied activity, but rather careful preparation matched by a sense of urgency. Only by skillfully planning your campaign ahead of time can you move confidently with blinding swiftness. Only by looking at all the possibilities in advance and then acting with a sense of urgency can you take advantage of fleeting opportunities as they arise. Therefore, you must plan far in advance of the contest to ensure that you can win All-under-Heaven.

For example, before Southwest Airlines opened a new route, they did a great deal of preparation. Everything was considered, and then the assault was launched. "We attack a city with a lot of flights," states CEO Herb Kelleher. "We won't go in with just 1 or 2 flights. We'll go in with 10 or 12." Once in, Southwest will launch eleven flights a day per gate, twice as much as other airlines can put out. Obviously, to launch such an attack on a new route takes significant preparation.[22]

■ To rely on rustics and not prepare is the greatest of crimes; to be prepared beforehand for any contingency is the greatest of virtues. (III.28 Ho Yen-hsi)

You must do everything you can to ensure you are properly prepared.

■ Now if the estimates made in the temple before hostilities indicate victory it is because calculations show one's strength to be superior to that of his enemy; if they indicate defeat, it is because calculations show that one is inferior. With many calculations, one can win; with few one cannot. How much less chance of victory has one who makes none at all! By this means I examine the situation and the outcome will be clearly apparent. (I.28)

For example, in 1854 in Crimea, Britain went to war with Russia over Russia's desire to expand at Turkey's expense. The most famous action in the war was the charge of the Light Brigade, whose reckless attack directly into Russian cannon made no military sense at all (but did make a great poem). Unfortunately for the British, their other planning, especially their logistics, was as bad as their tactics.

As the result of lack of coordination between the Army and Navy, little understanding of the Crimean climate, a dearth of planning for the requirements of the campaign, and a general disdain by British officers for any type of staff work, the British soldier in the Crimea was woefully ill equipped. Lacking the proper uniforms, food, and medical care he and his mates died by the hundreds of sickness and exposure. Had the Russians been better prepared, the result would have been even an greater disaster for the British. Luckily, however, the warring nations soon tired of the conflict and made peace.[23]

■ If we have made no plans we plunge in headlong. By braving the dangers and entering perilous places we face the calamity of being trapped or inundated. Marching as if drunk, we may run into an unexpected fight. When we stop at night we are worried by false alarms; if we hasten along unprepared we fall into ambushes. This is to plunge an army of bears and tigers into the land of death. (VII.11 Ho Yen-hsi)

Contrast the Crimean War fiasco with Desert Storm, a great achievement in logistics and planning. The movement of hundreds of thousands of troops and tons of equipment from all over the world to the Persian Gulf theater of operations in a few months was itself an amazing feat. Keeping these troops supplied with food, fuel, bullets, and bombs was yet another. Coordinating the air war in which airplanes and helicopters from different nations were flying from several dispersed airfields and aircraft carriers to strike targets all the way from Kuwait to Baghdad was still another planning achievement. And lastly, moving troops from several different nations deep into the vast Saudi desert for the lightning quick strike around the Iraqi right flank was the final coup. Some facts:

1. The U.S. Air Force deployed 46% of its U.S. combat force to the Iraqi theater.

2. The Civil Reserve Airfleet, in its first activation, airlifted the equivalent of the entire Berlin Airlift every six weeks.

3. In the first ninety days of the Gulf War, the Coalition put in more communications capability than it had placed in Europe in the prior forty years.

4. The U.S. Military Sealift Command delivered 3.4 million tons of cargo and 6.8 million tons of fuel to the theater, over four times the amount of cargo moved across the English Channel to support the D-Day assault.

5. In the attack, the combat units required 708 tons of food, 34,000 tons of ammo, 804 tons of other supplies, 5 million gallons of fuel and 1.3 million gallons of water—daily.

All this planning and preparation ensured victory within 100 hours of the beginning of the ground war along with minimal casualties.[24]

■ Those adept in waging war do not require a second levy of conscripts nor more than one provisioning. (II.9)

The key to such speedy success was superior preparation and planning. If you hope to be successful, you too must prepare. You must build a strategic plan that looks at the strengths and weaknesses of your company and understands those of your competitors, studies the trends in the marketplace, factors in new processes and technologies, and takes into account what customers are looking for.

- For a general unable to estimate his capabilities or comprehend the arts of expediency and flexibility when faced with the opportunity to engage the enemy will advance in a stumbling and hesitant manner, looking anxiously first to his right and then to his left, and be unable to produce a plan. Credulous, he will place confidence in unreliable reports, believing at one moment this and at another that. As timorous as a fox in advancing or retiring, his groups will be scattered about. What is the difference between this and driving innocent people into boiling water or fire? Is this not exactly like driving cows and sheep to feed wolves or tigers?   (IV.14 Tu Mu)

Once you know these things, once you have foreknowledge, you can plan where to strike, decide how you will utilize deception, and think through how you will deploy your resources.

- A victory gained before the situation has crystalized is one the common man does not comprehend. Thus its author gains no reputation for sagacity. Before he has bloodied his blade the enemy state has already submitted.   (IV.11 Tu Mu)

### Scenario Planning and Wargaming

In addition to basic strategic planning you must also do wargaming and scenario planning. The German Army, which created the first professional staff system, coined the saying, "No plan of battle survives first contact with the enemy." Therefore, they created the concept of the Kriegspiel, or wargame. They would create potential war scenarios by aligning themselves and a set of allies against a set of opponents. They would then develop their battle plans for that scenario and, using rules created to closely simulate actual battle conditions, play out the wargame on huge maps. After playing a scenario several times, the staff would be familiar with all the possibilities and could plan ways of countering the range of moves open to the enemy. When actual battle came and combat was heated, the situations played out earlier would appear and be familiar; there were few, if any, surprises. This gave the German officer a greater sense of confidence in his control over the situation, since he could harken back to the wargame and determine a proper response.

Prior to Desert Storm the U.S. Army played wargames deep in the Mojave Desert at a place called the National Training Center (NTC). Created as a result of research that showed troops in combat for the first time suffered much higher casualties than veteran units, the NTC provides a place where large-size units (battalion or higher) can practice fighting against specially trained opposing forces (OPFOR). Since the opponents of the U.S. Army are most likely to have been Soviet-trained and equipped, the OPFOR is skilled in former Red Army tactics and equipped with Soviet-style weaponry.

Battalions come to the NTC for roughly a month, where they execute a number of round-the-clock operations against the OPFOR. Enhanced realism is attained by equipping each person and vehicle with sensors that can be "hit" by laser simulators fired by personnel and weapons systems from the other side. When troopers are "hit," they become a casualty, and fellow soldiers must be assigned to evacuate them to the rear. Therefore, not only do the combat troops receive training, but so do the support troops.

All battles are monitored at the NTC control center, which tracks the movements of the battalion receiving training and the OPFOR. It also tracks all casualties and assigns a "winner" of each engagement. More important, after each "battle," every soldier from the commander on down is briefed on what they did right and what needs improvement.

These briefings, called "after-action reports," are crucial to improving the battalion's effectiveness and increasing the probability of success in the next engagement. These reports are a result of a structured discussion on what went right, what went wrong, what the strengths and weaknesses of the unit are, and how the battalion can do better in the next encounter. The findings are then written down for future reference and to track later progress.

Thus, through experiencing "combat" and making immediate, honest appraisals of the results, the entire month becomes one excellent learning experience that cannot be replicated.

The NTC is credited as having played a crucial role in the success of Desert Storm by preparing the Army's soldiers for the fast, chaotic tempo of battle, allowing them to be confident and bold in their attacks. The preparation at the NTC also was crucial in significantly reducing the number of casualties suffered by Allied forces during Desert Storm.[25]

Although many tools exist for businesses to "wargame" strategies, many business leaders prefer to wait until they are in crisis mode and then react. They do so without understanding possible alternative courses of action and their consequences. This is poor strategy.

- The Grand Duke said: "He who excels at resolving difficulties does so before they arise. He who excels in conquering his enemies triumphs before threats materialize." (III.4 Tu Mu)

To be successful, you must be able to see and stay several moves ahead of your competitor.

- If I wish to take advantage of the enemy I must perceive not just the advantage in doing so but must first consider the ways he can harm me if I do. (VIII.13 Tu Mu)

You can do the same by setting up a group of managers who serve as "shadow competitors." These teams of managers are assigned to track certain competitors and develop a deep understanding of their competitor's strategy and tactics. As discussed in Chapter 3, they must learn everything possible about the competition so they will know how their competitors will react under differing sets of circumstances. Once they are able to do so, they can then provide the intellectual pool of knowledge that allows you to wargame your strategic options.[26]

To actually perform the wargames, you can use simple yet effective tools, such as the "Implication Wheel" created by Joel Barker. As shown in Figure 4.4, you start in the middle with your strategic action and then have a shadow team determine the possible responses of their competitor. After seeing your competitor's potential responses, you write down how you might react to each response. There may be more than one possible reaction to each of your competitor's responses.

The simulation continues for an agreed-to number of moves and then you stop. At this point, everyone reviews the outcomes, discusses how the wargame played out (there will certainly be some surprises), and critiques the various strategic moves. The greatest learning occurs here.

Once the review is done, other strategic moves can be simulated in the same way. After all the moves have been played out and critiqued, it should be clear which moves have the best potential and which are most likely candidates for the strategy trash can.

Don't limit your use of the implication wheel. Put some of your

Counterpunch A

Counterpunch B

Mammoth retaliates with an ad campaign combined with rebates, targeted at your customers.
Time to Implement—3 months.
Probability = 20%

Mammoth takes no action at this time.
Probability = 10%

**STRATEGIC MOVE**

You can create a new distribution channel that reaches a small (5%) but lucrative segment of Mammoth's business.

Mammoth's response is something totally unexpected
Probability = 10%

Mammoth responds with a customer loyalty campaign, trading services for continued purchases. Time to implement is 6 months.
Probability = 20%

Mammoth attempts to replicate the new channel to better serve their customers.
Time to implement is 1 year.
Probability = 40%

Counterpunch C:
You start now on building your own customer loyalty program, so it is ready when Mammoth introduces theirs.

Counterpunch D:
You use the 1-year lead time to repackage your product so it can be distributed more cost effectively.

Counterpunch E:
You combine your product with services and "value price"

Counterpunch F:
You build another channel that targets Tiny Company

FIGURE 4.4  The Implication Wheel.

competitor's potential actions in the middle of the wheel and play them out. This exercise will prove insightful as well.

Rather than just have a wargame with one competitor, you could also choose to wargame with several. After your first strategic move is put in the center of the wheel, have the shadow teams determine the competitors' reactions. These actions are placed in the second ring. Each shadow team is then informed of the other's actions, they ponder the situation, and then state what the competitor would do next. These actions are put in the next ring of the wheel. Again, after a set number of periods, the wargame is ended, the results are critiqued, and the learning occurs.

The reason wargaming is so effective is that, unlike hearing or reading about examples, you actually *experience* the action. By experiencing it firsthand, you integrate the lessons much more deeply than you would with other methods of learning.

Another method of preparing is called "scenario planning." It has been used very successfully by Royal Dutch Shell to deal with major changes in the oil industry. The process created by Shell goes far beyond the what people usually think of when they hear the word "scenarios."

Instead of creating a set of scenarios that exist all along the same dimension (such as a high-revenue, medium-revenue and low-revenue scenarios), scenario planning seeks to create scenarios that are very different from one another. The goal is to stretch executives' minds by providing them with competitive "worlds" that reflect very different environments than those they are presently dealing with.

To be meaningful for the executive team, the scenarios that are created revolve around key decisions the team must make. Once these decisions are identified, the most important industry trends are culled out of all those that are occurring in the marketplace—such as the falling price of industry inputs or the maturing of the market. These trends are then understood in depth, and those that are almost certain to happen are left out. They are eliminated because they can be accounted and prepared for in advance. Thus, one is left with those trends that no one in the industry knows whether they will happen or not, but their presence or absence will dramatically alter the terrain of the competitive environment.

These key trends are then grouped together to create a pool of scenarios. Three to four scenarios are then selected from the pool, based on how different they are from one another and the degree with which they will expand the executive mindspace.

The chosen scenarios are then fleshed out with specific details of world events, economic trends, and competitive actions, written in prose. The executive team is then exposed to the scenarios, and they discuss implications of the scenarios for their existing strategy. At this point it becomes clear which strategies would be successful in all scenarios, which would be successful only in certain scenarios, and which would not be successful at all.

The last step is to determine "leading indicators" and "signposts" that will tell you in advance which scenario is happening, and therefore which strategies should be implemented. As you can imagine, this insight is very valuable.[27]

If you are willing to spend more money for more complex, indepth and perhaps exciting simulations, several computer-based business simulations are available. These run from the very simple and inexpensive, to the very customized, sophisticated, and high priced. Your choice depends on the number of people in your organization and the complexity of your business. Whatever tool you choose, the key is to understand the interplay of your competitors in response to different strategic actions.

- In planning, never a useless move; in strategy, no step taken in vain. (IV.12 Chen Hao)

## The Attack/Defend/Attack Cycle

- Invincibility lies in the defence; the possibility of victory in the attack. (IV.5)

In business competition, you will find that at times your company may not have the strength to attack. You may have just joined a company or division that is failing and needs to focus on survival. In these times, you must defend the markets and customers you do hold, buying time and husbanding your resources in preparation for attacks that will allow you to grow.

- Therefore it is said that one may know how to win, but cannot necessarily do so. (IV.4)

The other situation that calls for defense is when you have successfully carried out a business assault. The fast-paced, high-tempo operations you implement to throw a competitor off balance cannot continue forever. People tire out, the competition begins to respond more vigorously, and the marginal benefits of future assaults decline. At this point, you must go on the defensive, fortifying your new gains, resting your personnel, and preparing for competitive counterattacks. In this way you keep the market share you captured.

■ Anciently the skillful warriors first made themselves invincible and awaited the enemy's moment of vulnerability.  (IV.1)

### Organizational Learning

The final step in strategic preparation is continuous organizational learning.

■ If officers are unaccustomed to rigorous drilling they will be worried and hesitant in battle; if generals are not thoroughly trained they will inwardly quail when they face the enemy.  (I.12 Tu Yu)

Contrary to popular belief, the German Army in both world wars was not an army of mindless automatons, numbingly following orders from above. As compared to the British, French, and American officers, the German officer corps was significantly more educated in the art of war and innovative in its strategy and tactics. There were a number of reasons for this.

One is that in World War I the German Army was very decentralized. This decentralization was possible because the senior officers had a tremendous amount of trust in their junior officers. The junior officers were thereby allowed a great deal of latitude to experiment with tactics, and they readily did so in the front lines. As they found out what worked and what didn't, they informed their fellow officers via army-wide reports. The better ideas also bubbled to the top where the German High Command, eager for new concepts, could institute them in all units. Unlike the Allied armies, the German Army was not an army composed of two groups—the "thinkers" and the "doers." Instead, it was an army composed solely of "thinker/doers," men who could turn theory into action.

These junior officers were also not as "junior" as their counterparts in the Allied armies. They stayed at the same rank for several years, commanding the same unit, and were therefore accountable for the long-term improvement of that unit. There they had much time to learn, and their maturity motivated them toward self-education in military art.

All these characteristics were at the other extreme in the Allied armies in World War I. Junior officers were very young, and were switched from unit to unit. The high command was not interested in any new ideas. All tactics were determined in the rear areas, far from the front-line realities. Any serious study of the art of war was looked upon as ludicrous.[28]

The professionalism of World War I continued to serve the German Army in World War II, and it counted in combat.* Quantitative studies of sixty World War II battles found that, given comparable equipment, the relative combat effectiveness of German soldiers was 2.5 times that of Soviet soldiers and 1.2 times that of American and British soldiers. This superiority was not due to the ridiculous idea that Germans were a "master race"; the difference was determined to be solely the result of a much higher degree of military professionalism and organizational learning.[29]

To be innovative and creative, your company must encourage organizational learning. It too must be willing to consider new ideas, trust its junior managers, foster professional education, promote the sharing of ideas across organizational boundaries, and keep people in jobs long enough so that they actually know what they're doing,

This last point is especially important. New, quantitative business theories focused on improving shareholder value recommend that managers and executives stay in their positions longer in order both to learn their jobs better and force them to take a longer perspective than one or two years. These theories also state that executives should be compensated not only on their performance in the current job, but also on how well their previous business unit is performing. An executive is thus compensated for the results of their prior stewardship of a business unit, again motivating a longer-term view.[30]

Although many organizations say they support organizational learning, one must look at their actions instead of their words. It is much easier to micromanage people, stick to what worked in the past, and

*While you may rightly question how an army that was so professional participated in or allowed terrible atrocities to occur during World War II, that discussion is beyond the scope of this book. When I relate the results of the Germany Army's strategy and tactics, I am focusing solely on battlefield performance. I am in no way condoning any other actions that occurred.

cut educational spending to reduce expenses. This is the recipe for organizational sterility and decline.

■ If one ignorant of military matters is sent to participate in the administration of the army, then in every movement there will be disagreement and mutual frustration and the entire army will be hamstrung. (III.22 Wang Hsi)

Motorola, Inc. is one corporation that has followed through on organizational learning. In 1993, Motorola was investing the equivalent of 4% of its payroll in training, putting it near the top of the list with General Electric. It spends this money on such things as cycle-time reduction, first committing to reduce and then creating a class to help employees learn how. It has also created a fourteen-branch network of training centers called Motorola University. This institution not only teaches cross-functional skills such as creative problem-solving and specific skills such as robot operation, it also serves to spread the Motorola culture to all employees. The results: productivity that doubled between 1987 and 1993 and savings of $4 billion.[31]

## Summary

As I have shown, speed is crucial to victory.

■ Victory is the main object in war. If this is long delayed, weapons are blunted and morale depressed. When troops attack cities, their strength will be exhausted.

When the army engages in protracted campaigns the resources of the state will not suffice.

For there has never been a protracted war from which a country has benefited. (II.3–4; 7)

The key is to move with speed and end the battle quickly, before your competitor can react. Use speed to surprise and shock the competition, make up for scarce resources, exploit fleeting opportunities, and build momentum.

To move quickly, you must collect and analyze information rapidly, make decisions speedily, and then act with dispatch. You will have to reduce all your execution cycle times—product development, production, delivery, and customer service.

As a base for rapid movement, preparation is essential. Plan first, then act quickly. Develop possible scenarios and then wargame potential competitive responses. Be prepared in advance for competitive moves and short-lived opportunities.

Do not get bogged down in a war of attrition. Plan your campaigns to be of short duration. Meet your goals quickly before your competitor can respond. If you do not, you will either have to pull out and lose the resources you committed, or raise the ante, which forces you to commit even greater resources than you had planned.

- For he wins his victories without erring. "Without erring" means that whatever he does ensures his victory; he conquers an enemy already defeated. (IV.12)

At this point we have covered many ideas: the need to avoid strength and attack weakness, the benefits of deception and foreknowledge, the uses of speed and preparation. You have taken many steps along the path to becoming a master strategist. It is now time for the next step: putting these many concepts together by "shaping" your competitors and making them conform to your will, the lesson contained in the next chapter.

# 5 ■ Shape Your Opponent
## *Employing Strategy To Master the Competition*

■ Therefore, those skilled in war bring the enemy to the field of
battle and are not brought there by him.   (VI.2)

To defeat the competition, you must first make them conform to your
strategy, your rules, your will. You must seize the advantage and make
your competitor meet you at the time and place of your choosing. To
master the competition in this manner is what Sun Tzu meant by
"shaping."

■ When the enemy is at ease, be able to weary him: when well-
fed, to starve him, when at rest, to make him move.   (VI.4)

To shape your competition, you must first put together all you
have learned so far. You must know the situation.

■ And as water shapes its flow in accordance with the ground, so
an army manages its victory in accordance with the situation of
the enemy.   (VI.28)

Then you must be able to deceive your competitor as to your plans.

- Subtle and insubstantial, the expert leaves no trace; divinely mysterious, he is inaudible. Thus he is the master of his enemy's fate. (VI.9)

And do so with blinding speed!

- Appear at places to which he must hasten; move swiftly where he does not expect you. (VI.5)

These principles are the clay the master strategist works with. However, by themselves they are not enough. You must put them all together in a strategy that "shapes" your competition. Your strategy must attack not only the resources of your competitor, but, more important, the minds, thought processes, and wills of its executive team.

To begin, your strategy must employ both a direct and indirect force; these are important tools for shaping the perception, emotions, and actions of your competitor's managers. These forces work together to throw them off balance, making them easy to defeat.

To shape the competition, you must also gain and hold strategic positions in the marketplace, using technology, key buyers, and distribution channels to deny competitors access to key markets.

Shaping the competition is also performed by implementing strategic moves and sending market signals that bait your competition into committing strategic mistakes—either leading them to enter markets that will prove unprofitable or directing them away from markets you desire.

You must also understand the nature of alliances, how they are formed and maintained, and how to sever those of your competitor. Alliances allow you to increase your resources and diminish those of the competition. Used properly, they limit its possible moves and alternatives.

Shaping your competition consists of all these tactics. Let us discuss how you execute them.

### Cheng and Ch'i—Direct and Indirect Forces

To attack the mind and will of your competitor's CEO, you must employ both the direct force, Cheng, and the indirect force, Ch'i.

- The force which confronts the enemy is the normal [Cheng]; that which goes to his flanks the extraordinary [Ch'i]. No commander of an army can wrest the advantage from the enemy without extraordinary forces. (V.3 Li Ch'üan)

When you attack a competitor solely with a direct attack, you only strengthen its resistance, both physically and mentally. Your attack is landing where it is expected. There is no element of surprise and therefore the competition is balanced and prepared to receive your blows. You cannot succeed in this fashion.[1]

Thus, it is essential to mix both the direct attack and the indirect attack together to overcome your competitor. The direct attack is the one the competition expects, and it focuses the attention of its executives in the wrong place; the indirect attack then lands, surprising them and throwing them off balance. When off balance, they cannot respond effectively, allowing you to exploit the situation to achieve total victory.

There is a type of glass shaped like a tadpole and named "Prince Rupert drops." It is formed by allowing drops of molten glass to fall into a body of water or oil. Named after a seventeenth-century prince who was impressed with its attributes, one can smash these glasses on their heads with a hammer and they will not break. However, barely touch their tails and they explode into a million pieces.[2] In essence, this is the difference between the direct and the indirect approach. One can exert great force directly on your competitor and nothing happens, but hit the right spot indirectly and the result is victory. Remember, the goal of combining the direct and indirect forces is not to nibble away at your competitor's physical strength bit by bit, but to coordinate your forces most effectively to deliver a series of stunning psychological blows from which your competitor will not recover.

■ Generally, in battle, use the normal force to engage; use the extraordinary to win. (V.5)

In the fall of 1942, the German Sixth Army was attacking Stalingrad, hammering away at the Soviet forces who were tenaciously trying to hold the city. Hitler, fixated by the political and psychological importance of the place (after all, it was named after the Soviet dictator), ordered that all means necessary be taken to capture it. The Germans, giving up the superior mobility provided by their tank forces, concentrated their armored groups in the city for street-to-street fighting. The toll on the Sixth Army was enormous, and the direct attacks into fierce Soviet resistance bled the Germans dry. By November 1942, the Germans were exhausted.

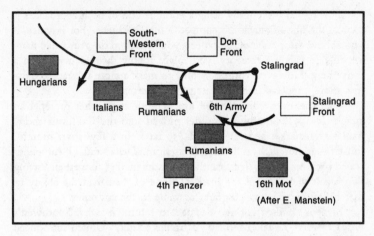

FIGURE 5.1   Soviet counterattack at Stalingrad.

Not so the Russians. On November 19, the Soviets unleashed a huge offensive aimed at destroying the Sixth Army. However, it did not attack directly through Stalingrad. Instead, the attack was indirect, unleashed at the German flanks, which the Nazis had weakened to support their direct attacks on the city (see Figure 5.1). Guarding these flanks were poorly led units from Rumania, Hungary, and Italy, Germany's allies. Unable to stand up to the Russian steamroller, they were overrun. Germany's Sixth Army was soon surrounded, and in early 1943 it surrendered. The 280,000 men, of which 200,000 were casualties, were a huge loss from which Germany would never recover.[3]

Examine the Soviet attack closely. In their offensive to relieve Stalingrad and destroy the German Sixth Army, the Soviets used the direct approach to fix the attention of the Germans and the indirect to finish them. They understood their enemy's preoccupation with Stalingrad and used it to lure them into a trap. With their opponents fixated, the Soviets sprung the trap with an indirect attack on the German flanks, gaining total victory.

■ He who wishes to snatch an advantage takes a devious and distant route and makes of it the short way. He turns misfortune to his advantage. He deceives and fools the enemy to make him dilatory and lax, and then marches on speedily.   (VII.3 Tu Mu)

The key to successfully using a combination of both approaches is to take the line of attack the competition least expects. For instance, if you believe your competitor expects your attack in the Australian market in one product category, you might follow through with such a movement. However, you do so only to mask a more substantial blow in a more important product category in Germany.

One can even combine the use of both approaches to repel an attack. In 1991, Southwest Airlines moved into the California short-haul travel market and introduced $59 fares. In a few short months, full-fare airlines such as United, American, Delta, and USAir either scaled back operations significantly or left the market altogether, leaving Southwest with 52% of the market. None of them had the ability to match Southwest's low-cost fares or value to the customer.

In 1994, United Airlines decided to return. In what Southwest's CEO Herbert Kelleher termed "a frontal assault," United introduced their U2 program, with the promise of low fares combined with better service and a broader frequent flyer program. That U2 plan called for United to reallocate Boeing 737s to the U2 campaign to increase the number of short-haul flights and then expand the short-haul service to other parts of the country should this attack on Southwest in California prove successful. United preferred not to heed the advice of America West Airlines President Maurice Meyers, who said, "Taking on Southwest head to head is unwise for anyone." Instead, United was betting that it could match Southwest's lower cost per mile.

Rather than responding directly to United's head-on assault by cutting fares even lower, Kelleher decided on a three-pronged counterattack plan that mixed direct attacks with indirect ones. First, he would reduce Southwest's costs further by utilizing the ticketless system of newly acquired Morris Air and making a deal with his pilots that exchanged stock options and profit-related bonuses for pay cuts. These moves cut Southwest's costs by hundreds of millions of dollars and would make it difficult, if not impossible, for United to match Southwest's cost structure. Next, Kelleher launched an indirect attack on United's full-fare short-haul routes in California. Finally, Kelleher released another indirect attack by starting new flights targeted at United's profitable long-haul routes.

"To the degree that U2 tries to take passengers from our short-haul, then we will certainly share with them some of their long-haul passengers. This is not a threat; it's a promise," said Ed Stewart, Southwest's spokesperson.

To better understand the effectiveness of Southwest's counterattack, it is best to look through the microscope at Sacramento's Metro Airport, where a key battle in the war between the two airlines was fought. Before the U2 attack, United had nineteen full-fare flights leaving Metro daily—four each to Los Angeles, Chicago, Denver, and Seattle and three to Portland.

Also in 1994, Southwest had thirty-one flights leaving Metro daily—all discounted. As Kelleher's strategy dictated, Southwest increased the number of its flights to forty-eight, targeting four against United's full-fare flights to Portland, three against United's full-fare flights to Seattle, and five against United's flights to Los Angeles.

The results? While United did increase its market share in 1995 at Metro and claimed to be making a profit on the short-haul flights, it killed two of its full-fare flights to Portland and two to Seattle. This dropped United back to nineteen flights, the same number it had in 1994. But rather than having nineteen full-fare flights as it did in 1994, United had only seven full-fare and twelve low-fare in 1995. Perhaps most important, United dropped its plans to expand the U2 program to the rest of the country.

Meanwhile, Southwest Airlines was flying twice as many passengers as United and grew its passenger volume at Metro faster than United (Southwest's increased 29% while United's grew 25%. Keep in mind that Southwest's growth came off a much larger base!)[4]

As this example illustrates, too often Western thought and logic builds off the idea that the shortest distance between two points is a straight line. However, in strategy, the shortest distance to achieving your business goal may end up being a more circuitous route.

In 1995, United Airlines was betting on bagging an additional $200 million in sales by gaining landing rights at London's Heathrow Airport from its Chicago terminal. Crucial to completing United's move was the success of the negotiations between the governments of the United States and the United Kingdom. The bargain traded Heathrow landing rights to United in exchange for Philadelphia landing rights for British Airways. Unfortunately for United, the negotiations broke down due to an indirect approach used by American Airlines. By asking for Heathrow landing rights as well, American changed the negotiated deal. In return for gaining additional landing rights for American, the U.S. negotiators offered to let U.S. government employees fly on British Airways. Feeling that this was not an equitable trade, the British backed out. When asked later, American executives stated that getting Heathrow landing rights was of less interest to them than stopping United from getting the additional $200 million dollars in revenue.[5]

One should also use the indirect approach to attack competing managers' emotions. On January 31, 1968, the North Vietnamese and the Viet Cong launched the Tet Offensive, named after the Vietnamese New Year. This massive offensive marked a shift in communist strategy, moving from a protracted guerilla hit-and-run war to trying for victory with one conventional attack composed of large units. Commando units attacked key government and American buildings in large cities and battalion-sized units attacked thirty major towns and seventy smaller ones. Roughly 60,000 troops were thrown at the South Vietnamese and their American allies.

It appears that a key goal of the communist offensive, in addition to dealing a physical blow to their enemies' armies, was to deal a mental blow to the minds of the American people. Without their support, the communists knew that South Viet Nam's war effort would fall apart.

The physical blow proved a total failure. American forces combined with the Army of the Republic of Viet Nam to savage the communists. Together they took back every major city and inflicted casualties large enough to keep the communist forces off the battlefield for months.

However, the communists' indirect attack on the mind and will of the American people was very successful. Even though their conventional forces had been destroyed militarily, the televised commando assault on the American embassy, combined with footage of heavy fighting, convinced Americans at home that the war would drag on indefinitely. This indirect, psychological assault on their opponent eventually led to the withdrawal of American forces and the final destruction of the South Vietnamese government.[6]

As the Tet Offensive example shows, the indirect approach can be used successfully to attack your competitor's mind. Therefore, to shape the competition, you must know how to use the emotions of its management to make them conform to your plans and commit errors in strategy.

For example, by moving into the network-operating-system business, Novell's main market, Microsoft was able to force Novell to react to its moves.

- Should one ask: "How do I cope with a well-ordered enemy host about to attack me?" I reply: "Seize something he cherishes and he will conform to your desires." (XI.28)

In early 1994, Novell's CEO made a series of acquisitions in a hodge-podge response to Microsoft's strategy. Novell purchased several software companies in order to battle Microsoft in both the application suite and operating systems businesses, two areas of strength for the latter company. These acquisitions totalled over $1.8 billion. "Without question, our major competition is Microsoft," said Novell's CEO.

However, many in the computer industry questioned Novell's strategy of focusing so heavily on Microsoft and acquiring a series of businesses to defeat it. Not only were people in the industry wondering aloud, but the stock market wondered as well. Novell's stock traded 16% lower immediately after one merger was announced.

- Anger his general and confuse him. If the general is obstinate and prone to anger, insult and enrage him, so that he will be irritated and confused, and without a plan will recklessly advance against you. (I.22 Sun Tzu and Chang Yü)

Why did Novell chose this path? It may be that Novell's CEO let bitterness left over from two failed merger attempts with Microsoft get the upper hand, leading emotion to overrule good business sense.

- Heart is that by which the general masters. Now order and confusion, bravery and cowardice, are qualities dominated by the heart. Therefore the expert at controlling his enemy frustrates him and then moves against him. He aggravates him to confuse him and harasses him to make him fearful. Thus he robs his enemy of his heart and of his ability to plan. (VII.20 Chang Yü)

Perhaps Microsoft's thrust at the heart of Novell's business forced Novell to respond in such a fashion. Perhaps it was the ability of Microsoft to anger Novell's CEO. Either way, it appears that Microsoft was able to shape Novell's strategy at will, to Novell's detriment.[7]

- A sovereign cannot raise an army because he is enraged, nor can a general fight because he is resentful. For while an angered man may again be happy, and a resentful man again be pleased, a state that has perished cannot be restored, nor can the dead be brought back to life.

  Therefore, the enlightened ruler is prudent and the good general is warned against rash action. Thus the state is kept secure and the army preserved. (XII.18–19)

Immediately after the retirement of Novell's CEO in 1994, Novell's new CEO, Robert Frankenburg, moved away from attacking Microsoft head-on. He discontinued work on a project to clone Microsoft's DOS operating system, sold off the recently purchased UNIX operating system business, and halted work on another project aimed at competing directly with Microsoft. The one-year purchase and sale of the UNIX business unit alone caused a $270 million write-off by Novell.[8]

To be most effective, the direct and the indirect approaches must be employed in endless combination. The master strategist's creativity must know no bounds.

> ■ In battle there are only the normal and extraordinary forces, but their combinations are limitless; none can comprehend them all. The musical notes are only five in number but their melodies are so numerous that one cannot hear them all.   (V.11; 8)

For example, you may combine indirect geographic assaults with psychological ones; by hitting a foreign competitor in their home market you may forestall their attack into your own.

Unfortunately, too often little time is spent on building a creative strategy. It is too easy to order a direct attack and then move on to another business problem. However, what executives are paid for is not only their ability to operate a company well on a day-to-day basis, but to build a strategy that will win in the long term.

> ■ Now the resources of those skilled in the use of extraordinary forces are as infinite as the heavens and earth; as inexhaustible as the flow of the great rivers.   (V.6)

What if your indirect approach fails to surprise the competition and its executives correctly perceive your indirect attack as the main blow? Move swiftly to change the weight and focus of the attack, turning Ch'i into Cheng.

> ■ I make the enemy conceive my normal force to be the extraordinary and my extraordinary to be the normal. Moreover, the normal may become the extraordinary and vice versa.   (V.3 Ho Yen- hsi)

If your indirect attack is failing yet your direct assault has met with success, put your resources behind the direct one. Reinforce success and starve failure! While you cannot completely control each individual engagement, you must influence and control the general course of the entire campaign. Thus, by combining direct and indirect forces, you present your competitor with no good options. They are left with no alternatives that have positive outcomes. If you use these approaches correctly, your competitor will have no choice but to submit.

- For these two forces are mutually reproductive: their interaction as endless as that of interlocked rings. Who can determine where one ends and the other begins? (V.12)

By utilizing Cheng and Ch'i interchangeably, you will be able to shape your competition and successfully destroy its ability to oppose you.

- He who knows the art of the direct [Cheng] and the indirect [Ch'i] approach will be victorious. (VII.16)

### Using Bait To Shape Your Competitor

Another way to shape your competitor and make it conform to your desires is to entice its executive team with bait.

- Thus, those skilled at making the enemy move do so by creating a situation to which he must conform; they entice him with something he is certain to take, and with lures of ostensible profit they await him in strength. (V.20)

In 1866, soldiers of the U.S. Army were in the process of building and defending a lonely outpost in Wyoming Territory named Fort Phil Kearny. In the midst of hostile Sioux, Cheyenne, and Arapaho warriors, the soldiers did their best to build and provision the fort. The detachment that went out to gather wood was often the target of attacks and the troopers that manned it were frustrated. They were being picked off one by one and the relief party was unable to retaliate effectively.

So it was with great glee on December 21 that the relief party from the fort saw a chance to get revenge. Hearing gunfire from the wood train and seeing ten of the enemy within reach, eighty-one troopers vied with each other to catch them. The ten warriors did their best to stay only a little way ahead of the cavalrymen, stopping when necessary to let them catch up.

When the soldiers crossed Peno Creek, the trap was sprung. Two thousand warriors under the command of the great Sioux leader, Crazy Horse, attacked the troopers. In bitter hand-to-hand fighting, not a single soldier was left alive. The Fetterman Massacre, named after the leader of the detachment, was history.[9]

From a business perspective you might use similar tactics. To lure away a competitor from attacking a market you are interested in, you could make statements to the effect that you find another market very alluring, even though you have no intention of entering it. Another tactic could be to withdraw from one market, allowing your competitor to reap a short-term profit there, in order to distract it from a larger, more profitable long-term market. Or you might even consider a small alliance with that competitor to enter the poorer market as a means of diverting it away from your chosen markets. Thus, by luring the competition toward other markets, you keep it out of your chosen ones.

- One able to make the enemy come of his own accord does so by offering him some advantage.

  Thus, march by an indirect route and divert the enemy by enticing him with a bait. So doing, you may set out after he does and arrive before him. One able to do this understands the strategy of the direct and the indirect. (VI.3; V.3)

### Holding Strategic Positions

Another way to shape your opponent's moves is to hold a strategic position in the industry.

- If you are able to hold critical points on his strategic roads the enemy cannot come. Therefore Master Wang said: "When a cat is at the rat hole, ten thousand rats dare not come out; when a tiger guards the ford, ten thousand deer cannot cross." (VI.3 Tu Yu)

There are several types of strategic high ground to hold. They can be positions that are the most profitable in the industry, allowing you to build resources. They could be technology chokepoints that ensure you competitive advantage. They may be positions on industry boards and organizations that enable you to influence the future direction of the industry. They may be strongholds created by attracting key decision-makers in the customer's buying process.

The positions that are the most profitable are those that provide the most value to the customer. For example, the explosive growth of the Internet in the mid-1990s offered several opportunities for companies to find positions of value. Companies that created user interfaces to search the Internet for information were seeking a place to provide value. Other companies focused on compressing huge amounts of data for travel over the infobahn, offering security to users of the data, supplying the information itself, or giving people with the ability the opportunity to conduct business electronically over the Internet.[10]

Owning key technology, such as controlling crucial patents, also allows you to shape your competitors. When the invention of "instant" photography created a new market segment, Polaroid was able to force Kodak out of it by owning and controlling ten crucial patents.[11]

Hewlett-Packard's success in inkjet printers was facilitated by holding numerous, important patents in that arena. Rigorous research and development combined with patenting as many findings as possible gave Hewlett-Packard control of a very strategic position. As Japanese competitors tried to catch up to Hewlett-Packard's lead in inkjet technology, they were stymied time and again by Hewlett-Packard's lock on key patents.

For example, as Citizen Watch Company moved to develop better print heads, they ran into fifty patents already held by Hewlett-Packard in that subtechnology, forcing them to go back to the drawing board several times to find a way around this strategic bottleneck. Obviously, this caused them to fall further and further behind as Hewlett-Packard continued to perform more research and capture new patents.[12]

- When one man defends a narrow mountain defile which is like sheep's intestines or the door of a dog house, he can withstand one thousand. (V.25 Chang Yü)

Another tactic for utilizing a strategic position is to capture a key decision-maker in the buying process. Federal Express does this by earning the loyalty of corporate secretaries through a periodical called "Via FedEx." The free magazine has over one million readers and is focused on helping secretaries improve their job performance. Corporate secretaries are a strategic customer set to capture, since they are often the ones who determine when a package should be sent overnight and which carrier to use. This move by FedEx appears to have paid off; a third of those who read it say they have increased their usage of Federal Express as a result of the magazine.[13]

Owning retailer shelf space is another way to hold a strategic position. Because of the strength of its brands, Anheuser-Busch sales representatives can often convince stores to shelve its products widthwise rather then lengthwise. This gives products such as Budweiser 50% more "facing" to the customer than its competitors.[14]

You can also box in your competition by repositioning them and turning their strengths into weaknesses. Coke's strength was its identity as the classic American soft drink, formed by decades of advertising and market presence. Pepsi turned this strength into a weakness by coming out with the "Pepsi Generation" theme. This positioned Pepsi as the drink of the young (and fashionable) and Coke as something that only older (and not so fashionable) people drank. Coke's reputation as America's traditional drink was used against it. By this method Pepsi was able to gain share at Coke's expense.[15]

Another means of controlling a strategic position is to hold a dominant place on a board or commission that influences the future of your industry. For instance, Herb Kelleher, CEO of Southwest Airlines, is the most prominent member of a congressional commission created to chart the future of the airline industry into the next century. Certainly this puts him in a position to fashion the future to the benefit of his company.[16]

- [The Hegemonic King] breaks up the alliances of All-under-Heaven and snatches the position of authority. He uses prestige and virtue to attain his ends. (XI.53 Ts'ao Ts'ao)

### Leaving A Way Out

A final consideration in shaping the competition is to consider leaving your competitor an easy way out of the market to avoid fighting over it with you.

- Do not press an enemy at bay. Prince Fu Ch'ai said: "Wild beasts, when at bay, fight desperately. How much more is this true of men! If they know there is no alternative they will fight to the death. (VII.32 Sun Tzu and Tu Yu)

Obviously, before launching an attack, you must determine how you would like events to play out. Do you intend to gain enough market share to control a new segment and push another competitor quietly out of the way? Or do you plan on totally defeating your competitor?

In January 1943, at the Casablanca Conference in Africa, Winston Churchill and Franklin D. Roosevelt, the two strongest Western Allied leaders, declared an "unconditional surrender" policy against Nazi Germany. This policy stated that no agreement short of total and complete surrender by the Germans was acceptable. While this declaration was very well received by the public, it is questionable whether it was good strategy.

Many prominent historians, supported by insights gained after World War II, have stated that the Allies' unconditional surrender policy made the Germany Army continue to fight for two and a half years longer than necessary. This is because the German Army saw no chance of negotiating a surrender that would allow Germany an honorable peace.

Had the Allies provided an offer that allowed more favorable terms, it is quite possible that the German Army may have overthrown Hitler and the Nazis in hopes of achieving good peace terms. This would have ended the war much earlier, with a great deal less death and destruction on all sides. Just as important, it would have avoided the projection of Soviet power into Central Europe, which resulted in the domination and subjection of those small countries by communism for fifty long years.[17]

Therefore, before launching any attack, you must consider this thought as well. Is total, public defeat of your competitor necessary or even desirable? Is it not logical that your competitor will instinctively fight harder if its executives know they are fighting for survival versus a few points of share?

Studies of the very competitive U.S. airline industry have borne out this logic. The research showed that the more public an attack was and the greater the defender relied on a market for survival, the more likely it was that the defender would respond and respond aggressively.[18]

In almost all cases, it is better to make it easy for your competitor to give up the share and exit as gracefully as possible, thereby reducing the amount of resources you must expend opposing it. Rarely is it worth the significant effort or resources to attempt to totally defeat a competitor.

■ To a surrounded enemy you must leave a way of escape.

When Ts'ao Ts'ao surrounded Hu Kuan he issued an order: "When the city is taken, the defenders will be buried." For month after month it did not fall. Ts'ao Jen said: "When a city is surrounded it is essential to show the besieged that there is a way to survival. Now, Sir, as you have told them they must fight to the death everyone will fight to save his own skin. The city is strong and has a plentiful supply of food. If we attack them, many officers and men will be wounded. If we persevere in this it will take many days. To encamp under the walls of a strong city and attack rebels determined to fight to the death is not a good plan!" Ts'ao Ts'ao followed this advice, and the city submitted.   (VII.31 Sun Tzu and Ho Yen-hsi)

## Alliances

There is more to shaping your competitor than knowing direct and indirect approaches. To weaken your competition and fortify your position, you must influence the dynamics of the alliances in your industry. By careful reading of *The Art of War*, one finds six rules to follow in the area of alliances (see Figure 5.2).

To increase your probability of success, you must prevent your competition from combining to oppose you. This can be done by forcing them to consider the consequences of opposing you.

■ Now when a Hegemonic King attacks a powerful state he makes it impossible for the enemy to concentrate. He overawes the enemy and prevents his allies from joining him.   (XI.52)

To illustrate, it is useful to compare two models of alliances from times past—those of the Romans and the Aztecs. The Romans were able to create and maintain an empire of client states very successfully for several hundred years. They achieved this through military prowess, sophisticated diplomacy, and by bestowing the benefits of civilization on those they ruled. This combination of power and progress served Rome well during its life-and-death struggles with the other Mediterranean power, Carthage.

When Hannibal, the Carthaginian general, came marching over the Alps into Italy, a key element of his strategy was to turn Rome's allies against her. Hannibal thought that if he could defeat the Roman legions

---

1. Prevent your competitors from combining to oppose you.
2. If powerful alliances exist, avoid attacking them.
3. If you must attack, first separate your competitor from his allies.
4. Make skillful use of your own allies.
5. Do not choose the wrong allies.
6. Know how to maintain an alliance and when to end one.

---

FIGURE 5.2   Six rules of alliances.

in the field, he would be successful in bringing Rome's allies over to his side.

Hannibal defeated Roman generals numerous times in battle, destroyed several Roman legions, and marched unhindered throughout Italy. At the battle of Cannae he defeated a disciplined Roman army of 86,000 men with an army only half its size, composed primarily of mercenaries. Of the 86,000 Romans he fought, 16,000 left the field alive. Hannibal's army suffered only 6,000 casualties, and in military history the Battle of Cannae became synonymous with total and crushing victory.

However, even with victories like Cannae, Hannibal could not convince Rome's allies to turn against her. He was unsuccessful because these allies weighed the balance of benefits Rome could provide against the potential damage she could inflict, and chose to stand by Rome. This ultimately led to Hannibal's lack of success in Italy and, eventually, the defeat and destruction of Carthage.[19]

The Aztec view of alliances was quite different from that of the Romans. When Hernando Cortez arrived in Mexico in 1519, the Aztec empire had existed for hundreds of years. However, the Aztecs maintained power not by a combination of power, diplomacy, and the benefits of an advanced civilization, but by dominating their tribal allies. For example, when the great pyramid temple of Tenochtitlan was dedicated, over 20,000 captives from the subordinated tribes were sacrificed to please the Aztec gods. Obviously, this type of behavior did not endear the Aztecs to their erstwhile allies.

Therefore, when Cortez arrived and demonstrated his prowess in battle, fierce tribes like the Tlaxcalans were only too eager to join him in challenging the Aztecs. Though formerly allies of the Aztecs, these tribes saw an enticing opportunity for retribution. Cortez was just as eager to use them to defeat the Aztecs, and combined with his tribal

allies for the final assault on and capture of the Aztec capitol of Tenochtitlan in 1521.

Roman policy included exuding power and bestowing benefits,
while Aztec policy was to dominate, thereby creating resentment. This
resentment led to Aztec allies combining with an outside force to fight
against Aztec domination. Thus, while it took several civil wars, numerous barbarian invasions, and hundreds of years for the Roman empire to decline and fall, it took only two years for the Aztec empire to
crumble.[20]

Microsoft in mid-1995 appeared to be at a similar position as the
Aztecs were when Cortez arrived. The perception of many executives
in the computer industry was that of a dominating Microsoft monop-
olizing the future of software and the information highway. This perception led to a backlash against the Redmond, Washington, company.
Although obviously there had been no human sacrifices at the opening
of a Microsoft building, many software, hardware, and online services
company executives did feel that Microsoft had in the past or was in
the future willing to sacrifice their firms in pursuit of its market growth.
This resentment resulted in a flurry of accusations and lawsuits between
Microsoft and its rivals, and eventually culminated in investigations and
antitrust suits by the Federal government of Microsoft's business practices.

The Justice Department began investigating Microsoft in 1993 and
in 1995 came to an agreement with them to change some of their
business practices. However, a new investigation was then begun into
Microsoft's plan to bundle its online service with its new Windows 95
product. Then, on April 27, 1995, the Justice Department also filed an
antitrust suit against Microsoft over their proposed acquisition of Intuit,
a provider of personal-finance software that held 80% of that market.
By May 22, Microsoft dropped its plans to acquire Intuit, losing $46
million on the deal.

Apple Computer piled on, filing suit against Microsoft in 1995 for
allegedly duplicating Apple's proprietary programming code. Apple also
charged Microsoft CEO Bill Gates with "bullying" its executives by
threatening to deny Apple access to critical Microsoft programming
code unless Apple dropped a prior suit against Microsoft. America Online, a company that provides online services to consumers, threatened
to bring a private antitrust suit against Microsoft over their plans to
bundle online services with their operating systems.

As a result of all this and the fact that other companies joined in
to complain about Microsoft's business practices, Microsoft was posi-

tioned negatively in numerous press articles. Furthermore, in at least one other instance, Microsoft dropped plans to make an acquisition to avoid another challenge from the Justice Department. All these attacks by former allies, combined with the Justice Department playing the role of Cortez, disrupted Microsoft's plans in the industry. As Mike Maples, Microsoft's executive vice president, said about the decision to give up pursuing Intuit, "Over the last seven months, we have been hamstrung in our ability to work with partners and develop a strategy. The prospect of being limited for another 12 months didn't seem like a rational decision."

The lesson to be learned from these examples is, in your quest for market share growth and determining the evolution of your industry, you should avoid acting in a manner that allows alliances of your competitors to form in the process.[21]

The second rule of alliances is, if you are faced with a competitor that has strong allies, you must avoid attacking them.

> ■ It follows that he does not contend against powerful combinations nor does he foster the power of other states.   (XI.53)

In two world wars, Germany took on almost all the other major powers essentially by herself. In World War I, Germany was opposed by Britain, France, Russia, the United States, and Italy. Her major allies were very weak; Austria and Turkey were more of a hindrance than a help. Only in the spring of 1918, when the Allied strength had ebbed (Russia had been knocked out of the war and America had yet to make her presence felt) did Germany come close to winning the war.

In World War II, Germany was one of the Axis Powers, along with Italy and Japan. However, the Axis was not much of a working alliance. Italy only attacked France once Mussolini realized that Germany was going to defeat the French Army, and Germany never coordinated her moves with Japan to any degree. Had Germany chosen to work closely with Japan, they could have cooperated to knock the Soviet Union out of the war, perhaps forcing Britain to capitulate before the United States could enter the fray. However, rather than coordinating with her allies to defeat their opponents one by one, Germany instead chose to create a new enemy and a stronger enemy alliance by declaring war on the United States immediately after Japan attacked Pearl Harbor. You must not make the same mistake; avoid attacking powerful alliances at all times.

It follows that, before launching an attack, you should find ways to separate your competitor from its allies.

- Next best is to disrupt his alliance:

  Do not allow your enemies to get together.

  Look into the matter of his alliances and cause them to be severed and dissolved. If an enemy has alliances the problem is grave and the enemy's position is strong; if he has no alliances the the problem is minor and the enemy's position weak. (III.5 Sun Tzu, Tu Yu, and Wang Hsi)

In the Persian Gulf War, the United States and Great Britain performed an amazing feat in creating the Coalition to defeat Saddam Hussein. Working bilaterally and through the United Nations, they created an alliance of forty-six countries; eighteen provided military forces and twenty-eight provided nonmilitary support and/or financial aid. The former included such countries as France, Saudi Arabia, and Syria, while the latter included the likes of Japan, Finland, and Sierra Leone. Keeping this very diverse group of countries together, each with very different national interests and varying levels of public support for the war, was extremely difficult. The leader of Iraq knew this.

Saddam Hussein also knew that, if he could break up the Coalition, he would have a chance at avoiding war and keeping Kuwait. Therefore, in one of the few strategic moves Hussein performed that made sense, Saddam focused on splitting the alliance.

Hussein's plan to break up the Coalition was based on bringing Israel into the war. If he could do that, many of the Coalition's Arab nations would have to seriously consider ending their participation in the war, since they could not be seen as being allies of Israel. Saddam realized that this was the weak spot of the Coalition.

Hussein's tool to bring Israel into the war was the Scud missile. By firing forty Scuds at Israel, Hussein hoped to force the Israelis to retaliate against Iraq.

As Scuds fell in Israeli cities, sirens screamed as their warheads detonated. Israeli women and children were filmed donning gas masks to protect themselves from the possibility of toxic chemicals being released from the warheads. The pressure on the Israeli government to retaliate was enormous. It was only by putting the destruction of the Scud launchers as a top priority, quickly deploying Patriot missiles to Israel to shoot down incoming Scuds, and practicing fancy diplomatic footwork that the Coalition was able to keep Israel out of the war and the alliance together. Saddam was almost successful in his effort to "disrupt" his enemy's alliance.

In the business world, BMW was more successful than Saddam Hussein. BMW's surprise takeover of Britain's Rover Group in 1994 severed Honda's close alliance with Rover. Honda owned a 20% stake in the company and its long-term strategy was to use Rover as a springboard into Europe. In this manner, Honda would grow its low-share position in Europe. Instead, when BMW moved quickly to merge with Rover, it was BMW that increased its share of the European car market, instantly doubling it. Honda executives were left aghast; its European strategy was in shambles. In the end, Honda wound up selling its stake in Rover and was forced into rethinking its European strategy.[22]

- When he is united, divide him.

  Sometimes drive a wedge between a sovereign and his ministers; on other occasions separate his allies from him. Make them mutually suspicious so that they drift apart. Then you can plot against them.   (I.25 Sun Tzu and Chang Yü)

You may even consider making allies of former competitors. The U.S. railroad industry has recovered partly because of its ability to create an alliance with its former rival, the trucking industry. The emergence of intercity trucking almost drove the railroads out of business, due to its greater flexibility and lower costs. However, the railroad industry made a comeback. In 1994, the railroad industry was back to carrying 40% of the country's intercity freight, improved productivity 157% between 1983 and 1992, had seven record years of freight shipments in a row, and was earning more than it had in the past sixty years. In 1993, the railroads hired 1,300 locomotive engineers and bought 600 new locomotives, twice the number of the year before. Many actions conspired to bring this about, but a major one was the introduction of "intermodal freight" carrying, the use of railroads to ship truck trailers on flatbed cars. Between 1983 and 1993 it had grown 60% and had reduced expenses for both industries.[23]

In the late 1960s the National Football League utilized a similar strategy to deal with their competitor, the American Football League. Instead of continuing to compete, the two leagues combined to create the spectacle of the Superbowl. In the process, they propelled football past baseball to become America's number one sport. Both these examples show that it is possible to make successful alliances with former rivals. Therefore, do not limit who you consider as a potential ally.

Once you have created an alliance, you must make skillful use of your allies.

- If one neither covenants for the help of neighbors nor develops plans based on expediency but in furtherance of his personal aims relies only on his own military strength to overawe the enemy country then his own cities can be captured and his own state overthrown. (XI.53 Tu Mu)

In contrast to the Germans, Great Britain has always sought allies to help her win her wars (perhaps this is why there has not been a successful invasion of Britain since William the Conqueror in 1066). In World War II, Britain first allied with France. When France was knocked out of the war, Britain appealed to the United States for war materiel and received it through the Lend/Lease program. When Britain learned of Germany's impending invasion of the Soviet Union, it passed the information along to Stalin, along with offers of an alliance. Although Stalin didn't take the British offer at the time, he gladly accepted it when the German blitzkrieg sliced through Russian defenses and drove toward Moscow.

Also in contrast to Germany and the Axis, the major Allied powers (the United States, Britain, the Soviet Union, France and China) coordinated several times on war policy and strategy. High-level discussions between the very highest political and military leadership, combined with joint operations at the small-unit level, led to a synergistic effort to defeat the Axis.

In 1989, KLM Royal Dutch Airlines bought a 20% stake in the American carrier Northwest Airlines. The goal of the alliance was to link the routes of the two airlines to offer greater flexibility to worldwide travelers and gain access to each other's markets.

By 1995, it was clear that the alliance had paid off for both carriers. After signing the open-skies agreement with the U.S. government, KLM and Northwest were able to jointly set prices, perform joint ticketing, and market together. Combined revenues of KLM and Northwest made it the world's third largest carrier in 1994. By this alliance, KLM doubled its market share in Europe and achieved double-digit growth in Asia and Latin America, increasing the amount of passengers it carries without increasing the number of its employees. Even more impressive, it was able to earn excellent profits without laying off a single employee. Northwest became profitable again, gaining access to markets, such as Rome, that were off limits before the alliance. "We sit down and conspire, we set prices, we share routes—it's wonderful," said Michael E. Levine, Northwest's marketing executive vice president.[24]

Although one must make allies to survive and prosper, do not chose poor allies just to have allies. A bad alliance is worse than none at all. Germany's alliance with Italy in World War II led to disastrous consequences for Germany. Mussolini's bungled invasion of Greece, done without Hitler's knowledge, forced Germany to divert troops to bail out the Italians precisely at the time the German Army should have been preparing for its assault on the Soviet Union. The time it took for Germany to complete its ally's failed attack and conquer Greece set the Russian campaign back two months. This delay made it impossible for the German Army to destroy the Red Army before the Russian winter came, which in turn led to the terrible German defeat and retreat from Moscow in 1941.[25]

Choosing poor allies is disastrous in business as well. September 1993 brought the announcement of a merger between Sweden's Volvo and the French car manufacturer Renault. It was the result of a three-year effort to fashion a $40 billion European car company that could take on the American and Japanese giants. However, in December 1993, only three months later, the deal fell apart. Why?

There were several contributing factors but a major one was that the existing alliance between the two firms wasn't working. Problems existed in shared R&D and engineering. For example, one source said that Renault and Volvo engineers could not even agree on which way the engine would face on a car they were building together. In addition, top managers below the Volvo Chairman had no confidence in the effort.

When Volvo stockholders found out about the real situation and the poor terms of the merger, they rebelled, forcing the abandonment of the deal and resignation of Volvo's CEO. This left Volvo unsure of where its required capital would come from and its strategy of diversification and merger in a shambles. This situation illustrates that, while it is critical to have allies, one must ensure that they are the right allies and not ones who will bring more pain than profit.[26]

Choosing the right allies is only the beginning; you must also know how to maintain your alliances and how to end them when they are no long useful.

> ■ I reward my prospective allies with valuables and silks and bind them with solemn covenants. I abide firmly by the treaties and then my allies will certainly aid me.   (XI.19 Chang Yü)

An alliance works when there is trust between the allies, true cooperation, perceived fairness, and, most important, a mutual interest. It is the mutual interest that should be the seed of the alliance.

Mutual interest results from having a good fit between the goals and strategies of two or more companies. For example, they may both want to band together in defense from an attack by another company. They may want to ally because they have potentially synergistic capabilities that allow them to cut the costs of differentiating themselves from competitors. Or they may want to work together to develop an emerging market. Whatever the reason, for the alliance to flourish and prosper, the mutual interest must be strong and lasting. If it is not, the problems of having an ally will quickly overcome the benefits and the alliance will fail.

In World War II, the mutual interest of the Soviet Union and the Western Allies in seeing Nazi Germany defeated overcame problems of mistrust, difficulties in long-distance cooperation, and perceptions of unfairness in carrying the load. Given their past histories, each side had reason to mistrust the other, coordination and cooperation was difficult because of distances and differences in language and history, and the Soviet Union felt it unfair that they were carrying the bulk of the burden of the land war with Germany (roughly 80% of Germany's land forces were fighting against the Soviets from 1941 on). However, mutual interest, supported by constant discussions and good-faith efforts, kept the alliance intact.

Mutual interest was the driving force behind several mergers and alliances between telecommunications companies and computer companies to build the infrastructure and content for the information superhighway. Mutual interest was also the driver behind mergers between companies who have strong balance sheets combining with companies with weaker balance sheets to "deleverage" the latter and create new value.

On September 30, 1993, Hanson PLC combined with Quantum

Chemical Corporation. Quantum, which was losing money and had only a BB debt rating, was a prime acquisition for Hanson, whose debt rating was A. By refinancing Quantum's 8 to 11% debt at Hanson's 4 to 5% rates, Hanson saved about $70 million. Although there were other parts of the deal that made it attractive, the debt reduction was an essential part of making it pay off.[27]

One must also know when to end an alliance. This is actually very simple. You must do so when the mutual interest that created the alliance no longer exists. If mutual interest fades, yet the alliance is continued, the arrangement will still eventually end, often with acrimony and bitterness. As in all business deals, one should end an alliance as gracefully as possible but end it nonetheless.

When considering making and breaking alliances, business leaders would do well to follow the example of Great Britain. Britain's overarching aim for hundreds of years was to keep any power from becoming so dominant in continental Europe that they could threaten the British Isles. This led Britain to make a number of alliances, each lasting long enough to defeat the country that was attempting to become dominant. For example, in the 1820s Britain supported the Greek efforts for independence from the Ottoman Empire but in the early 1840s she allied herself with the Ottomans against Russia when Russia threatened Britain's interests. However, 1848 found Britain supportive of Russia's efforts to put down a rebellion in Hungary that threatened the status quo. Later in the 1800s, Britain stood by when Prussia defeated Britain's former ally, Austria, because Austria's weakness made her useless as an ally. However, when Prussia threatened to gain primacy in Europe in the early 1900s, Britain allied herself with France and Russia to stop her.[28]

In business, even the major Japanese corporations, known for their close alliances, are recognizing that alliances that worked in the past might not be right for the future. Forged before World War II, "keiretsu" alliances were made illegal by the Allies after the war, but then reformed again. These alliances, composed of several large and small Japanese firms, are combined with a major bank and export company to form a constellation of companies aimed at increasing exports. The tight keiretsu alliances have served Japanese industry very well by providing the capital and resources to drive exports. However, the advent of increased international competition is beginning to make the benefits of these locally oriented alliances questionable. More and more Japanese firms, such as those in electronics and autos, are making alliances with

American companies and forsaking their partnership with other Japanese companies to be part of the global alliances required to compete internationally.[29]

To shape your competitor you must know the six rules of alliances and follow them. Break them at your peril.

### Avoid Being Shaped

We have talked much about shaping your competition. It is also critical that you avoid being shaped by your competition.

■ The ultimate in disposing one's troops is to be without ascertainable shape. Then the most penetrating spies cannot pry in nor can the wise lay plans against you.   (VI.24)

To avoid being shaped by your rivals, you must avoid two things: using the same tactic twice in succession and telling people how you accomplished your success.

Using the same methods twice in a row is a cardinal sin in small-unit tactics. For example, when a patrol is sent out into enemy territory to scout, it should never come back to friendly lines using the same path—it should return a different way. It should also avoid patrolling an area using the same route at the same time every day. If it does, the enemy will discern the pattern from observing its movements and execute an ambush with deadly results.

You must learn from this. Do not do the same thing over and over. Do not get into patterns or routines with your strategy or your tactics. Otherwise, you will be an easy target for a corporate ambush.

Although he was in many ways great, Henry Ford, the founder of the Ford Motor Company, relied too long on old formulas for success. The Model T, the car that built Ford, was first produced in mass quantities when Henry Ford introduced the assembly-line concept in his factories in 1914. Although only 6,000 Model T Fords were sold in 1909, in 1914 Ford sold about 200,000. They sold for up to $1,000 in 1909; because of mass production, a Model T could be had for $260 by 1924.

To enable the miracle of the assembly process as well as produce more cars faster, it was necessary to use black paint. Black paint dried much more quickly than any other color; therefore, every car manufacturer used it. This fact led to Henry Ford's famous statement, "You can have any color car you want, as long as it's black."

The invention of quick-drying paint by DuPont Company and its instant adoption by General Motors in the early 1920s changed the playing field. Using its wide variety of car models, introducing new models each year, and capitalizing on new colors, GM's new approach put Ford's venerable single-product strategy in the back seat. Even though Ford Motor Company had produced more cars than the rest of the world's manufacturers in 1914, by 1927 General Motors had taken away Ford's lead in market share. Ford never regained it.[30]

- Therefore, when I have won a victory I do not repeat my tactics but respond to circumstances in an infinite variety of ways. (VI.26)

You also must not disclose the means by which you have been successful. Be obtuse and unclear when people ask you for your methods. In this way no one can discern your strategy for winning:

- It is according to the shapes that I lay the plans for victory, but the multitude does not comprehend this. Although everyone can see the outward aspects, none understands the way in which I have created victory. (VI.25)

Remember, you do not owe it to your competitors to tell them how you achieved success!

Finally, do your best not to let people know how successful you have been. Keep a low profile and downplay your achievements; if competitors see the fruits of your labors, they will most certainly come after them. If you start playing up your own success, it may even lead to a change in your behavior. It can be easy to become overconfident when people tell you what a great job you have done and you will become less open to ideas from others, thinking instead that you have all the answers. Remember, when your hands are raised in victory and self-congratulation, it is easy for someone to hit you where it hurts the most.

### Summary

To shape your competition, your strategy must utilize both direct and indirect approaches, make the proper use of alliances, limit your competitor's moves, and take advantage of their executives' emotions. You must also ensure that you do not allow your company to be shaped.

By combining direct and indirect approaches you can misdirect the attention of your competitor's managers, take them by surprise, put them off balance, and then exploit your advantage. You must be very creative and take the route least expected.

You can limit your competitor's movements and make them conform to your desires by seizing key markets, customers, or patents, or enticing that firm with bait. These moves, performed properly, will play off the emotions of your competitor's executives, leading them to make mistakes.

By properly utilizing alliances, you can increase your strength while decreasing that of the competition. You must sever or disable your competitor's alliances, bring their allies over to your side, choose the right allies, and then maintain those alliances. Avoid attacking competitors who have strong alliances that are not easily broken. To enter into battle with poor allies against a strong array of foes is folly.

To ensure success, you must avoid being shaped. You should never use the same tactic too long. You must avoid getting into routines or patterns with your strategy.

- The flavors are only five in number but their blends are so various that one cannot taste them all.   (V.10)

All this requires leadership, which is the subject of the next chapter.

# 6 ■ Character-Based Leadership
## *Providing Effective Leadership in Turbulent Times*

■ And therefore the general who in advancing does not seek personal fame, and in withdrawing is not concerned with avoiding punishment, but whose only purpose is to protect the people and promote the best interests of his sovereign, is the precious jewel of the state. . . . Few such are to be had.   (X.19)

Truly, leaders of this caliber are unique and hard to find. As the passage suggests, they are desirable because of their willingness to put the needs of others before their own; they have strong, well-developed characters. To become such a leader, to put others before yourself, is not an easy task. It demands sacrifice. You must be willing to:

- Build your character, not just your image
- Lead with actions, not just words.
- Share employee's trials, not just their triumphs.
- Motivate emotionally, not just materially.
- Assign clearly defined missions to all, avoiding mission overlap and confusion.
- Make your strategy drive your organization, not the reverse.

As you can see, Sun Tzu does not support a martinet-style of leadership. Instead, he states that a leader must be strong enough to impose the strategy on the organization, but also confident and trusting enough to allow subordinates to carry it out successfully. Let's examine each of his leadership imperatives in more detail.

### Build Your Character, Not Just Your Image

Much has been written in the last few decades about management methods, devices, and tricks one can learn to manipulate people to do what one wants.[1] However, little has been said about what true leadership is really based on—character. *The Art of War* recognizes that, to lead and command properly, a person must have certain character traits and virtues.

- By command I mean the general's qualities of wisdom, sincerity, humanity, courage and strictness. . . . If wise, a commander is able to recognize changing circumstances and to act expediently. If sincere, his men will have no doubt of the certainty of rewards and punishments. If humane, he loves mankind, sympathizes with others, and appreciates their industry and toil. If courageous, he gains victory by seizing opportunity without hesitation. If strict, his troops are disciplined because they are in awe of him and are afraid of punishment.   (I.7 Sun Tzu and Tu Mu)

In business there are many unknowns. Therefore, wisdom is important, for it allows a leader to clearly divine the company's strengths, weaknesses, and opportunities to build a strategy. Courage is essential because, without it, a leader cannot take advantage of wisdom with bold action when the time requires it. Sincerity and humanity are crucial because, at the heart of it, leading a team, department, division, or company means accomplishing success through other human beings. Discipline is necessary, for it is required to ensure that strategy is executed successfully. All these traits are a manifestation of a strong, positive, and well-developed character.

- Now the general is the protector of the state. If this protection is all-embracing, the state will surely be strong; if defective, the state will certainly be weak.  (III.18)

| | |
|---|---|
| Integrity | Justice |
| Maturity | Self-improvement |
| Will | Assertiveness |
| Self-discipline | Empathy |
| Flexibility | Sense of humor |
| Confidence | Creativity |
| Endurance | Bearing |
| Decisiveness | Humility |
| Coolness under stress | Tact |
| Initiative | |

FIGURE 6.1  Leadership traits desired by U.S. Army.

Just as it is important to be sincere and humane, leaders must appear to be in control of the situation, exuding confidence and assurance. This appearance of confidence cannot be a facade, but must be based on true confidence built on wisdom, sincerity, humanity, and courage. If the leader has even one doubt, his followers will have several.

- Shen Pao-hsu . . . said: "If a general is not courageous he will be unable to conquer doubts or to create great plans."

  It is the business of a general to be serene and inscrutable, impartial and self-controlled. If serene, he is not vexed; if inscrutable, unfathomable; if upright, not improper; if self-controlled, not confused.   (I.7 Tu Mu; XI.42 Sun Tzu and Wang Hsi)

After the leadership problems it experienced in Viet Nam, the U.S. Army regained interest in creating leaders with character. Field Manual 22-100, titled *Military Leadership,*was written specifically to communicate to the ranks what leadership is and how one becomes a leader. Chapter Five of the manual discusses character traits desirable in a leader and developed a list somewhat longer, but very similar to that of Sun Tzu's (see Figure 6.1).

What business would not want its executives and managers to possess all these traits? A company peopled with leaders who have these abilities and business acumen as well would be extremely successful and a boon to society. Its products and services would be successful, its customer relations positive, and its ethical dealings an example for other companies and organizations.

- Those who excel in war first cultivate their own humanity and justice and maintain their laws and institutions. By these means they make their governments invincible.   (IV.15 Tu Mu)

As *Military Leadership* further states, a good leader is one who not only has the above traits, but also has the self-discipline to adhere to personal values and whose actions are consistent with those values. Just as important, good leaders do not exhibit character flaws that hurt the organization, such as indecision, deceit, cowardice, and selfishness. *The Art of War* agrees.

- There are five qualities which are dangerous in the character of a general.
  - If reckless, he can be killed; A general who is stupid and courageous is a calamity.
  - If cowardly, captured; One who esteems life above all will be overcome with hesitancy. Hesitancy in a general is a great calamity.
  - If quick-tempered you can make a fool of him: An impulsive man can be provoked to rage and brought to his death.
  - If he has too delicate a sense of honour you can calumniate him; One anxious to defend his reputation pays no regard to anything else.
  - If he is of compassionate nature you can harass him; He who is humanitarian and compassionate and fears only casualties cannot give up temporary advantage for a long-term gain and is unable to let go this in order to seize that.

  Now these five traits of character are serious faults in a general and in military operations are calamitous. The ruin of the army and the death of the general are inevitable results of these shortcomings.   (VIII.17–24, including Tu Mu, Ho Yen-hsi, Tu Yu, and Mei Yao-ch'en)

Unfortunately, although there are many examples of good business leaders throughout time, instances of business owners, executives, and managers who lack good character seem to outnumber them. Evidence of this begins in Roman times, where the saying "caveat emptor" (the buyer beware) originated, through the mistreatment of employees during the early stages of capitalism, down to the business and labor battles earlier this century. Current business issues, such as the Bhopal and

Exxon Valdez incidents and poorly handled corporate downsizings, continue. To be successful and improve their image and contribution to society, it is incumbent on businesses to expect executives, managers, and employees to have good character and to invest resources assisting them in developing it.

- When the general is morally weak and his discipline not strict, when his instructions and guidance are not enlightened, when there are no consistent rules to guide the officers and men and when the formations are slovenly, the army is in disorder. (X.14)

### Lead with Actions, Not Just Words

- When one treats people with benevolence, justice, and righteousness, and reposes confidence in them, the army will be united in mind and all will be happy to serve their leaders. (I.4 Chang Yü)

The best way to prove your leadership, to show character, is not to talk about it, but set the example. Leading by example means that you lead not primarily with words but by action. Visions, missions, and daily communications are important, yet they must be followed and supported by actions that are consistent in order to be meaningful. Nothing sends a truer, clearer message to employees about you than your behavior.

The old adage that "talk is cheap" is correct. Many employees have been burned by believing in new programs their bosses have sold them, only to find that program go quietly away as soon as the next one is announced. They have seen executives say one thing and do another so often that they have become jaundiced and cynical whenever pronouncements come from on high. Employees have thus learned to notice the difference between what their leaders say and what they do and take their cue from the latter. If you as leader say that strategy is important, but then spend all your time on tactical operations, your employees will focus on these. If you say that it is critical to listen to customers but then you never have time to meet with any, your employees will ignore them as well. Therefore, spend your time on what is truly important and you can rest assured your people will do likewise. To gain their trust, make your words and actions consistent.

■ When orders are consistently trustworthy and observed, the relationship of a commander with his troops is satisfactory. (IX.50)

The CEO of Southwest Airlines, Herbert D. Kelleher, is an excellent example of an executive who matches actions with words. An essential part of Southwest's success is maintaining its low-cost advantage over other airlines. In Southwest's first national TV ad, Kelleher stated publicly, "Southwest Airlines will not lose a fare war. We have low operating costs, so we can offer you low fares on a regular basis. It's not a gimmick, it's not a promotion with us. It's something we believe in with all of our fiber. It's every seat, every flight, everywhere we fly."

Kelleher supports his public statements by paying careful attention to even the smallest costs. Kelleher himself approves every purchase over $1,000. He says it's "not because I don't trust our people, but because I know if they know I'm watching, they'll be just that much more careful."

Herb Kelleher also claims his people are his most important asset. However, unlike many other CEOs who say the same thing and then lay off thousands of employees without a second thought, Kelleher really means it. "Southwest has its customers, the passengers, and I have my customers, the airline's employees. If the passengers aren't satisfied, they won't fly with us. If the employees aren't satisfied, they won't provide the product we need. The front office is there to support the working troops, not vice versa."

This thinking is reflected in Southwest's relationship with its employees and customers. When hiring, Southwest is looking for employees who enjoy providing service to customers. Says Kelleher, "What we are looking for, first and foremost, is a sense of humor. Then we are looking for people who have to excel to satisfy themselves and who work well in a collegial environment. We don't care that much about education and expertise, because we can train people to do whatever they have to do. We hire attitudes."

This philosophy pays off in customer service. Customers enjoy the antics of Southwest employees, such as flight attendants hiding in overhead bins, having an airplane painted like Shamu the killer whale, or seeing Kelleher himself dress up like Elvis to greet customers during Halloween. Deborah Franklin, a Southwest flight attendant with twenty-three years of service with the company, says, "At Southwest everyone can be themselves. They don't try to put you in a mold."

Measurements of customer satisfaction include 3,500 favorable letters per month and ranking second in the nation in telephone customer service, ahead of Disney, Saturn and Nordstrom. To understand how customer needs are changing, Kelleher reads every letter sent in, both favorable and unfavorable.

The "employee is important" philosophy also pays off in reduced costs, helping to create Southwest's cost advantage. Although 80% of Southwest's employees are unionized and their compensation is tops in the industry, their higher productivity drives down Southwest's costs. This productivity is enabled by a positive company/union relationship, fostered by honest dealing and a no-layoff policy, that allows Southwest to utilize more flexible work rules, leverage high employee morale, and avoid crippling strikes.

Kelleher is truly an executive who leads by example. Southwest employees see their CEO stating what is important and then observe him following through. They understand from their leader how Southwest makes a profit and how they contribute to the bottom line. This enables them to act in a manner that supports Southwest's strategy, and to trust Kelleher when he tells them something.[2]

- Without extorting their support the general obtains it; without inviting their affection he gains it; without demanding their trust he wins it.   (XI.34)

To gain your employees' trust and respect and have their actions support your strategy, you should never say one thing is important and then focus your efforts on something else. It is easy to concentrate on the "something else" if you know how to do it better or enjoy it more. However, if a gap exists between what you say is important and what you actually do, two things will happen: your employees will focus on the less important item, because they see you doing it, and you will destroy your credibility with your employees as they compare what you say to what you do.

Therefore, you must ensure that what you are spending the majority of your time on is what is important to the business—determine what tasks are critical and focus on them. Then you can rest assured that your people will spend their time on the important things and your credibility will remain intact.

### Share Employees' Trials, Not Just Their Triumphs

■ The general must be the first in the toils and fatigues of the army. In the heat of summer he does not spread his parasol nor in the cold of winter don thick clothing. In dangerous places he must dismount and walk. He waits until the army's wells have been dug and only then drinks; until the army's food is cooked before he eats; until the army's fortifications have been completed, to shelter himself.   (X.20 Chang Yü)

A leader "must be first in the toils and fatigues of the army." As the leader, you must show your people that you are willing to share not only their triumphs but also their tribulations. If you expect your team to work late, you must be there with them. If you are asking them to take a pay freeze, then you should too. You cannot and should not expect your employees to do things you are not willing to do. Show your employees that you are in the battle with them, supporting them, helping them, and leading them. Prove to them you do not think yourself special or above them. In this way, you can establish a bond with them that will improve team performance and take you through the toughest times.

In warfare, one of the most compelling stories of a leader sharing the trials and struggles of his followers is that of Admiral Matome Ugaki. Ugaki was the naval commander of the Japanese kamikaze force in World War II, Japan's last-ditch attempt to prevent the total defeat of their nation. After having supervised the effort that sent so many young Japanese men to their fate, Ugaki felt he owed it to them to join them. On hearing of the surrender of Japan to the Allies, he flew out on the last day of the war to attack American ships and pay his debt to his men. Enroute he was shot down and killed. This is a very extreme example of a leader sharing the fate of his men, yet it shows the depth of the bond good leaders form with their followers.[3]

Contrast this devotion to followers with the scene found by General H. Norman Schwartzkopf when he reported to the headquarters of the Americal division at Chu Lai in Viet Nam to serve as a battalion commander:

The place was almost worthy of a Club Med—a spacious building with screened porches and low tropical eaves, nestled on a hilltop with a gorgeous view of the South China Sea. We were seated at a long, U-shaped table with white tablecloth, china and wineglasses—

Major General Lloyd B. Ramsey, his deputy commanders, his staff, and me—as soldiers waited on us. At the end of the meal came what I was told was the nightly ritual: a staff officer stood and recited a poem he'd written about the day's events at headquarters. Everybody laughed and applauded. Then another officer stood and with a lot of joking asides announced the movie for the evening. I was heartsick. We had men—about eighteen thousand men—out in the mud and the jungle, maybe fighting the enemy, maybe dying at that moment, while their senior officers ate off fine china and recited cutesy little poems.[4]

Leadership starts at the top and both good and poor examples of leadership trickle all the way down the chain of command. It is interesting to note that a unit from the Americal division had been responsible for the My Lai incident two years earlier.

As a business leader, you must follow a different path.

■ During the Warring States [period] when Wu Ch'i was a general he took the same food and wore the same clothes as the lowliest of his troops. On his bed there was no mat; on the march he did not mount his horse; he himself carried his reserve rations. He shared exhaustion and bitter toil with his troops.　(X.20 Tu Mu)

For example, the CEO of Northwest Airlines, John Dasburg, returned a $750,000 bonus he received in 1993 from the board for restructuring Northwest's finances. Dasburg gave back the money because he did not want to lose the trust of his employees, especially since the restructuring included wage cuts of 11%. "In order for this airline to be successful, it has to be well led," said Dasburg. "Employees don't follow leaders they don't trust. Money isn't everything."

Northwest Airline union officials were very supportive of Dasburg's move, with one saying that the return of the bonus "will go a long way toward building back the confidence employees need."[5]

Another example involves the chief executive and the chairman of Cabletron Systems, Inc., makers of computer networking equipment. S. Robert Levine, chief executive, and Chairman Craig R. Benson each make $52,000 for running the $3.5 billion company.

"I find it extremely distasteful the way many CEOs pay themselves. The numbers are pretty revolting, and we don't want to be part of it," is the way Levine views the situation. Although the two are co-founders of Cabletron and together own $927 million of its stock, they forego giving themselves salaries in the millions because they believe that their compensation should come from driving up the stock price. In fact, Levine actually reimbursed Cabletron $70,000 in 1994 because his travel expenses exceeded the spartan limits he and Benson set for the company.[6]

Contrast these examples to that provided by the former CEO of Borden, who was asked to resign by his board on December 9, 1993. Even though his flawed acquisition strategy and poor operating tactics left Borden with over $1 billion in losses, burdened with high debt and a stock that had fallen from a high of $35 to a low of around $12, the ex-CEO would be able to collect an annual salary of $900,000 until November 1997.[7]

This area—executive pay and executive perks—tends to drive apart employees and senior management. Perks for executives, such as corporate jets and helicopters, private dining rooms and elevators, country club memberships, company apartments, condos, and ski lodges isolate executives from employees, creating upper and lower classes within the company. Huge pay differentials, combined with excessive perks, thrown on top of massive downsizing by large corporations, have exacerbated the feeling of employees at many companies that their senior management has nothing in common with them and cares little about their fate. General Motors, despite massive layoffs and the loss of almost thirty points of market share, had one more vice-president in 1990 than the company had in 1980. Small wonder, then, that there is not a sense of teamwork and cooperation at some corporations.[8]

Obviously, the reality of business is that in tough times, people get laid off and lose their jobs. However, these realities don't preclude good leaders from building close bonds with their employees by sharing in their efforts and the pains of cost reductions. If a general can give up creature comforts and risk personal safety during wartime to lead his troops, certainly executives can limit excessive compensation to create team spirit. Recall that the word "company" is derived from the Latin "companio," which means "to companion." To truly be a companion, yet still be a leader, you must reduce as many barriers as possible between yourself and your team.

- Because such a general regards his men as infants they will march with him into the deepest valleys. He treats them as his own beloved sons and they will die with him. (X.20)

You don't have to send bonuses back to lead by example. However, if you do want to become more effective as a leader, you should consider doing the following:

- Eliminate or severely reduce executive perks, especially those viewed by employees as blatantly excessive or extravagant. Most certainly there should be no perks that are not only divisive but ethically questionable. For instance, the former CEO of Morrison Knudsen used the company jet for personal travel, got a life-size painting of himself and his wife painted at company expense, and even charged his firm for installing petunia beds at his Pebble Beach home.[9]

  If you feel it necessary to maintain the same level of compensation to retain executive talent, replace perks with additional pay. Then allow your executives to pay for the perks that they want with their own money. Make it clear to employees that this is your policy.

- Tie executive compensation to company performance so that executives only receive bonuses when company finances improve, not when they decline. Similarly, tie executive compensation to employee profit-sharing plans, so that when the company does well, employees and executives are rewarded simultaneously. In 1987, GM gave $157 million in bonuses to its top executives. Not bad money, except that GM's North American operations made so little money its employees received no profit-sharing payout. Obviously, morale did not improve.

- Take time to meet with employees to understand their issues and see them in their own environment, not just in your office. You cannot expect to lead people you know nothing about, nor fix problems you do not know exist. For example, CEO Herb Kelleher and every other Southwest manager spend one day every quarter working in another job. This enables them to get a better perspective of the total company operations and see what is really happening while they are at their office. Kelleher himself once received an employee letter stating that cargo-bay doors often came undone, hitting cargo-handlers on the head. Kelleher went to examine the situation himself—and got hit in the head by a cargo door.

The door mechanism was immediately fixed on all planes. "I knew we had a problem. I'd seen it. The more time I spend with our people, the more I learn about our company," says Kelleher.[10]

■ Pay heed to nourishing the troops; do not unnecessarily fatigue them. Unite them in spirit; conserve their strength.   (XI.32)

### Motivate Emotionally, Not Just Materially

To beat your competition, the morale of your company must be excellent. Therefore, an essential part of leadership is motivation, for the morale of any organization begins at the top.

■ The responsibility for a martial host of a million lies in one man. He is the trigger of its spirit.   (VII.20 Ho Yen-hsi)

*The Art of War* describes many of the methods of motivation, including material rewards.

■ They take booty from the enemy because they desire wealth.   (II.17)

The offer of material incentives is the customary way companies motivate their employees. Almost everyone in the corporate world desires money to maintain or improve their standard of living and it is a traditional means of recognizing achievement. Therefore, it is important to show employees the material benefits and rewards they will receive by helping the company win in the marketplace and reward them accordingly. To take excellent employees for granted is a severe mistake.

■ One who confronts his enemy for many years in order to struggle for victory in a decisive battle yet who, because he begrudges rank, honors, and a few hundred pieces of gold, remains ignorant of his enemy's situation, is completely devoid of humanity. Such a man is no general; no support to his sovereign; no master of victory.   (XIII.2)

Financial rewards are crucial. However, they are a necessary but not sufficient condition for excellent morale. Material incentives must be accompanied by other incentives. Just as there are many ways to win an engagement, there are also many ways to motivate employees.

For example, winning in the marketplace itself motivates employees. Success feeds on itself, instilling greater confidence and further increasing morale.

- When the general is contemptuous of his enemy and his officers love to fight, their ambitions soaring as high as the azure clouds and their spirits as fierce as hurricanes, this is the situation with respect to morale.   (V.25 Chang Yü)

When Louis V. Gerstner arrived at IBM in 1993, morale was at an all-time low. IBM had been losing money since 1991 and the company had downsized thousands of employees. Many of the company's human resource policies, which were very paternalistic, had been eliminated to enable IBM to reduce costs. Employees were very uncertain of the future.

Gerstner received a great deal of advice on different means of improving employee morale; reinstitute the old policies, promise no more layoffs, reassure the employees. Gerstner instead chose to make it plain to employees that his method of improving morale was to help them win again in the marketplace. "Success can be a powerful motivator. Nothing makes people feel better than to be part of a winning team" said Gerstner in *Think* magazine, IBM's employee newsletter. Only by winning customers, increasing revenue, and restoring profit could IBMers begin to feel more positive.

- Now when troops gain a favorable situation the coward is brave; if it be lost, the brave become cowards.   (V.19 Li Ch'üan)

Another means a leader may use to improve morale is empowering employees and delegating authority and responsibility to them.

- A sovereign of high character and intelligence must be able to know the right man, should place the responsibility on him, and expect results.   (III.29 Wang Hsi)

You must select the right people and then delegate authority and responsibility to them to enable them to implement strategy—it comes down to trusting people to do the right thing. Refusing to delegate and empower in a dynamic, fast-changing, and geographically dispersed environment, where a change in supply in China can affect market prices in Germany, will lead you to disaster. None of *The Art of War*'s principles, such as acting with speed, can be effectively carried out if you do not trust people to act in concert with the strategy.

> ■ Now in war there may be one hundred changes in each step. When one sees he can, he advances; when he sees that things are difficult, he retires. To say that a general must await commands of the sovereign in such circumstances is like informing a superior that you wish to put out a fire. Before the order to do so arrives the ashes are cold. And it is said one must consult the Army Supervisor in these matters! This is as if in building a house beside the road one took advice from those who pass by. Of course the work would never be completed. (III.29 Ho Yen-hsi)

This philosophy is consistent with current military doctrine in the Marine Corps. Orders in the Marines state that the procurement or use of any equipment that allows a commander to overcontrol sub-unit commanders in battle is unjustifiable and forbidden. This thinking is the direct result of generals in Viet Nam directing the movement of platoons on the ground while cruising the battlefield in a helicopter overhead.[11]

The ability to act as one feels appropriate, make a difference, and be responsible are often work's greatest motivators. In contrast, micromanagement, lack of authority, and being second-guessed on every move are demoralizing and debilitating to subordinates. In that environment, proper risk-taking, commitment, and setting high personal objectives and standards will quickly disappear from the organization. Therefore, it is imperative that you trust your subordinates and give them room to maneuver within guidelines.

> ■ To put a rein on an able general while at the same time asking him to suppress a cunning enemy is like tying up the Black Hound of Han and then ordering him to catch elusive hares. What is the difference?   (III.29 Ho Yen-hsi)

Someone who was not allowed to do as he saw fit was Zenith Electronics Chairman and CEO Jerry K. Pearlman. Due to losses of about $330 million from 1989 to 1993 Pearlman was held on "a short leash," according to Zenith outside director T. Kimball Booker. The

Zenith board exercised heavy oversight and more than doubled the number of times it met in order to practice that oversight. The board began monitoring twenty areas of business performance, such as sales and financial ratios, and even took a hand in operational matters, such as reducing capacity at assembly plants. They also hired Albin F. Moschner as president and chief operating officer to help Pearlman. Despite all this, Booker stated at the time that Pearlman was "a first rate CEO."

Having Zenith pay a large salary and bonuses to its CEO and then not let him run the business was the worst of both worlds. How willing do you think Pearlman felt about taking risks with the board looking over his shoulder and someone waiting in the wings to take his place? For the Zenith board to create such a situation and expect results made little sense, not to mention the fact that paying Pearlman's salary was a waste of stockholders' money if he was not being allowed to run the company. Major stockholder NYCOR was so dissatisfied with the situation that it tried in 1991 to replace some of Zenith's board members.

This situation continued until 1995 when Pearlman, after six straight years of losses, finally agreed to step down. Zenith's board immediately promoted Moschner.[12]

Now I am not saying to give all the power to employees and let them do whatever they want. I am saying that if you select capable, creative, and committed people, and you provide them with the tools and knowledge necessary to meet the challenges they face, you can trust them to do what is right given the situation they face. Proper empowerment and delegation allow managers and employees to act on their best judgment, after deciding how their decisions would impact the whole company and affect the implementation of its strategy. Before you can delegate, you not only must have the right people, you must also make sure they know the strategic objectives the organization is trying to achieve.

In the U.S. Army this is called understanding your "commander's intent." The basic idea behind commander's intent is that a subordinate commander does not follow orders from a superior exactly to the letter but instead uses personal initiative and a solid understanding of the situation to carry out the mission and achieve what the leader intended to accomplish.

To communicate your intent clearly, for major actions you should consider writing down precisely what needs to be accomplished, provide background on the subject, give a due date, and detail any resources you are making available to carry out the task. Although this method may seem bureaucratic, it actually is more efficient in the long run since it reduces confusion and miscommunication early in the process and ensures that important tasks receive the proper focus.

The eventual goal you would like your team to achieve over time is to know you and each other so well that actual time spent communicating is reduced while the team's shared understanding increases. Teammates who have worked together closely for an extended period of time, have built a wealth of trust, and operate with a consistent business philosophy will learn to "read each others' minds" and anticipate how their leader and team members respond in certain situations. They can then act accordingly. This is the ultimate attainment of commander's intent.

In the first world war, the German Army had a concept very similar to that of commander's intent, called Weisungsfuhrung. Translated as "leadership guidance," the Weisungsfuhrung concept materialized in parallel with the creation of the stormtrooper concept. As you'll recall, the idea of the stormtrooper arose from the effort to break out of the trench warfare of World War I, where long lines of foot soldiers advanced directly into strong defenses bolstered by machine-gun fire, artillery shells, and barbed wire. Gaining a few yards of ground at tremendous cost became unaffordable and unpalatable, not to mention ineffective.

In response to the stalemate, the German Army formed "Sturmtruppen" units. These were small groups of highly trained, highly motivated soldiers who were very capable of acting independently and combined a mix of skills in different weapons systems (essentially a self-sufficient cross-functional team).

Individual initiative was highly prized, as stormtroopers advanced not in long lines, but independently in dispersed fashion. Their mission was to avoid enemy strongpoints and attack the enemy's rear areas, where they were the weakest. In this highly dynamic and fluid situation, when it might not be possible to stay in contact with one's leader, following the exact orders of a commander made no sense—hence the Weisungsfuhrung concept. Weisungsfuhrung demanded the type of soldier who could think for himself, interpret the intent of his leader, and then take the necessary steps to make that intent a reality. The combination of the Weisungsfuhrung and stormtrooper concepts formed the foundation for the new tactics that provided the breakthroughs Germany had sought and allowed Germany to come within a hairsbreadth of winning the war.[13]

In a sense, the Weisungsfuhrung and stormtrooper concepts of

World War I proved to be the precursors for the current-day in-formation-age employee. Bypassing the "trench warfare" of the pro-duction line for which industrial-era skills were suitable, the information-age worker must be highly skilled, highly motivated, and able to interpret the leader's intent in order to survive and carry out the company's mission in today's more dynamic business battlefield. Therefore, leaders must supply their employees not with exact orders to be carried out to the letter, but with strategic objectives to be met, and the means and maneuvering room to achieve the leader's intent as they see fit.

The payoff of delegation and empowerment properly implemented is to instill boldness of action to enable dramatic breakthroughs. To harness this power and obtain the payoff, you must be able to say to your employees (and mean it):

- When you see the correct course, act; do not wait for orders. (VIII.8 Chang Yü)

American Freightways' CEO Sheridan Garrison believes in trusting his employees to do the right thing. "Don't treat people like idiots," is the way Garrison, an entrepreneur from Arkansas, sums up his phi-losophy. Providing his truckers with the technology such as laptops to help them plan better routes and control inventory, Garrison also looks to his people to think on their own about ways to save the company money. Even little things, such as turning off engines instead of idling them when loading a truck, are appreciated.

Garrison's approach has paid off for his firm. He started American Freightways in 1982 with $1.5 million and by 1993 the firm was worth $532 million. Its 5,000 employees have rejected efforts to unionize them four times, each by a 2-to-1 vote ratio. Notes one former union trucker, "American Freightways treats us with respect."[4]

Since you must find the right person and "place responsibility on him and expect results," there must be both positive and negative con-sequences for behaviors and results. Leaders hold heavy responsibility for the success of the company and the fate of the all the people de-pendent on it. If you find they cannot take the proper action, then you must admit you selected the wrong person for that job and replace them. Success must be rapidly followed by reward and failure must be first understood, then addressed.

- If a general indulges his troops but is unable to employ them; if he loves them but cannot enforce his commands; if the troops are disorderly and he is unable to control them, they may be compared to spoiled children, and are useless. . . . Good commanders are both loved and feared.   (X.21 Sun Tzu and Chang Yü)

If you have been named to head a new area, you must be especially careful to set the correct tone right away. Be sure not to overstep one way or the other. Take time to learn your employees' strengths and weaknesses and how they operate before you take action.

- If troops are punished before their loyalty is secured they will be disobedient. If not obedient, it is difficult to employ them. If troops are loyal, but punishments are not enforced, you cannot employ them.   (IX.47)

You must be both fair and consistent, all the while using what we've discussed to build toward success.

- Thus, command them with civility and imbue them uniformly with martial ardor and it may be said that victory is certain.   (IX.48)

You will know soon enough if what you are doing is working or not working.

- When the troops continually gather together in small groups and whisper together the general has lost the confidence of the army.   (IX.48)

In the end, it comes down to truly caring for people, trusting them to carry out the strategy, and providing both positive and negative incentives for behavior and results.

- Too frequent rewards indicate that the general is at the end of his resources; too frequent punishments that he is in acute distress. [A good general] administers rewards and punishments in a more enlightened manner. Neither should be excessive.   (I.13 Tu Mu)

There is one final way to motivate employees, as the following passage indicates.

■ Throw the troops into a position from which there is no escape and even when faced with death they will not flee. In a desperate situation they fear nothing; when there is no way out they stand firm. (XI.33)

There may be times when extreme circumstances for the firm can be used to motivate and bond your employees. At these times, monetary rewards may be insufficient and even get in the way. These are the times when people want to be involved in something bigger than themselves. It might be turning around a business, it could be starting a company from scratch, it could be bringing out a new product. Whatever it is, find a way to add meaning beyond material incentives. Do not be afraid to challenge people to their limits.

### Assign Clearly Defined Missions; Do Not Tolerate Confusion

For your employees to know your intent and carry out the strategy, they must know the general strategy and their mission within it.

■ He whose ranks are united in purpose will be victorious. (III.27)

To perform their jobs effectively, employees must first understand how their efforts fit into the overall picture. Similarly, divisions within the company and functions within each division must understand their missions and how they support each other.

Unfortunately, executives and managers often assign vague or overlapping missions to organizations and individuals. Two product divisions build similar products for the same market because no one at headquarters decided which division was best suited to serve that market. Two functions within a division both perform the same work, because their executives do not work well together or mistrust one another. A manager gives two employees the same task, figuring that by assigning two people, at least one will get it done. Each of these lead to waste, confusion, and demoralization.

■ If the army is confused and suspicious, neighboring rulers will cause trouble. This is what is meant by the saying, "A confused army leads to another's victory." (III.23)

If the goal is to maximize profits, what company can afford having two divisions building similar products for the same market? Within a division, how can functions work together properly when people in one function think that people in the other are encroaching on their jobs? How can functions organize and perform well when they don't have a clear mission? How can a person do a task with speed, motivation, and effectiveness once he or she finds out that someone else in their area has been given the same task?

■ To manage a host one must first assign responsibilities to the generals and their assistants, and establish the strengths of ranks and files. (V.1 Chang Yü)

Through the 1980s and early 1990s, General Motors had great lack of clarity in the missions of their divisions. When Alfred P. Sloan created the division structure in GM in the 1920s, he set it up with the idea that each division built a certain kind of product for a certain market. Chevrolet would build cars for the common person or the one just starting out, but as one progressed in a job and status a brand new Pontiac might be desirable, then an Oldsmobile, followed by a Buick, and then perhaps even a Cadillac.[15]

However, over time the missions assigned to the divisions were not followed and boundaries became blurred. Each division started building a wider line of cars. Differentiation between cars produced by each division dissolved and the names that used to mean something, such as Buick or Cadillac, meant less. Clear direction and control over the divisions was not maintained at corporate headquarters. Each division tried to become all things to all people and the result was wasted resources, reduced differentiation, confusion for customers, and lost market share.

To avoid this situation, a company must first decide its overall strategy, then assign clear missions and markets to its divisions to eliminate product overlap and confusion. It must then rigorously police these boundaries to ensure that clarity of purpose and original focus are maintained.

Similar situations occur with functions. Division executives reorganize and create new functions before they figure out how those functions are to work together. They believe that the people in the functions will together determine the process by which they will complete their work after they have been reorganized. This is a recipe for disaster. The people in these functions will spend their time fighting each other as they try to protect their turf and job. Just as a company must decide its strategy first and then assign missions, when reorganizing, leaders must first design the process and then form the organization.

- **Generally, management of many is the same as management of few. It is a matter of organization.   (V.1)**

Once you have decided on a strategy and assigned missions, you must ensure that this information doesn't just end up in your desk but that everyone knows the high-level game plan and where they fit in. This requires a communications plan.

- **And to control many is the same as to control few. This is a matter of formations and signals.**

  **The Book of Military Administration says, "As the voice cannot be heard in battle, drums and bells are used. As troops cannot see each other clearly in battle, flags and banners are used."   (V.2; VII.17)**

Newsletters, posters, slides, and videos have replaced Sun Tzu's drums, bells, flags, and banners but the intent is the same. Clear direction must be given to large numbers of people in a timely fashion. Each of these media can be used effectively to allow that direction to make an impact on employees, give them better understanding of the strategy, reach the broadest audience, and continually reinforce your message.

### Make Your Strategy Drive Your Organization

Beyond the setting and communication of your strategy, another major part of leadership is the proper staffing and organization of your staff. Crucial to your success is selecting a management team for your organization that is composed of the best people available. Getting the best people is essential, for they will carry out the strategy and greatly influence your other employees.

- [The wise general] selects his men and they exploit the situation. (V.22)

Often more attention is put toward reacting to crises that arise daily than longer-range issues such as hiring the right people. This is a crucial mistake that happens with leaders who enjoy fire-fighting over planning and doing projects themselves over delegation. If you put in the time necessary to select the right people, give them the proper guidance, and then let them carry out their mission, the majority of the fire-fighting will go away. Unfortunately, Western society prefers and rewards the glamor of crisis management over the more mundane and less visible necessity of planning and solving little problems before they become big ones.

- **He who excels at resolving difficulties does so before they arise. By taking into account the favorable factors, he makes his plan feasible; by taking into account the unfavorable, he may resolve the difficulties. (III.4 Tu Mu, X.13)**

I once heard an executive speak to a group of employees on the topic of leadership. He related how he and his family were on his boat, which got caught in a storm. The executive went on to tell in detail how he, the captain, overcame the difficulties and brought his family safely to shore. Although the story makes an engaging and dramatic anecdote, I do not believe it reflects true leadership. A true leader would have been continually looking for signs of a storm, watching the sky, and listening to weather reports. When trouble was seen brewing, the true leader would have brought the boat and the family in before the storm even hit. A good leader isn't one who reacts dramatically to a problem once it has gotten out of control; a good leader solves little problems before they become big ones.

Therefore, you must populate your ranks with people who can "resolve difficulties before they arise" and "exploit the situation."

- **The Grand Duke said: "A sovereign who obtains the right person prospers. One who fails to do so will be ruined." (III.18 Chang Yü)**

There may be times you do not get to choose your staff; they are chosen for you or they come with the job. If this is the case, you must ensure that you use everyone to the best of their ability until you can replace them.

- ■ Now the method of employing men is to use the avaricious and the stupid, the wise and the brave, and to give responsibility to each in situations that suit him. Do not charge people to do what they cannot do. Select them and give them responsibilities commensurate with their abilities. (V.22 Chang Yü)

You must find out their special abilities and use them. Take time to learn about each person who reports to you—their strengths and their weaknesses, their desires and their fears, what they do well and what they do poorly. Only in this way can you use them to the best of their ability.

- ■ Now the valiant can fight, the cautious defend, and the wise counsel. Thus there is none whose talent is wasted. (V.22 Li Ch'üan)

### Summary

Do not forget that the leader is responsible for everything that happens in the organization. If there are problems, you must first look within yourself to see if there is something you have done incorrectly, then look at those who report to you, then look down the management chain. The last place you should look to find the root cause of any problem is at employees, for the strengths and weaknesses of any organization flow from the top down.

- ■ Now when troops flee, are insubordinate, distressed, collapse in disorder or are routed, it is the fault of the general. None of these disasters can be attributed to natural causes. (X.9)

You must lead by example. Get to know your people and share in their bad times as well as the good. Say what's important and then follow through.

Communicate your strategy so effectively that your employees will be able to carry it out even in your absence by knowing your intent. To help them operate, you must assign clear and distinct missions, then select the right people to achieve those missions. Empower them within limits so that they can respond as circumstances dictate. As you get to know your people, you will find the best ways to motivate them and will learn to use each according to their abilities.

Finally, work on your own character. Read widely on many subjects, listen well to others and seek their counsel, and take time to think in order to increase your wisdom. Realize that having courage means not only that you can take risks but also that you have the courage to do what is ethically right. Be sincere and humane in your dealings with subordinates, and when you must enforce discipline, do it in a manner that is consistent and fair.

- Now, the supreme requirements of generalship are a clear perception, the harmony of his host, a profound strategy coupled with far-reaching plans, an understanding of the seasons, and an ability to examine the human factors. (IV.14 Tu Mu)

In these ways, you will lead so that your people will gladly follow you and your organization will value you. Sun Tzu calls this "moral influence."

- By moral influence I mean that which causes people to be in harmony with their leaders, so that they will accompany them in life and unto death without fear of mortal peril. (I.4)

Now that we have discussed leadership, the capstone of the six principles, we move to the last stage: putting these principles into action. By learning to apply Sun Tzu's principles, you move from student to practitioner. This is the final step toward becoming a master strategist, and is the subject of the next and final chapter.

# 7 ▪ *Putting* The Art of Business *into Practice*

Now that you have read and contemplated Sun Tzu's approach to strategy, it is time to apply it. This chapter helps you to do that by providing a process you can use in your company. This process, *The Art of Business Approach*™, has six steps that follow naturally from the six principles. Although parts of the six principles may apply to more than one step, for simplicity's sake I have made them correspond directly.

1. *Win All Without Fighting:*
   *Prioritize Markets and Determine Competitor Focus*
   To win all without fighting you must first decide which markets you want to win and whom you must defeat in those markets to do so. Therefore, in this step, you must first prioritize your markets and then select a competitor in those markets on whom to focus your efforts.

2. *Avoid Strength, Attack Weakness:*
   *Develop Attacks Against Competitor's Weakness*
   Once you've selected a competitor to focus on, you must determine that firm's strengths and weaknesses, as well as understanding your own. Prioritize your competitor's weaknesses by elevating in importance those weaknesses that, if attacked successfully, would severely unbalance your com-

petitor. Take the four most critical weaknesses and develop two to three potential attacks against each that could be used successfully.

3. *Deception and Foreknowledge:*
   *Wargame and Plan for Surprise*
   Now use your knowledge of your competitor to wargame each attack, playing out the moves and countermoves that could occur. It is especially important to forecast how your competitor might leverage its strengths in a counterattack. As you wargame your attacks, think through how you might achieve surprise against your competitor by disguising the attacks with deceptive moves.

4. *Shape Your Competitor:*
   *Integrate Best Attacks to Unbalance Your Competition*
   This is the point to select the one or two key weaknesses of your competitor that you will exploit. The results of your wargaming will provide the insight to do so and will also assist you in deciding which set of attacks to utilize and how they can best be integrated for maximum impact on your competitor. This becomes your strategy.

5. *Speed and Preparation:*
   *Ready Your Attacks and Release Them*
   Determine what preparations are required for successfully executing your integrated set of attacks, your strategy. Then execute your attacks with speed and shockpower.

6. *Leadership:*
   *Reinforce Success, Starve Failure*
   Support your strategy with prompt action, determining quickly which attacks are succeeding and which are not. Ruthlessly reinforce success and starve failure.

These are the essential steps in your strategy process. While there is obviously no "recipe" with which you can cook up strategic success, this process provides the structure for organizing your strategic knowledge and creativity. In the end, your knowledge and your creativity in thinking about your competitor and developing strategies are what will ultimately determine your success.

One additional point: I believe that a key cause of the failure of

| MARKET | YOUR COMPANY |
| --- | --- |
| • Revenue | • Revenue share |
| • Units | • Unit share |
| • Growth | • Product/service fit |
| • Profitability | • Marketing, manufacturing, |
| • Sophistication | financial, and development |
| | capabilities |

FIGURE 7.1   Market prioritization factors.

strategic planning within corporations is unnecessary complexity. In the attempt to factor in every detail and view the market several different ways, planners lose a high-level view and participants in the process get frustrated. Therefore, my goal has been to keep this process as simple as possible. Likewise, as you use this process I would urge you to strive for simplicity in creating your strategy; details should be added later.

### Win All Without Fighting:
### Prioritize Markets and Determine Competitor Focus

The first decision you must make in the process is to determine the markets that are critical to your company's future success. This decision must be made first because market opportunity, not competitive reaction, should drive your strategy. Once you have selected your key markets, then you can select from those competitors you face in those markets.

Therefore, think about which markets are the fastest growing, which are the largest, and which you already have a substantial share of. You must balance each market's opportunity against your ability to meet its demands and prioritize your markets accordingly. The factors in Figure 7.1 should be studied and understood in depth to successfully complete this step of the process.

Obviously, those markets with good opportunity and good fit for your company would be at the top of your market priority list.

Next, focus on a competitor in your key markets. One approach is to target your most successful and strongest competitor. This approach is useful because you know you are taking on the company that can do you the most damage and has significant market share that you can gain. Although attacking your strongest competitor appears to be a less subtle and more direct approach, as long as you attack its weaknesses with an indirect approach, you will be successful.

Another option is to target one or two of your weaker competitors, with the idea that their weaknesses will be more easily exploited. This approach allows you to pick up market share and encircle your strongest competitor without attacking them directly.

If you are well entrenched in a market, you may choose to focus on an emerging competitor in order to prevent its growth into a future rival.

Obviously, in this stage, market and competitor foreknowledge are crucial. You must collect the data you have available, augment it where necessary, and study it in detail to truly divine the correct competitor to concentrate against.

Conclude this step by selecting a competitor on which to focus.

### Avoid Strength/Attack Weakness: Develop Attacks Against Competitor's Weakness

Now that you have selected a competitor to focus on, you must determine its strengths and weaknesses. Look at its value chain; are there weak parts of it that could be attacked? Are there niches in the market that it is not addressing? Are its alliances weak and suffering? Does it have a customer set that it has been ignoring?

Think of these areas and others and list all the weaknesses you can develop. Shorten the list to four to six major weakness areas that, when attacked, will throw your competitor significantly off balance.

In addition, determine your competitor's strengths and list four to six major ones. Finally, complete this step by listing the strengths and weaknesses of your own company (see Figure 7.2).

For each weakness of your competitor, think of two to three attacks that you could use to take advantage of it. To help you, you may want to fill in the matrix in Figure 7.3.

In Quadrant I, list both your company's and your competitor's strengths. In Quadrant II, list your strengths and your competitor's weaknesses and so on until the matrix is complete.

Quadrant II will be the most useful in helping you leverage your firm's strengths against your competitor's weaknesses. Quadrant I features strengths against strengths and should be avoided. Quadrant III is

**WEAKNESSES**

1. _____
2. _____
3. _____
4. _____
5. _____
6. _____

**STRENGTHS**

1. _____
2. _____
3. _____
4. _____
5. _____
6. _____

FIGURE 7.2 Weaknesses and strengths template.

useful in illuminating areas your competitor may choose to counterattack. Quadrant IV is null. Now use Figure 7.4 to list your attacks for each weakness.

You may choose to complete this step and the next two in group mode, since having more people involved allows you to generate more ideas and options. These people should have a mix of backgrounds—managers and key specialists, technical people and businesspeople, as many disciplines as possible. This mix will bring many perspectives to the table, and provide the fresh approaches necessary in brainstorming.

|  | **Competition** | |
|---|---|---|
|  | Strengths | Weaknesses |
| **Your Company** Strengths | I | II |
| Weaknesses | III | IV |

FIGURE 7.3 Strength/weakness matrix.

**WEAKNESS 1**
_____

Attacks
A. _____
B. _____
C. _____


**WEAKNESS 2**
_____

Attacks
A. _____
B. _____
C. _____


**WEAKNESS 3**
_____

Attacks
A. _____
B. _____
C. _____


**WEAKNESS 4**
_____

Attacks
A. _____
B. _____
C. _____


**WEAKNESS 5**
_____

Attacks
A. _____
B. _____
C. _____

FIGURE 7.4  Weakness and attacks format.

### Deception and Foreknowledge:
### Wargame and Plan for Surprise

If you have been able to come up with five weaknesses and three attacks
for each weaknesses, you have eighteen attacks to wargame. This may
seem like too many; however, if you do wargame these attacks thor-

oughly you will cover much strategic ground. Think of how well you will have thought out potential actions by your competitor. Imagine the new options you might uncover for yourself! This effort will provide great foreknowledge.

As discussed earlier, one can use either a simple yet effective method such as the Implication Wheel or get very sophisticated and detailed business strategy simulation software to carry out this phase. The Implication Wheel can be created very effectively in brainstorming mode. One wheel should be done for each unique attack, as shown in Figure 7.5.

As you wargame, think creatively about how you might use the direct and indirect approaches to surprise and deceive your competitor. Remember: surprise is crucial to success. Is there something your competitor's executives desire that you could seize and thus control their emotions? Is there a feint toward a market that you could use that would force your competitor off balance for your major thrust?

Also think through, as countermove follows countermove, how your alliances and those of your competitor might be affected and come into play. Is there a way to leverage your allies to take advantage of your competitor's weaknesses? Will a shift in the balance of power cause your competitor's allies to desert to your side?

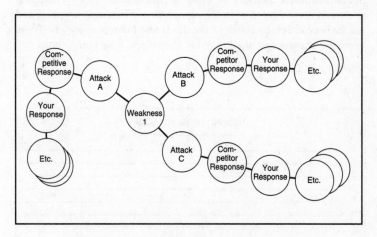

FIGURE 7.5  Wargaming with the Implication Wheel.

As you think through your competitor's potential responses, remember to take into account the firm's strengths, since your competitor will likely rely heavily on its strengths to repel your assaults.

Continue to wargame until you determine which of your attacks plays out most successfully. Again, this is a lot of work, but the depth of strategic understanding you receive will be the reward.

To help wargame, you may even want to set up a "Red Flag" team whose job it is to think like the competition and come up with viable counterattacks. This team should be staffed with personnel who know your chosen competitor well enough to simulate its moves with a high degree of authenticity.

### Shape Your Competitor:
### Integrate Best Attacks To Unbalance the Competition

After wargaming, you will have had the opportunity to look at several different approaches to attacking your competitor and also have a good idea about which would be the most successful. Take the six or seven with the highest probability for success and list them again (Figure 7.6).

From this list, pick the three or four attacks that, when used in synergy, will yield the best integrated strategy for attacking your competitor. Look for attacks that build on one another, use overlapping resources, cause confusion in the competition when used together, and can be used as combinations of the direct and indirect approach. These become your strategy; used together they shape your competitor.

---

**HIGH POTENTIAL ATTACKS**

1. _____
2. _____
3. _____
4. _____
5. _____
6. _____
7. _____

FIGURE 7.6  Determining high potential attacks.

### *Speed and Preparation:*
### *Ready Your Attacks and Release Them*

Now that you have a strategy, it must become more detailed to be implemented. Lay out the specific actions of each attack on a timeline and determine how best to coordinate them (see Figure 7.7).

In addition to laying out the specific actions on the timeline, you must also determine the following for the combined strategy (see Figure 7.8):

- Investments in physical and human capital required
- Organizational changes necessary
- Process improvements
- Skills required

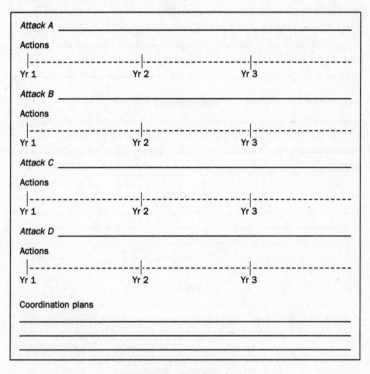

FIGURE 7.7   Timeline format.

From the information in Figure 7.8 you then must build the financial model that corresponds to your strategy, ensuring that the plan meets your business goals (Figure 7.9).

Finally, you must create a contingency plan in case your strategy does not bear its expected fruit. The wargaming just completed should provide ample information to build a credible contingency plan (see Figure 7.10).

You have found your competitor's weaknesses, laid out a myriad of attacks to take advantage of them, wargamed possible outcomes, selected the best strategies, and lined up the resources. You must now execute your plans with speed and shock. Release them in a timed series of moves, with blow following blow. Do not allow your competitor to regain balance once your attacks have started; they must follow in rapid succession to achieve maximum effect.

**INVESTMENTS**

**ORGANIZATION**

**PROCESSES**

**SKILLS**

FIGURE 7.8   Required changes.

|  | Yr 1 | Yr 2 | Yr 3 |
|---|---|---|---|
| Revenue |  |  |  |
| Expenses |  |  |  |
|   Manufacturing |  |  |  |
|   Development |  |  |  |
|   SG&A |  |  |  |
| Total Expenses |  |  |  |
| Profit |  |  |  |

FIGURE 7.9 Business model.

### Leadership: Reinforce Success, Starve Failure

Soon after launching your attacks, you will begin to see signs of whether they are working. Assuming you have set up the proper intelligence network, information will be coming in that tells you how your competitor is reacting, where your attacks have been successful, and where they have been stymied. This is the time to exercise true leadership.

Do not allow yourself to fall into the trap of ignoring successful attacks by trying to prop up failing ones. Do not lose your nerve as the situation develops. Keep a clear head and groom your successful attacks; funnel resources to them. They will pay off in orders of magnitude when compared to throwing resources at failing ones.

You must also stop investing in attacks that appear to be failing. You may want to delude yourself that perhaps you just had the wrong plan of attack, that maybe you still have the right plan but just have not executed it properly. Do not be fooled. Once an attack is launched and unsuccessful, the element of surprise is gone. The resources that must now be committed to revive an attack once the surprise and

Plan to scale back or shut down investments if attack is not progressing _____

Plan to switch resources between attacks as circumstances dictate _____

Plan to react to competitor's most threatening responses _____

FIGURE 7.10 Contingency plan.

momentum are lost are huge and must be weighed against the small probability of success.

One final word of advice: Sun Tzu counsels us to apply his concepts in an integrated and synergistic manner for victory. One cannot assure success by using only one or two separately.

■ The primary colors are only five in number but their combinations are so infinite that one cannot visualize them all. The flavors are only five in number but their blends are so various that one cannot taste them all. (V.9 and 10)

## *Summary*

Business strategy has been a much discussed topic in recent years, and corporations have invested millions in hiring management consultants, creating strategic planning organizations, and developing visions, missions, goals, and, finally, strategies. Given this huge investment and, at times, meager results, many executives have begun to question if the return on investment is truly there for strategic planning. The bottom-line question being asked is: "Since my environment changes so drastically and so quickly, should I really spend any time on strategy or should I just focus on improving my tactics and operations? Is the world changing so fast that the concept of strategy is outdated and no longer possible or useful to pursue?"

My response is that strategy has not deserted us; we have deserted strategy. In the rush to invest in the latest management fads, companies have overlooked time-honored strategic principles. They have poured money into programs that run for one year and then abandoned them the next, seeking the quick fix and losing focus on the long term.

While business competition is proliferating, and new technology is constantly changing the playing field, the basics of business and business strategy remain essentially unchanged. Although new products and services emerge daily, the key to success involves providing unique and superior value for customers, giving them something they cannot get elsewhere. Constant improvement of operations is critical to corporate survival, yet maximum profits and return on investment are attained by leveraging the smallest amount of resources into the largest amount of revenues. Achieving this requires a strategic focus, for to give up on strategy and focus solely on operational and tactical excellence is to invite disaster. The preference of operational over strategic is precisely the recipe that led Germany to lose two world wars.

Blinded by paranoia and consciously avoiding efforts to diplomatically break up the allies arrayed against her, Germany entered the first world war with a strategy that had two major flaws. The first was that it depended on a single decisive battle to defeat France and Britain in the West before turning to the East to destroy Russia. No strategy or contingency plan existed if victory was not achieved in the decisive battle.

The second strategic error Germany's generals made was ignoring their lack of military resources necessary for winning the decisive battle. Prior wargaming had concluded that the German Army required thirteen corps to achieve victory in the decisive attack on the Allies' left flank. However, in reality, only five corps were available. The German general staff's excellent strategic plan was based totally on soldiers who did not exist!

After Germany failed to achieve success in the "decisive battle" and the war dragged on, focus turned to operational excellence, encapsulated in the stormtrooper concept. In fact, General Ludendorff, the leader of the German Army, forbade the use of the term "strategy" at headquarters, and only allowed his staff to discuss and use the word "tactics." In the end, excellent operational execution failed to achieve a favorable strategic outcome.[1]

World War II again found Germany favoring operational excellence over strategy. In their haste to rearm Germany's forces with the latest in weaponry, her military leaders focused on tactical, not strategic requirements. As a result, they did not select the proper arms to match Germany's political goals, they did not coordinate weapons selection between the navy, army, and air force, and their rapid build-up of Germany's military might created enemies of countries that were initially supportive of Germany (e.g., Britain).

Next, even though Germany's main political goal was living space in the east, German diplomacy failed at keeping the Western Powers from entering the war against her. Once the war began, the German Luftwaffe was unable to defeat Britain because its aircraft had not been designed for that task. Instead of finishing off Britain, Germany attacked the Soviet Union, forcing herself into fighting a two-front war that she lacked the resources to complete. The final folly was Germany's choice to declare war on the United States after Pearl Harbor, recklessly adding to the list of enemies arrayed against her.

In the end, the operational and tactical excellence of Germany's armed forces, exemplified by the prowess of the Wehrmacht's armored divisions, the Luftwaffe's jet fighter planes and rockets, and the Kriegsmarine's technologically advanced submarines, was insufficient for victory. It only extended the length of the war and increased the human and physical destruction endured by all.[2]

Unfortunately, business leaders make similar mistakes, creating plans they lack the resources to complete, focusing on improving processes without questioning the need for the processes themselves, and ignoring strategy to focus on the day-to-day crises of the business.

The lesson to be learned is that neither strategic nor tactical excellence is sufficient by itself; the two must accompany one another for decisive victory. If you have the right strategy but execute it poorly, your company will not be profitable. Similarly, if you execute a poor strategy with excellence, your company will also fail; it makes no sense to focus on shortening the manufacturing lead-time of a product for which there is no demand. You must have a creative, powerful strategy and carry it out with will, dispatch, and force.

Therefore, business leaders cannot give up the strategic lever in hopes of simplifying their lives. Focusing on strategy is essential to success, and you must have a set of principles to guide your strategy. I believe those principles are the ones outlined in this book.

With the creative power of these principles, one can transcend old barriers and achieve great goals once thought unachievable. Used together, the principles provide the ability to find opportunities previously unseen and create offerings that will benefit people around the world.

Your value-add as a leader and master strategist comes in integrating the six principles for the maximum synergistic effect on the marketplace and the competition. To integrate these principles effectively, you must be both creative and disciplined, open to new ideas, yet able to ruthlessly pare those ideas down to a few good ones and execute them, able to logically assess the environment and the strategy, yet have the heart, will, and sense of urgency to motivate yourself and your team to implement that strategy expeditiously.

- Therefore when those experienced in war move they make no mistakes; when they act, their resources are limitless. (X.25)

With this immense, new strength also comes the duty to use it wisely, for the benefit of all. Employ the power of your new knowledge appropriately.

- And therefore the general who understands war is the Minister of the people's fate and arbiter of the nation's destiny. (II.21)

# NOTES

## Introduction

1. Sterling Seagrave, *Lords of the Rim* (New York: G.P. Putnam's Sons, 1995), 20–25.

2. R. W. L. Guisso, Catherine Pagani, with David Miller, *The First Emperor of China* (New York: Birch Lane Press, 1989), 47.

3. Samuel B. Griffith, *Sun Tzu: The Art of War* (New York and Oxford: Oxford University Press, 1963), 169–183.

4. B. H. Liddell Hart, forward to *Sun Tzu: The Art of War* by Samuel B. Griffith (New York and Oxford: Oxford University Press, 1963).

5. Rick Atkinson, *Crusade* (Boston and New York: Houghton Mifflin Company, 1993), 330–335 and 405.

6. Seagrave, *Lords of the Rim*, 33.

7. Richard Gibson, "Burger King Overhaul Includes Refocus on Whopper," *Wall Street Journal*, 15 December 1993.

8. Larry Light and Julie Tilsner, "This Painkiller Gives Rivals a Headache," *Business Week*, 31 October 1994, 6.

9. Michael E. Porter, *The Competitive Advantage of Nations* (New York: Free Press, 1990).

10. Philip Kotler and Ravi Singh, "Marketing Warfare in the 1980s," *Journal of Business Strategy*, vol 1(3) (1981), 30–41.

11. Lee Smith, "New Ideas From the Army (Really)," *Fortune*, 19 September 1994, 203–212.

12. In order to make this book meet my objective of being more readable, I have combined some of *The Art of War* quotations. I have also included quotations from the other commentators in *The Art of War* such as Tu Mu, Ho Yen-hsi, and others where they make a useful point. All quotations are

annotated and can be looked up in the original translation of *The Art of War* by Samuel B. Griffith included in this book.

13. Brian Gardner, *The East India Company* (New York: Dorset Press, 1971), 11–17.

## Chapter 1

1. Robert D. Buzzell and Bradley T. Gale, *The PIMS Principles: Profit Impact of Market Strategy* (New York: Free Press, 1987).

Since a firm's market share is dependent on the definition of the market it is in, a market share number can be jockeyed to a certain extent. Therefore, what is most important is to define the business you are in, stick to that definition to measure your market share, then drive for dominance.

2. Wendy Zellner, Robert D. Hof, Richard Brandt, Stephen Baker, and David Greising, "Go-Go Goliaths," *Business Week*, 13 February 1995, 66.

3. C. Y. Woo and A. C. Cooper, "The Surprising Case for Low Market Share," *Harvard Business Review*, no. 59 (1982) 106–113.

4. Andrew Erdman, "Fall for Philip Morris," *Fortune*, 3 May, 1993, 68–69. Laura Zinn, "Marlboro Country Blues," *Business Week*, 13 December, 1993, 46. Laura Zinn, "Unemployed–and Loving It," *Business Week*, 18 July 1994, 32.

5. Nuala Beck and Associates, "The 20 Worst Industries for Jobs," *Fortune*, 18 September 1995, 54. See also: Jonathan Dahl, "Airlines Shoehorn Passengers into Skinnier Jets," *Wall Street Journal*, 17 February 1995; Kevin Kelly, Aaron Bernstein, and Seth Payne, "Rumble on the Runway, *Business Week*, 29 November 1993, 36–37; James Ott, "Employee Takeovers Set World Airline Trend," *Aviation Week & Space Technology*, 1 November 1993, 24; Tim Smart, Julia Flynn, and Dori Jones Yang, "Clash of the Flying Titans, *Business Week*, 22 November 1993, 64–65.

6. Richard Bozulich, *The Second Book of Go* (Tokyo: Ishi Press, 1987), iii; Lester and Elizabeth Morris, *The Game of Go* (board game instruction booklet) (The American Go Association, 1951), 1–10.

7. Ming-Jer Chen and Ian C. MacMillan, "Nonresponse and Delayed Response to Competitive Moves: The Roles of Competitor Dependence and Action Irreversibility," *Academy of Management Journal*, no. 35 (1992), 359–370. Ming-Jer Chen and Danny Miller, "Competitive Attack, Retaliation, and Performance: An Expectancy-Valence Framework," *Strategic Management Journal*, no. 15 (1994), 85–102. Ian C. MacMillan and Mary Lynn McCaffery, "Strategy for Financial Services: Cashing in on Competitive Inertia," *Journal of Business Strategy* no. 4 (1983), 58–65. Ian C. MacMillan, "Controlling Competitive Dynamics by Taking Strategic Initiative," *The Academy of Management Executive Issue*, no. 11(2) (1988) 111–118.

8. George Day, *Market-Driven Strategy* (New York: Free Press, 1990), 21.

## Chapter 2

1. Atkinson, *Crusade*, 333–335; Watson et al., *Military Lessons of the Gulf War*, 246.

2. Christina Duff and Bob Ortega, "How Wal-Mart Outdid a Once-Touted Kmart in Discount-Store Race," *Wall Street Journal*, 24 March 1995; Keith H. Hammonds, "Wal-Mart Picks Up the Pace," *Business Week*, 15 November 1993, 45; Keith H. Hammonds, "Attention, Kmart President," *Business Week*, 30 January 1995, 42; Bill Saporito, "The High Cost of Second Best," *Fortune*, 26 July 1993, 99–102; David Woodruff and Judith H. Dobrzynski, "Revolt? What Revolt?," *Business Week*, 20 June 1994, 42.

3. Bill Saporito, "The High Cost of Second Best," *Fortune*, 26 July 1993, 99–102.

4. Catherine Arnst, Leah Nathans Spiro, and Peter Burrows, "Divide and Conquer?," *Business Week*, 2 October 1995, 56–57; John J. Keller, "AT&T Plans Further Cuts in Work Force," *Wall Street Journal*, 1 December 1993; John J. Keller, "Why AT&T Takeover of NCR Hasn't Been a Real Bell Ringer," *Wall Street Journal*, 19 September 1995; John J. Keller, "Defying Merger Trend, AT&T Plans to Split into Three Companies," *Wall Street Journal*, 21 September, 1995; Larry Light and Julie Tilsner, "AT&T to NCR: R.I.P.," *Business Week*, 25 October 1993, 6; John W. Verity with Bart Ziegler, "NCR, Phone Home," *Business Week*, 8 November 1993, 90–92.

5. Al Ries and Jack Trout, *Positioning: The Battle For Your Mind* (New York: Warner Books, 1986) 97–99; John Sculley, *Odyssey* (New York: Harper & Row, 1987), 161–162.

6. Tim Smart, Pete Engardio, and Geri Smith, "GE's Brave New World," *Business Week*, 8 November 1993, 65–70.

7. Ian C. MacMillan, "Preemptive Strategies," *Journal of Business Strategy*, no. 4(2) (1984), 16–26.

8. Zellner et al., "Go-Go Goliaths," 66.

9. Watson et al., *Military Lessons of the Gulf War*, 64.

10. Watson et al., *Military Lessons of the Gulf War*, 101–102.

11. Jennifer Lawrence, "Integrated Mix Makes Expansion Fly," *Advertising Age*, 8 November 1993, S–10; Edward O. Welles, "Captain Marvel," *INC.* January 1992, 44–47.

## Chapter 3

1. William M. Carley, "A Chip Comes in from the Cold: Tales of High-Tech Spying," *Wall Street Journal*, 19 January 1995.

2. John G. Hubbell, *P.O.W.—A Definitive History of the American Prisoner-of-War Experience in Vietnam, 1964–1973* (New York: Reader's Digest Press, 1976), 536–538.

3. Kathy Blomstrom, "IBM, HP Lock Swords in Battle for the Midrange," *NEWS 3X/400*, December 1994, 28; Donald Davis, "Mid-range Magic," *Manufacturing Systems*, January 1995, 30–34; Lee Kroon, "The HP 'AS/sault?'," *Midrange Computing*, January 1995, 10–11.

4. Charles W. L. Hill and Gareth R. Jones, *Strategic Management: An Integrated Approach* (Boston: Houghton Mifflin Company, 1992), 764–783.

5. U.S. Department of Commerce, *Malcolm Baldrige National Quality Award: 1995 Criteria.*

6. David H. Feedman, "An Unusual Way to Run a Ski Business," *Forbes ASAP*, 27–32; Gene C. Marcial, "Where S-K-I Is Getting Its Lift," *Business Week*, 3 October 1994, 116.

7. Gary Hoover, Alta Campbell and Patrick J. Spain, *Hoover's Handbook of American Business—1995* (Austin: The Reference Press, Inc., 1994), 292–293; Suein L. Hwang, "Borden's Board Mulls Placing Firm on Block," *Wall Street Journal*, 20 December 1993; Elizabeth Lesly, "Why Things Are So Sour at Borden," *Business Week*, 22 November 1993, 78–85.

8. Alvin Toffler, *Powershift: Knowledge, Wealth and Violence at the Edge of the 21st Century* (New York: Bantam Books, 1990), 89–153.

9. Rick Atkinson, *Crusade*, 234.

10. James A. Belasco, "Scanning the Present to Discover the Future," *Planning Review*, March/April 1994, 14–19.

11. Charles W. L. Hill and Gareth R. Jones, *Strategic Management: An Integrated Approach*, 764–783.

12. Ames Nelson, "Running Again," *Think*, February/March 1995, 5–6 and special *Think* insert, "Postmark Armonk."

13. Gabriella Stern, "P&G Mulls Plan To Cut Costs of Distribution," *Wall Street Journal*, 8 November 1993.

## Chapter 4

1. Editors of American Heritage, *The Civil War* (New York: Golden Press, 1960), 55. Editors of Time-Life Books, *Brother Against Brother* (New York: Prentice Hall Press, 1990), 109.

2. Jonathan B. Levine, "IBM Is Teaching the Scots How To Pinch Pennies," *Business Week*, 29 November 1993, 126.

3. Tim R.V. Davis, "The Distribution Revolution," *Planning Review*, March/April 1994, 46–47.

4. George Stalk, Jr., and Thomas M. Hout, *Competing Against Time* (New York: The Free Press, 1990), 2.

5. Welles, "Captain Marvel," 44–47.

6. B. H. Liddell Hart, *History of Second World War* (New York: G.P. Putnam's Sons, 1970), 65–74.

7. Hill and Jones, *Strategic Management: An Integrated Approach*, 764–783.

8. Eric Morris, *Tanks* (London: Octopus Books, 1975), 20–32.

9. Anthony Livesey, *Great Battles of World War I* (New York: Macmillan Publishing Company, 1989), 144–153.

10. David Woodruff with Kathleen Kerwin, "Suddenly, Saturn's Orbit Is Getting Wobbly," *Business Week*, 28 February 1994, 34.

11. David Woodruff, James B. Treece, Sunita Wadekar Bhargara, and Karen Lowry Miller, "Saturn," *Business Week*, 17 August 1992, 86–91.

12. Laura Zinn, "Does Pepsi Have Too Many Products?," *Business Week*, 14 February 1994, 64–67.

13. Oliver Morton, "The Information Advantage," *Economist*, 10 June 1995, 5–20.

14. James B. Treece, "Here Comes GM's Saturn," *Business Week*, 9 April 1990, 56–62.

15. Welles, "Captain Marvel," 44–47.

16. John Walcott, "The Man To Watch," *U.S. News & World Report*, 21 August 1995, 19–22.

17. Steve Gessner, Mark McNeilly, and Bill Leskee, "Using Electronic Meeting Systems for Collaborative Planning at IBM Rochester," *The Planning Review*, January/February 1994, 34–39.

18. Davis, "The Distribution Revolution," 46–47.

19. Welles, "Captain Marvel," 44–47.

20. IBM Rochester, Malcolm Baldrige Quality Showcase, 1991.

21. John W. Verity, "The Gold Mine of Data in Customer Service," *Business Week*, 21 March 1991, 114.

22. Subrata N. Chakravarty, "Hit 'em Hardest with the Mostest," 48–51; Welles, "Captain Marvel," 44–47.

23. Byron Farwell, *Queen Victoria's Little Wars* (New York and London: W. W. Norton & Company, 1972), 68–72.

24. Watson et al., *Military Lessons of the Gulf War*, 61, 71, 75, 123, 171.

25. Tom Clancy, *Armored Cav: A Guided Tour of an Armored Cavalry Regiment* (New York: Berkley Press, 1994), 202–209.

26. Ian C. MacMillan, "Seizing the Competitive Initiative,." *Journal of Business Strategy* no. 3(1) (1982), 43–57.

27. Peter Schwartz, *The Art of the Long View* (New York: Doubleday, 1991), 226–233.

28. Bruce I. Gudmundsson, *Stormtroop Tactics: Innovation in the German Army, 1914–1918* (New York: Praeger, 1989), 171–178.

29. Colonel Trevor N. Dupuy, *Future Wars: The World's Most Dangerous Flashpoints* (New York: Warner Books, 1993), 325.

30. Joel M. Stern, "EVA and Strategic Financial Management." paper presented at 1995 International Strategic Management Conference, Dallas, TX, April 1994.

31. Kevin Kelly with Peter Burrows, "Motorola, Training for the Millennium," *Business Week*, 28 March 1994, 158–162.

## Chapter 5

1. B. H. Liddell Hart, *Strategy* (London: Faber & Faber, Ltd, 1954, 1967) 5–6.

2 William S. Ellis, "Glass: Capturing the Dance of Light," *National Geographic*, vol. 184, no. 6, December 1993, 51.

3 Matthew Cooper, *The German Army: 1933–1945* (Chelsea: Scarborough House, 1978) 434; B. H. Liddell Hart, *History of the Second World War*, 255–265.

4. Thomas Jaffe, "When The Going Gets Tough . . . ," *Forbes*, 2 January 1995, 16; Mark Larson, "United To Take on Southwest," *The Business Journal Serving Greater Sacramento*, vol. 11, no. 6, 2 May 1994, 1–3; Mark Larson, "United Takes on Southwest for Low-Fare Market," *The Business Journal Serving Greater Sacramento*, vol. 11, no. 40, 26 December 1994, 37; Mark Larson, "Southwest, United Slug It Out," *The Business Journal Serving Greater Sacramento*, vol. 12, no. 19, 2.; Jennifer Lawrence, "No Frills Airline Prepares To Go Toe to Toe Against Giant United," *Advertising Age*, 11 July 1994, 1; Jennifer Lawrence, "Airlines Give Fliers Fleet of New Choices," *Advertising Age*, 12 September 1994, 59; James T. McKenna, "Southwest To Raise Ante in United Markets," *Aviation Week & Space Technology*, 18 July 1994, 22; James T. McKenna, "Southwest Adopts Ticketless Travel Plan," *Aviation Week & Space Technology*, 7 November 1994, 39; Wendy Zellner, Eric Schine, and Susan Chandler, "Dogfight Over California," *Business Week*, 15 August 1994, 32; Viewpoint, "Southwest's Gamble," *Advertising Age*, 18 July 1994, 16.

5. Larry Light, "The Second Battle of Britain," *Business Week*, 15 May 1995, 6.

6. Robert B. Asprey, *War in the Shadows*, Vol II (New York: Doubleday, 1975), 1216–1240.

7. Richard Brandt, "How Sweet a Deal for Novell?," *Business Week*, 4 April 1994, 38.

8. Don Clark, "Novell Planning a New System for Networks," *Wall Street Journal*, 12 September 1994; Don Clark, "Novell Redraws Lines of Battle over Business Software: By Selling UNIX System, It Ceases Fighting Microsoft Across a Broad Front," *Wall Street Journal*, 21 September 1995.

9. Dee Brown, *Bury My Heart At Wounded Knee* (New York: Holt, Rinehart & Winston, Inc., 1970), 128–133.

10. Jack Egan with Kenan Pollack, "Gold Rush in Cyberspace," *U.S. News & World Report*, 13 November 1995, 72–83.

11. Bradley A. Forest, "Inventions," *IBM Rochester Technical Awareness Journal*, Vol. 7, No. 2, 11 2Q, 1993.

12. Stephen Kreider Yoder, "How H-P Used Tactics of the Japanese to Beat Them at Their Game," *Wall Street Journal*, 8 September 1994.

13. Tibbett Speer, "How To Keep Customers Loyal? Try a Magazine." *American Demographics*, November 1993, 23.

14. Seth Lubove, "Get 'em Before They Get You," *Forbes*, 31 July 1995, 88–93.

15. Sculley, *Odyssey*, 25–30.

16. "Plane Sense," *The Economist*, 26 June 1993, 71.

17. Liddell Hart, *History of the Second World War*, 588 and 712–713.

18. Chen and Ian MacMillan, "Nonresponse and Delayed Response to Competitive Moves: The Roles of Competitor Dependence and Action Irreversibility," 359–370; Chen and Miller, "Competitive Attack, Retaliation, and Performance: An Expectancy-Valence Framework," 85–102.

19. Edward N. Luttwak, *The Grand Strategy of the Roman Empire* (Baltimore: John Hopkins University Press, 1976), 1–5; William Weir, *Fatal Victories* (Hamden, CT: Shoe String Press, Inc, 1993), 3–14.

20. *Compton's Interactive Encyclopedia* (Carlsbad, CA: Compton's New-Media, Inc., 1992).

There are two additional points about both empires: (1) The idea of the Roman Empire lived on long after the fall of Rome itself, through both the Byzantine Empire in Constantinople (originally called "New Rome") and the Holy Roman Empire in Europe. A further tribute to the longevity of the Imperial Roman idea is the fact that the last time two rulers with the title of Caesar did battle was in World War I—the German Kaiser and the Russian Czar. (2) Cortez did have both the power of technology and mythology on his side. Cortez had firearms, ships and horses; none of which the Aztecs had ever seen. Also, it was originally thought by the Aztecs that Cortez was the incarnation of an Aztec god who had been prophesized to return in the year 1519. However, even with these assets, Cortez could never have beaten the tens of thousands of Aztec warriors without having tribal allies. They were just too numerous.

21. Don Clark, "Apple Alleges Gates Bullied It on Lawsuits" *Wall Street Journal*, 23 January 1995; Don Clark, "Microsoft Sticks by Its Tactics, Despite Uproar," *Wall Street Journal*, 1 May 1995; Mark Halper, Stuart J. Johnson, and Mitch Betts, "Apple, Microsoft Barbs Stoke Feud," *Computerworld*, vol. 29, no. 9, 27 February 1995, 1; G. Christian Hill and Don Clark, "Microsoft Drops Its Bid for Intuit, Giving the Justice Department an Antitrust Victory," *Wall Street Journal*, 22 May 1995.

22. Larry Light and Julie Tilsner, "Mass Matrimony for Carmakers?," *Business Week*, 7 March 1994, 6.

23. David Hage, "On the Right Track: America's Resurgent Railroads Are Chugging Their Way Back to Prosperity." *U.S. News & World Report*, 21 March 1994, 46–53.

24. Stewart Toy, Susan Chandler, Robert Neff, and Margaret Dawson, "Flying High: Why KLM's Global Strategy Is Working," *Business Week*, 27 February 1995, 90–91.

25. Liddell Hart, *History of the Second World War*, 145–152.

26. Paula Dwyer, "Why Volvo Kissed Renault Goodbye," *Business Week*, 20 December 1993, 54–55.

27. Phillip L. Zweig and Leah Nathans Spiro, "It's Instant Financial Synergy," *Business Week*, 29 November 1993, 120–121.

28. Henry Kissinger, *Diplomacy* (New York: Simon & Schuster, 1994), 97–100.

29. Larry Holyoke, William Spindle and Neil Gross, "Doing the Unthinkable: Japan Inc's Suppliers Gasp as It Buys Abroad," *Business Week*, 10 January 1994, 52–53.

30. Jennifer Hawthorne, *The Open Road: A History of the Popular Car* (Cambridge: Impressions, 1994), 17–32.

## Chapter 6

1. See primarily Stephen R. Covey in *The 7 Habits of Highly Effective People* (New York, Simon & Schuster, 1990).

2. David A. Brown, "Southwest's Success, Growth Tied to Maintaining Original Concept," *Aviation Week & Space Technology*, 27 May 1991, 75–77; Subrata N. Chakravarty, "Hit 'em Hardest with the Mostest," *Forbes*, 16 September 1991, 48–51; Linda Himmelsteing with Olumwabunmi Shabi, "To Scream, Press 'O'," *Business Week*, 29 May 1995, 4; Kenneth Labich, "America's Best CEO?," *Fortune*, 2 May 1994, 44–52; Susan Reed and Anne Maier, "Cleared For Takeoff," *People*, 2 May 1994, 67–70; Richard Woodbury, "Prince of Midair," *Time*, 25 January 1993, 55; Editorial, "Lighten Up and Treat Passengers to Some Fun," *Aviation Week & Space Technology*, 14 March 1994, 130.

3. Edwin P. Hoyt, *The Last Kamikaze—The Story of Admiral Matome Ugaki* (Westport, CT: Praeger, 1993), vii–xvi.

4. General H. Norman Schwartzkopf, *It Doesn't Take A Hero* (New York: Bantam Books, 1992), 173.

5. Associated Press, "NWA Executive Gives Back Bonus," *Rochester Post-Bulletin*, 28 February 1994, 1.

6. John A. Byrne, "Are You Guys Crazy or Something?" *Business Week*, 24 April 1995, 92.

7. Larry Light and Julie Tilsner, "What's the Worst They Can Do—Fire Me?," *Business Week*, 17 January 1994, 6.

8. James B. Treece, "Will GM Learn froms Its Own Role Models?," *Business Week*, 9 April 1990, 62; Graef S. Crystal, *In Search of Excess: The Overcompensation of American Executives* (New York & London: W. W. Norton & Company, 1991), 28.

9. News Roundup, "In a Cost-Cutting Era, Many CEOs Enjoy Imperial Perks," *Wall Street Journal*, 7 March 1995.

10. Charles A. Jaffe, "Moving Fast by Standing Still," *Nation's Business*, October 1991, 57–59.

11. U.S. Marine Corps, *Warfighting* (New York: Doubleday, 1989), 68.

12. Judith H. Dobrzynski, "How to Handle a CEO," *Business Week*, 21

February 1994, 64–65; Thane Peterson, "Zenith Dials Up a New CEO," *Business Week*, 13 March 1995, 46.

13 Richard A. Melcher and Judith H. Dobrzynski, " 'A Short Leash' at Zenith," *Business Week*, 31 January 1994; Hoover et al., *Hoover's Handbook of American Business—1995*, pg 1136–1137.

14. Gudmundsson, *Stormtroop Tactics—Innovation in the German Army, 1914–1918*, 150.

15. William Stern, "A Lesson Learned Early," *Forbes*, 8 November 1993, 220–21.

16. Alfred P. Sloan, *My Years With General Motors* (New York: Doubleday, 1963), 160.

## Chapter 7

1. Williamson Murray, MacGregor Knox, and Alvin Bernstein, *The Making of Strategy: Rulers, States and War* (New York: Cambridge University Press, 1994), 242–277.

2. Ibid., 352–392.

# Suggested Readings

If you are interested in reading further about either business or military strategy, a quick perusal of the notes is a good place to start from. To avoid overwhelming you with a list of several books, I have chosen to mention just a few that have particularly resonated with me and seem to have stood the test of time. My apologies to the many authors whose books are just as excellent but which I may have overlooked or am not aware of.

*Lords of the Rim*, by Sterling Seagrave, is an excellent combination of both the military and business history and culture of the overseas Chinese and their impact on today's global marketplace. Extremely readable, insightful, and interesting, it discusses the impact of Sun Tzu on the business philosophy of the influential merchants and financers and gives excellent examples of how they implement his concepts.

For pure business strategy, one should have read Michael Porter's *Competitive Strategy* (New York: Free Press, 1980), which provides an excellent base for understanding all business strategy and competitive analysis. Another classic, with more of a marketing bent, is *Positioning, The Battle for Your Mind* by Jack Trout and Al Ries, which discusses at length how to capture a strong and defensible position in your prospect's mind. For a viewpoint on effective leadership, I would suggest Stephen R. Covey's *The 7 Habits of Highly Effective People*, which illustrates character-based leadership in depth. *My Years With General Motors*, by Alfred P. Sloan, is the highly readable and timeless view of how to make a business organization effective. Finally, the numerous articles listed in the notes by Ian C. MacMillan, Mary Lynn McCaffery, Ming-

Jer Chen, and Danny Miller are excellent for understanding more about using an indirect strategic approach.

For military strategy, one should start with the classic *Strategy* by B. H. Liddell Hart. This work describes how military leaders across time have successfully used the indirect approach to defeat their enemies. *Warfighting*, the official fighting manual of the U.S. Marine Corps, is available to the public and provides a short, concise, and illuminating view of how to implement military strategy. Both *Diplomacy* by Henry Kissinger and *The Making of Strategy: Rulers, States and War*, edited by Williamson Murray, MacGregor Knox, and Alvin Bernstein, offer great insight on the strategies countries have employed, either to rise to power or fall from it. Xenophon's *The Persian Expedition* provides a timeless view of leadership that mixes discipline with innovation to achieve one's objectives in a near hopeless situation. If you are interested in the Gulf War. I am aware of two excellent books on the subject: *Military Lessons of the Gulf War* by Bruce W. Watson, Bruce George, Peter Tsouras, and B. L. Cyr and *Crusade* by Rick Atkinson. These two books are very readable and explain how the lessons America's military learned in Viet Nam were successfully applied in this conflict. Finally, if you would like to know more about the innovations the Germany Army introduced in World War I and exploited in World War II, I would recommend *Stormtroop Tactics* by Bruce I. Gudmundsson and *Steel Wind* by David T. Zabecki. The latter describes the innovations in artillery tactics created by a little-known German colonel named Georg Bruchmuller. Bruchmuller's tactics form the basis of those still used today by the world's most sophisticated armies.

Beyond reading, I would urge you to utilize strategy games. These include Go and military strategy simulation games, either very simple ones like Risk or much more elaborate ones that replicate specific battles such as Agincourt, Waterloo, or Stalingrad. Beyond the military strategy games are business simulation games, which put you in the role of CEO and allow you to make the marketing, production, engineering, and personnel decisions that will lead to business success or failure. Such games, which are available in computer form, allow you to practice your strategic moves in a risk-free environment and learn from your successes and mistakes.

*Original Translation of The Art of War*

**by Samuel B. Griffith**

# LIST OF ABBREVIATIONS OF WORKS
## MENTIONED SEVERAL TIMES IN NOTES

| | |
|---|---|
| BLS | Book of Lord Shang (Duyvendak) |
| CA | *La Chine Antique* (Maspero) |
| CC | Chinese Classics (Legge) |
| CKS | *Chan Kuo Shih* (Yang K'uan) |
| Dubs | *Hsün Tzu* |
| Duy | *Tao Te Ching* (Duyvendak) |
| GS | *Grammata Serica Recensa* (Karlgren) |
| HIWC | *Han (Shu) I Wen Chih* |
| HCP | *History of Chinese Philosophy* (Fung Yü-lan) (Bodde) |
| HFHD | *History of the Former Han Dynasty* (Dubs) |
| HFT | *Han Fei Tzu* (Liao) |
| Mao | *Collected Works of Mao Tse-tung* |
| OPW | *On the Protracted War* (Mao Tse-tung) |
| PTSC | *Pei T'ang Shu Ch'ao* |
| San I | *Japan, A Short Cultural History* (Sansom) |
| San II | *A History of Japan to 1334* (Sansom) |
| SC | *Shih Chi* |
| TC | *Tso Chuan* |
| TPYL | *T'ai P'ing Yü Lan* |
| TT | *T'ung Tien* |
| WSTK | *Wei Shu T'ung K'ao* |

# I

# ESTIMATES†

SUN TZU said:

1. War is a matter of vital importance to the State; the province of life or death; the road to survival or ruin.* It is mandatory that it be thoroughly studied.

> *Li Ch'üan*: "Weapons are tools of ill omen." War is a grave matter; one is apprehensive lest men embark upon it without due reflection.

2. Therefore, appraise it in terms of the five fundamental factors and make comparisons of the seven elements later named.†† So you may assess its essentials.

3. The first of these factors is moral influence; the second, weather; the third, terrain; the fourth, command; and the fifth, doctrine.**

---

†The title means "reckoning," "plans," or "calculations." In the Seven Military Classics edition the title is "Preliminary Calculations." The subject first discussed is the process we define as an Estimate (or Appreciation) of the Situation.

*Or "for [the field of battle] is the place of life and death [and war] the road to survival or ruin."

††Sun Hsing-yen follows the *T'ung T'ien* here and drops the character *shih* (事): "matters," "factors," or "affairs." Without it the verse does not make much sense.

**Here *Tao* (道) is translated "moral influence." It is usually rendered as "The Way," or "The Right Way." Here it refers to the morality of government; specifically to that of the sovereign. If the sovereign governs justly, benevolently, and righteously, he follows the Right Path or the Right Way, and thus exerts a superior degree of moral influence. The character *fa* (法), here rendered "doctrine," has as a primary meaning

*Chang Yü*: The systematic order above is perfectly clear. When troops are raised to chastise transgressors, the temple council first considers the adequacy of the rulers' benevolence and the confidence of their peoples; next, the appropriateness of nature's seasons, and finally the difficulties of the topography. After thorough deliberation of these three matters, a general is appointed to launch the attack.[†] After troops have crossed the borders, responsibility for laws and orders devolves upon the general.

4. By moral influence I mean that which causes the people to be in harmony with their leaders, so that they will accompany them in life and unto death without fear of mortal peril.[*]

*Chang Yü*: When one treats people with benevolence, justice, and righteousness, and reposes confidence in them, the army will be united in mind and all will be happy to serve their leaders. The Book of Changes says: "In happiness at overcoming difficulties, people forget the danger of death."

5. By weather I mean the interaction of natural forces; the effects of winter's cold and summer's heat and the conduct of military operations in accordance with the seasons.[††]

6. By terrain I mean distances, whether the ground is traversed with ease or difficulty, whether it is open or constricted, and the chances of life or death.

*Mei Yao-ch'en*: . . . When employing troops, it is essential to know beforehand the conditions of the terrain. Knowing the distances, one can make use of an indirect or a direct plan. If he knows the degree of ease or difficulty of traversing the ground, he can estimate the advantages of using infantry or cavalry. If he knows where the

"law" or "method." In the title of the work it is translated "Art." But in v. 8 Sun Tzu makes it clear that here he is talking about what we call doctrine.

[†]There are precise terms in Chinese that cannot be uniformly rendered by our word "attack." Chang Yü here uses a phrase that literally means "to chastise criminals," an expression applied to attack of rebels. Other characters have such precise meanings as "to attack by stealth," "to attack suddenly," "to suppress the rebellious," "to reduce to submission," &c.

[*]Or "Moral influence is that which causes the people to be in accord with their superiors. . . ." Ts'ao Ts'ao says the people are guided in the right way (of conduct) by "instructing" them.

[††]It is clear that the character *t'ien* (天) (Heaven) is used in this verse in the sense of "weather," as it is today.

ground is constricted and where open he can calculate the size of force appropriate. If he knows where he will give battle he knows when to concentrate or divide his forces.[†]

7. By command I mean the general's qualities of wisdom, sincerity, humanity, courage, and strictness.

*Li Ch'üan*: These five are the virtues of the general. Hence the army refers to him as "The Respected One."

*Tu Mu*: . . . If wise, a commander is able to recognize changing circumstances and to act expediently. If sincere, his men will have no doubt of the certainty of rewards and punishments. If humane, he loves mankind, sympathizes with others, and appreciates their industry and toil. If courageous, he gains victory by seizing opportunity without hesitation. If strict, his troops are disciplined because they are in awe of him and are afraid of punishment.

Shen Pao-hsu . . . said: "If a general is not courageous he will be unable to conquer doubts or to create great plans."

8. By doctrine I mean organization, control, assignment of appropriate ranks to officers, regulation of supply routes, and the provision of principal items used by the army.

9. There is no general who has not heard of these five matters. Those who master them win; those who do not are defeated.

10. Therefore in laying plans compare the following elements, appraising them with the utmost care.

11. If you say which ruler possesses moral influence, which commander is the more able, which army obtains the advantages of nature and the terrain, in which regulations and instructions are better carried out, which troops are the stronger;[*]

*Chang Yü*: Chariots strong, horses fast, troops valiant, weapons sharp—so that when they hear the drums beat the attack they are happy, and when they hear the gongs sound the retirement they are enraged. He who is like this is strong.

12. Which has the better trained officers and men;

[†]"Knowing the ground of life and death . . ." is here rendered "If he knows where he will give battle."

[*]In this and the following two verses the seven elements referred to in v. 2 are named.

*Tu Yu*: ... Therefore Master Wang said: "If officers are unaccustomed to rigorous drilling they will be worried and hesitant in battle; if generals are not thoroughly trained they will inwardly quail when they face the enemy."

13. And which administers rewards and punishments in a more enlightened manner;

*Tu Mu*: Neither should be excessive.

14. I will be able to forecast which side will be victorious and which defeated.

15. If a general who heeds my strategy is employed he is certain to win. Retain him! When one who refuses to listen to my strategy is employed, he is certain to be defeated. Dismiss him!

16. Having paid heed to the advantages of my plans, the general must create situations which will contribute to their accomplishment.[†] By "situations" I mean that he should act expediently in accordance with what is advantageous and so control the balance.

17. All warfare is based on deception.

18. Therefore, when capable, feign incapacity; when active, inactivity.

19. When near, make it appear that you are far away; when far away, that you are near.

20. Offer the enemy a bait to lure him; feign disorder and strike him.

*Tu Mu*: The Chao general Li Mu released herds of cattle with their shepherds; when the Hsiung Nu had advanced a short distance he feigned a retirement, leaving behind several thousand men as if abandoning them. When the Khan heard this news he was delighted, and at the head of a strong force marched to the place. Li Mu put most of his troops into formations on the right and left wings, made a horning attack, crushed the Huns and slaughtered over one hundred thousand of their horsemen.[*]

21. When he concentrates, prepare against him; where he is strong, avoid him.

[†]Emending *i* (以) to *i* (已). The commentators do not agree on an interpretation of this verse.

[*]The Hsiung Nu were nomads who caused the Chinese trouble for centuries. The Great Wall was constructed to protect China from their incursions.

22. Anger his general and confuse him.

*Li Ch'üan:* If the general is choleric his authority can easily be upset. His character is not firm.

*Chang Yü:* If the enemy general is obstinate and prone to anger, insult and enrage him, so that he will be irritated and confused, and without a plan will recklessly advance against you.

23. Pretend inferiority and encourage his arrogance.

*Tu Mu:* Toward the end of the Ch'in dynasty, Mo Tun of the Hsiung Nu first established his power. The Eastern Hu were strong and sent ambassadors to parley. They said: "We wish to obtain T'ou Ma's thousand-*li* horse." Mo Tun consulted his advisers, who all exclaimed: "The thousand-*li* horse! The most precious thing in this country! Do not give them that!" Mo Tun replied: "Why begrudge a horse to a neighbor?" So he sent the horse.[†]

Shortly after, the Eastern Hu sent envoys who said: "We wish one of the Khan's princesses." Mo Tun asked advice of his ministers who all angrily said: "The Eastern Hu are unrighteous! Now they even ask for a princess! We implore you to attack them!" Mo Tun said: "How can one begrudge his neighbor a young woman?" So he gave the woman.

A short time later, the Eastern Hu returned and said: "You have a thousand *li* of unused land which we want." Mo Tun consulted his advisers. Some said it would be reasonable to cede the land, others that it would not. Mo Tun was enraged and said: "Land is the foundation of the State. How could one give it away?" All those who had advised doing so were beheaded.

Mo Tun then sprang on his horse, ordered that all who remained behind were to be beheaded, and made a surprise attack on the Eastern Hu. The Eastern Hu were contemptuous of him and had made no preparations. When he attacked he annihilated them. Mo Tun then turned westward and attacked the Yueh Ti. To the south he annexed Lou Fan . . . and invaded Yen. He completely recovered the ancestral lands of the Hsiung Nu previously conquered by the Ch'in general Meng T'ien.[*]

[†]Mo Tun, or T'ou Ma or T'ouman, was the first leader to unite the Hsiung Nu. The thousand-*li* horse was a stallion reputedly able to travel a thousand *li* (about three hundred miles) without grass or water. The term indicates a horse of exceptional quality, undoubtedly reserved for breeding.

[*]Meng T'ien subdued the border nomads during the Ch'in, and began the con-

*Ch'ên Hao*: Give the enemy young boys and women to infatuate him, and jades and silks to excite his ambitions.

24. Keep him under a strain and wear him down.

*Li Ch'üan*: When the enemy is at ease, tire him.

*Tu Mu*: . . . Toward the end of the Later Han, after Ts'ao Ts'ao had defeated Liu Pei, Pei fled to Yuan Shao, who then led out his troops intending to engage Ts'ao Ts'ao. T'ien Fang, one of Yuan Shao's staff officers, said: "Ts'ao Ts'ao is expert at employing troops; one cannot go against him heedlessly. Nothing is better than to protract things and keep him at a distance. You, General, should fortify along the mountains and rivers and hold the four prefectures. Externally, make alliances with powerful leaders; internally, pursue an agro-military policy.†† Later, select crack troops and form them into extraordinary units. Taking advantage of spots where he is unprepared, make repeated sorties and disturb the country south of the river. When he comes to aid the right, attack his left; when he goes to succor the left, attack the right; exhaust him by causing him continually to run about. . . . Now if you reject this victorious strategy and decide instead to risk all on one battle, it will be too late for regrets." Yuan Shao did not follow this advice and therefore was defeated.**

25. When he is united, divide him.

*Chang Yü*: Sometimes drive a wedge between a sovereign and his ministers; on other occasions separate his allies from him. Make them mutually suspicious so that they drift apart. Then you can plot against them.

26. Attack where he is unprepared; sally out when he does not expect you.

*Ho Yen-hsi*: . . . Li Ching of the T'ang proposed ten plans to be used against Hsiao Hsieh, and the entire responsibility of com-

struction of the Great Wall. It is said that he invented the writing-brush. This is probably not correct, but he may have improved the existing brush in some way.

††This refers to agricultural military colonies in remote areas in which soldiers and their families were settled. A portion of the time was spent cultivating the land, the remainder in drilling, training, and fighting when necessary. The Russians used this policy in colonizing Siberia. And it is in effect now in Chinese borderlands.

**During the period known as "The Three Kingdoms," Wei in the north and west, Shu in the south-west, and Wu in the Yangtze valley contested for empire.

manding the armies was entrusted to him. In the eighth month he collected his forces at K'uei Chou.[†]

As it was the season of the autumn floods the waters of the Yangtze were overflowing and the roads by the three gorges were perilous, Hsiao Hsieh thought it certain that Li Ching would not advance against him. Consequently he made no preparations.

In the ninth month Li Ching took command of the troops and addressed them as follows: "What is of the greatest importance in war is extraordinary speed; one cannot afford to neglect opportunity. Now we are concentrated and Hsiao Hsieh does not yet know of it. Taking advantage of the fact that the river is in flood, we will appear unexpectedly under the walls of his capital. As is said: 'When the thunder-clap comes, there is no time to cover the ears.' Even if he should discover us, he cannot on the spur of the moment devise a plan to counter us, and surely we can capture him."

He advanced to I Ling, and Hsiao Hsieh began to be afraid and summoned reinforcements from south of the river, but these were unable to arrive in time. Li Ching laid siege to the city and Hsieh surrendered.

"To sally forth where he does not expect you" means as when, toward its close, the Wei dynasty sent Generals Chung Hui and Teng Ai to attack Shu.[*] . . . In winter, in the tenth month, Ai left Yin P'ing and marched through uninhabited country for over seven hundred *li*, chiselling roads through the mountains and building suspension bridges. The mountains were high, the valleys deep, and this task was extremely difficult and dangerous. Also, the army, about to run out of provisions, was on the verge of perishing. Teng Ai wrapped himself in felt carpets and rolled down the steep mountain slopes; generals and officers clambered up by grasping limbs of trees. Scaling the precipices like strings of fish, the army advanced.

Teng Ai appeared first at Chiang Yu in Shu, and Ma Mou, the general charged with its defence, surrendered. Teng Ai beheaded Chu-ko Chan, who resisted at Mien-chu, and marched on Ch'eng Tu. The King of Shu, Liu Shan, surrendered.

27. These are the strategist's keys to victory. It is not possible to discuss them beforehand.

---

[†]K'uei Chou is in Ssu Ch'uan.
[*]This campaign was conducted about A.D. 255.

*Mei Yao-ch'en*: When confronted by the enemy, respond to changing circumstances and devise expedients. How can these be discussed beforehand?

28. Now if the estimates made in the temple before hostilities indicate victory it is because calculations show one's strength to be superior to that of his enemy; if they indicate defeat, it is because calculations show that one is inferior. With many calculations, one can win; with few one cannot. How much less chance of victory has one who makes none at all! By this means I examine the situation and the outcome will be clearly apparent.[†]

[†]A confusing verse difficult to render into English. In the preliminary calculations, some sort of counting devices were used. The operative character represents such a device, possibly a primitive abacus. We do not know how the various "factors" and "elements" named were weighted, but obviously the process of comparison of relative strengths was a rational one. It appears also that two separate calculations were made, the first on a national level, the second on a strategic level. In the former, the five basic elements named in v. 3 were compared; we may suppose that if the results of this were favorable, the military experts compared strengths, training, equity in administering rewards and punishments, and so on (the seven factors).

# II

# WAGING WAR

Sun Tzu said:

1. Generally, operations of war require one thousand fast four-horse chariots, one thousand four-horse wagons covered in leather, and one hundred thousand mailed troops.

> *Tu Mu:* . . . In ancient chariot fighting, "leather-covered chariots" were both light and heavy. The latter were used for carrying halberds, weapons, military equipment, valuables, and uniforms. The *Ssu-ma Fa* said: "One chariot carries three mailed officers; seventy-two foot troops accompany it. Additionally, there are ten cooks and servants, five men to take care of uniforms, five grooms in charge of fodder, and five men to collect firewood and draw water. Seventy-five men to one light chariot, twenty-five to one baggage wagon, so that taking the two together one hundred men compose a company."[†]

2. When provisions are transported for a thousand *li* expenditures at home and in the field, stipends for the entertainment of advisers and visitors, the cost of materials such as glue and lacquer, and of chariots and armor, will amount to one thousand pieces of gold a day. After this money is in hand, one hundred thousand troops may be raised.[*]

---

[†]The ratio of combat to administrative troops was thus 3:1.

[*]Gold money was coined in Ch'u as early as 400 B.C., but actually Sun Tzu does not use the term "gold." He uses a term that meant "metallic currency."

*Li Ch'üan:* Now when the army marches abroad, the treasury will be emptied at home.

*Tu Mu:* In the army there is a ritual of friendly visits from vassal lords. That is why Sun Tzu mentions "advisers and visitors."

3. Victory is the main object in war.[†] If this is long delayed, weapons are blunted and morale depressed. When troops attack cities, their strength will be exhausted.

4. When the army engages in protracted campaigns the resources of the state will not suffice.

*Chang Yü:* ... The campaigns of the Emperor Wu of the Han dragged on with no result and after the treasury was emptied he issued a mournful edict.

5. When your weapons are dulled and ardor damped, your strength exhausted and treasure spent, neighboring rulers will take advantage of your distress to act. And even though you have wise counsellors, none will be able to lay good plans for the future.

6. Thus, while we have heard of blundering swiftness in war, we have not yet seen a clever operation that was prolonged.

*Tu Yu:* An attack may lack ingenuity, but it must be delivered with supernatural speed.

7. For there has never been a protracted war from which a country has benefited.

*Li Ch'üan:* The Spring and Autumn Annals says: "War is like unto fire; those who will not put aside weapons are themselves consumed by them."

8. Thus those unable to understand the dangers inherent in employing troops are equally unable to understand the advantageous ways of doing so.

9. Those adept in waging war do not require a second levy of conscripts nor more than one provisioning.[*]

---

[†]I insert the character *kuei* (貴) following the "Seven Martial Classics." In the context the character has the sense of "what is valued" or "what is prized."

[*]The commentators indulge in lengthy discussions as to the number of provisionings. This version reads "they do not require three." That is, they require only two, that is, one when they depart and the second when they return. In the meanwhile they

10. They carry equipment from the homeland; they rely for provisions on the enemy. Thus the army is plentifully provided with food.

11. When a country is impoverished by military operations it is due to distant transportation; carriage of supplies for great distances renders the people destitute.

> *Chang Yü:* ... If the army had to be supplied with grain over a distance of one thousand *li,* the troops would have a hungry look.[†]

12. Where the army is, prices are high; when prices rise the wealth of the people is exhausted. When wealth is exhausted the peasantry will be afflicted with urgent exactions.[*]

> *Chia Lin:* ... Where troops are gathered the price of every commodity goes up because everyone covets the extraordinary profits to be made.[††]

13. With strength thus depleted and wealth consumed the households in the central plains will be utterly impoverished and seven-tenths of their wealth dissipated.

> *Li Ch'üan:* If war drags on without cessation, men and women will resent not being able to marry, and will be distressed by the burdens of transportation.

14. As to government expenditures, those due to broken-down chariots, worn-out horses, armor and helmets, arrows and crossbows, lances, hand and body shields, draft animals and supply wagons will amount to sixty percent of the total.[**]

15. Hence the wise general sees to it that his troops feed on the enemy, for one bushel of the enemy's provisions is equivalent to twenty of his; one hundredweight of enemy fodder to twenty hundredweight of his.

> *Chang Yü:* ... In transporting provisions for a distance of one thousand *li,* twenty bushels will be consumed in delivering one to

---

live on the enemy. The TPYL version (following Ts'ao Ts'ao) reads: 'They do not require to be *again* provisioned," that is, during a campaign. I adopt this.

[†]This comment appears under V. 10 but seems more appropriate here.

[*]Or, "close to [where] the army [is]," (i.e., in the zone of operations) "buying is expensive; when buying is expensive..." The "urgent [or 'heavy'] exactions" refers to special taxes, forced contributions of animals and grain, and porterage.

[††]This comment, which appears under the previous verse, has been transposed.

[**]Here Sun Tzu uses the specific character for "crossbow."

the army. . . . If difficult terrain must be crossed even more is required.

16. The reason troops slay the enemy is because they are enraged.[†]

*Ho Yen-hsi*: When the Yen army surrounded Chi Mo in Ch'i, they cut off the noses of all the Ch'i prisoners.[*] The men of Ch'i were enraged and conducted a desperate defense. T'ien Tan sent a secret agent to say: "We are terrified that you people of Yen will exhume the bodies of our ancestors from their graves. How this will freeze our hearts!"

The Yen army immediately began despoiling the tombs and burning the corpses. The defenders of Chi Mo witnessed this from the city walls and with tears flowing wished to go forth to give battle, for rage had multiplied their strength by ten. T'ien Tan knew then that his troops were ready, and inflicted a ruinous defeat on Yen.

17. They take booty from the enemy because they desire wealth.

*Tu Mu*: . . . In the Later Han, Tu Hsiang, Prefect of Chin Chou, attacked the Kuei Chou rebels Pu Yang, P'an Hung, and others. He entered Nan Hai, destroyed three of their camps, and captured much treasure. However, P'an Hung and his followers were still strong and numerous, while Tu Hsiang's troops, now rich and arrogant, no longer had the slightest desire to fight.

Hsiang said: "Pu Yang and P'an Hung have been rebels for ten years. Both are well-versed in attack and defense. What we should really do is unite the strength of all the prefectures and then attack them. For the present the troops shall be encouraged to go hunting." Whereupon the troops both high and low went together to snare game.

As soon as they had left, Tu Hsiang secretly sent people to burn down their barracks. The treasures they had accumulated were completely destroyed. When the hunters returned there was not one who did not weep.

Tu Hsiang said: "The wealth and goods of Pu Yang and those with him are sufficient to enrich several generations. You gentlemen did not do your best. What you have lost is but a small bit of what is there. Why worry about it?"

---

[†]This seems out of place.
[*]This siege took place in 279 B.C.

---

When the troops heard this, they were all enraged and wished to fight. Tu Hsiang ordered the horses fed and everyone to eat in his bed, and early in the morning they marched on the rebels' camp.[†] Yang and Hung had not made preparations, and Tu Hsiang's troops made a spirited attack and destroyed them.

*Chang Yü:* ... In this Imperial Dynasty, when the Eminent Founder ordered his generals to attack Shu, he decreed: "In all the cities and prefectures taken, you should, in my name, empty the treasuries and public storehouses to entertain the officers and troops. What the State wants is only the land."

18. Therefore, when in chariot fighting more than ten chariots are captured, reward those who take the first. Replace the enemy's flags and banners with your own, mix the captured chariots with yours, and mount them.

19. Treat the captives well, and care for them.

*Chang Yü:* All the soldiers taken must be cared for with magnanimity and sincerity so that they may be used by us.

20. This is called "winning a battle and becoming stronger."

21. Hence what is essential in war is victory, not prolonged operations. And therefore the general who understands war is the Minister of the people's fate and arbiter of the nation's destiny.

*Ho Yen-hsi:* The difficulties in the appointment of a commander are the same today as they were in ancient times.[*]

---

[†]They ate a pre-cooked meal in order to avoid building fires to prepare breakfast.
[*]Ho Yen-hsi probably wrote this about A.D. 1050.

# III

## OFFENSIVE STRATEGY

SUN TZU said:

1. Generally in war the best policy is to take a state intact; to ruin it is inferior to this.

> Li Ch'üan: Do not put a premium on killing.

2. To capture the enemy's army is better than to destroy it; to take intact a battalion, a company or a five-man squad is better than to destroy them.

3. For to win one hundred victories in one hundred battles is not the acme of skill. To subdue the enemy without fighting is the acme of skill.

4. Thus, what is of supreme importance in war is to attack the enemy's strategy;[†]

> Tu Mu: ... The Grand Duke said: "He who excels at resolving difficulties does so before they arise. He who excels in conquering his enemies triumphs before threats materialize."
> Li Ch'üan: Attack plans at their inception. In the Later Han, K'ou Hsün surrounded Kao Chun.* Chun sent his Planning Officer, Huang-fu Wen, to parley. Huang-fu Wen was stubborn and rude and K'ou Hsün beheaded him, and informed Kao Chun: "Your staff

---

[†]Not, as Giles translates, "to balk the enemy's plans."
*This took place during the first century A.D.

officer was without propriety. I have beheaded him. If you wish to submit, do so immediately. Otherwise defend yourself." On the same day, Chun threw open his fortifications and surrendered.

All K'ou Hsün's generals said: "May we ask, you killed his envoy, but yet forced him to surrender his city. How is this?"

K'ou Hsün said: "Huang-fu Wen was Kao Chun's heart and guts, his intimate counsellor. If I had spared Huang-fu Wen's life, he would have accomplished his schemes, but when I killed him, Kao Chun lost his guts. It is said: 'The supreme excellence in war is to attack the enemy's plans.' "

All the generals said: "This is beyond our comprehension."

5. Next best is to disrupt his alliances:[†]

> *Tu Yu*: Do not allow your enemies to get together.
> *Wang Hsi*: . . . Look into the matter of his alliances and cause them to be severed and dissolved. If an enemy has alliances, the problem is grave and the enemy's position strong; if he has no alliances the problem is minor and the enemy's position weak.

6. The next best is to attack his army.

> *Chia Lin*: . . . The Grand Duke said: "He who struggles for victory with naked blades is not a good general."
> *Wang Hsi*: Battles are dangerous affairs.
> *Chang Yü*: If you cannot nip his plans in the bud, or disrupt his alliances when they are about to be consummated, sharpen your weapons to gain the victory.

7. The worst policy is to attack cities. Attack cities only when there is no alternative.[*]

8. To prepare the shielded wagons and make ready the necessary arms and equipment requires at least three months; to pile up earthen ramps against the walls an additional three months will be needed.

9. If the general is unable to control his impatience and orders his troops to swarm up the wall like ants, one-third of them will be killed without taking the city. Such is the calamity of these attacks.

---

[†]Not, as Giles translates, "to prevent the junction of the enemy's forces."

[*]In this series of verses Sun Tzu is not discussing the art of generalship as Giles apparently thought. These are objectives or policies—*cheng* (政)—in order of relative merit.

*Tu Mu*: ... In the later Wei, the Emperor T'ai Wu led one hundred thousand troops to attack the Sung general Tsang Chih at Yu T'ai. The Emperor first asked Tsang Chih for some wine.[†] Tsang Chih sealed up a pot full of urine and sent it to him. T'ai Wu was transported with rage and immediately attacked the city, ordering his troops to scale the walls and engage in close combat. Corpses piled up to the top of the walls and after thirty days of this the dead exceeded half his force.

10. Thus, those skilled in war subdue the enemy's army without battle. They capture his cities without assaulting them and overthrow his state without protracted operations.

*Li Ch'üan*: They conquer by strategy. In the Later Han the Marquis of Tsan, Tsang Kung, surrounded the "Yao" rebels at Yüan Wu, but during a succession of months was unable to take the city.[*] His officers and men were ill and covered with ulcers. The King of Tung Hai spoke to Tsang Kung, saying: "Now you have massed troops and encircled the enemy, who is determined to fight to the death. This is no strategy! You should lift the siege. Let them know that an escape route is open and they will flee and disperse. Then any village constable will be able to capture them!" Tsang Kung followed this advice and took Yüan Wu.

11. Your aim must be to take All-under-Heaven intact. Thus your troops are not worn out and your gains will be complete. This is the art of offensive strategy.

12. Consequently, the art of using troops is this: When ten to the enemy's one, surround him;

13. When five times his strength, attack him;

*Chang Yü*: If my force is five times that of the enemy I alarm him to the front, surprise him to the rear, create an uproar in the east and strike in the west.

---

[†]Exchange of gifts and compliments was a normal preliminary to battle.

[*]*Yao* (妖) connotes the supernatural. The Boxers, who believed themselves impervious to foreign lead, could be so described.

---

14. If double his strength, divide him.[†]

> *Tu Yu:* . . . If a two-to-one superiority is insufficient to manipulate the situation, we use a distracting force to divide his army. Therefore the Grand Duke said: "If one is unable to influence the enemy to divide his forces, he cannot discuss unusual tactics."

15. If equally matched you may engage him.

> *Ho Yen-hsi:* . . . In these circumstances only the able general can win.

16. If weaker numerically, be capable of withdrawing;

> *Tu Mu:* If your troops do not equal his, temporarily avoid his initial onrush. Probably later you can take advantage of a soft spot. Then rouse yourself and seek victory with determined spirit.
>
> *Chang Yü:* If the enemy is strong and I am weak, I temporarily withdraw and do not engage.[*] This is the case when the abilities and courage of the generals and the efficiency of troops are equal.
>
> If I am in good order and the enemy in disarray, if I am energetic and he careless, then, even if he be numerically stronger, I can give battle.

17. And if in all respects unequal, be capable of eluding him, for a small force is but booty for one more powerful.[††]

> *Chang Yü:* . . . Mencius said: "The small certainly cannot equal the large, nor can the weak match the strong, nor the few the many."[**]

18. Now the general is the protector of the state. If this protection is all-embracing, the state will surely be strong; if defective, the state will certainly be weak.

---

[†]Some commentators think this verse "means to divide one's own force," but that seems a less satisfactory interpretation, as the character *chih* (之) used in the two previous verses refers to the enemy.

[*]Tu Mu and Chang Yü both counsel "temporary" withdrawal, thus emphasizing the point that offensive action is to be resumed when circumstances are propitious.

[††]Lit. "the strength of a small force is. . . ." This apparently refers to its weapons and equipment.

[**]CC II (Mencius), i, ch. 7.

*Chang Yü:* ... The Grand Duke said: "A sovereign who obtains the right person prospers. One who fails to do so will be ruined."

19. Now there are three ways in which a ruler can bring misfortune upon his army:[†]

20. When ignorant that the army should not advance, to order an advance or ignorant that it should not retire, to order a retirement. This is described as "hobbling the army."

*Chia Lin:* The advance and retirement of the army can be controlled by the general in accordance with prevailing circumstances. No evil is greater than commands of the sovereign from the court.

21. When ignorant of military affairs, to participate in their administration. This causes the officers to be perplexed.

*Ts'ao Ts'ao:* ... An army cannot be run according to rules of etiquette.
*Tu Mu:* As far as propriety, laws, and decrees are concerned, the army has its own code, which it ordinarily follows. If these are made identical with those used in governing a state the officers will be bewildered.
*Chang Yü:* Benevolence and righteousness may be used to govern a state but cannot be used to administer an army. Expediency and flexibility are used in administering an army, but cannot be used in governing a state.

22. When ignorant of command problems to share in the exercise of responsibilities. This engenders doubts in the minds of the officers.[*]

*Wang Hsi:* ... If one ignorant of military matters is sent to participate in the administration of the army, then in every movement there will be disagreement and mutual frustration and the entire army will be hamstrung. That is why Pei Tu memorialized the

---

[†]Here I have transposed the characters meaning "ruler" and "army," otherwise the verse would read that there are three ways in which an army can bring misfortune upon the sovereign.
[*]Lit. "Not knowing [or "not understanding" or "ignorant of"] [where] authority [lies] in the army"; or "ignorant of [matters relating to exercise of] military authority. ..." The operative character is "authority" or "power."

throne to withdraw the Army Supervisor; only then was he able to pacify Ts'ao Chou.[†]

*Chang Yü*: In recent times court officials have been used as Supervisors of the Army and this is precisely what is wrong.

23. If the army is confused and suspicious, neighboring rulers will cause trouble. This is what is meant by the saying: "A confused army leads to another's victory."[*]

*Meng*: ... The Grand Duke said: "One who is confused in purpose cannot respond to his enemy."
*Li Ch'üan*: ... The wrong person cannot be appointed to command. ... Lin Hsiang-ju, the Prime Minister of Chao, said: "Chao Kua is merely able to read his father's books, and is as yet ignorant of correlating changing circumstances. Now Your Majesty, on account of his name, makes him the commander-in-chief. This is like glueing the pegs of a lute and then trying to tune it."

24. Now there are five circumstances in which victory may be predicted.

25. He who knows when he can fight and when he cannot will be victorious.

26. He who understands how to use both large and small forces will be victorious.

*Tu Yu*: There are circumstances in war when many cannot attack few, and others when the weak can master the strong. One able to manipulate such circumstances will be victorious.

27. He whose ranks are united in purpose will be victorious.

*Tu Yu*: Therefore Mencius said: "The appropriate season is not as important as the advantages of the ground; these are not as important as harmonious human relations."[††]

---

[†]The "Army Supervisors" of the T'ang were in fact political commissars. Pei Tu became Prime Minister in A.D. 815 and in 817 requested the throne to recall the supervisor assigned him, who must have been interfering in army operations.

[*]"Feudal Lords" is rendered "neighboring rulers." The commentators agree that a confused army robs itself of victory.

[††]CC II (Mencius), ii, ch. I, p. 85.

28. He who is prudent and lies in wait for an enemy who is not, will be victorious.

> *Ch'ên Hao*: Create an invincible army and await the enemy's moment of vulnerability.
>
> *Ho Yen-hsi*: ... A gentleman said: "To rely on rustics and not prepare is the greatest of crimes; to be prepared beforehand for any contingency is the greatest of virtues."

29. He whose generals are able and not interfered with by the sovereign will be victorious.

> *Tu Yu*: ... Therefore Master Wang said: "To make appointments is the province of the sovereign; to decide on battle, that of the general."
>
> *Wang Hsi*: ... A sovereign of high character and intelligence must be able to know the right man, should place the responsibility on him, and expect results.
>
> *Ho Yen-hsi*: ... Now in war there may be one hundred changes in each step. When one sees he can, he advances; when he sees that things are difficult, he retires. To say that a general must await commands of the sovereign in such circumstances is like informing a superior that you wish to put out a fire. Before the order to do so arrives the ashes are cold. And it is said one must consult the Army Supervisor in these matters! This is as if in building a house beside the road one took advice from those who pass by. Of course the work would never be completed![†]
>
> To put a rein on an able general while at the same time asking him to suppress a cunning enemy is like tying up the Black Hound of Han and then ordering him to catch elusive hares. What is the difference?

30. It is in these five matters that the way to victory is known.

31. Therefore I say: "Know the enemy and know yourself; in a hundred battles you will never be in peril.

---

[†]A paraphrase of an ode that Legge renders:
> They are like one taking counsel with wayfarers about building a house
> Which consequently will never come to completion.

(CC IV, ii, p. 332, Ode I.)

---

32. When you are ignorant of the enemy but know yourself, your chances of winning or losing are equal.

33. If ignorant both of your enemy and of yourself, you are certain in every battle to be in peril."

> *Li Ch'üan*: Such people are called "mad bandits." What can they expect if not defeat?

# IV

## DISPOSITIONS†

SUN TZU said:

1. Anciently the skillful warriors first made themselves invincible and awaited the enemy's moment of vulnerability.

2. Invincibility depends on one's self; the enemy's vulnerability on him.

3. It follows that those skilled in war can make themselves invincible but cannot cause an enemy to be certainly vulnerable.

> *Mei Yao-ch'en*: That which depends on me, I can do; that which depends on the enemy cannot be certain.

4. Therefore it is said that one may know how to win, but cannot necessarily do so.

5. Invincibility lies in the defense; the possibility of victory in the attack.*

6. One defends when his strength is inadequate; he attacks when it is abundant.

7. The experts in defense conceal themselves as under the ninefold

---

†The character *hsing* (形) means "shape," "form," or "appearance" or in a more restricted sense, "disposition" or "formation." The Martial Classics edition apparently followed Ts'ao Ts'ao and titled the chapter *Chun Hsing* (軍形), "Shape [or "Dispositions"] of the Army." As will appear, the character connotes more than mere physical dispositions.

*"Invincibility is [means] defense; the ability to conquer is [means] attack."

earth; those skilled in attack move as from above the ninefold heavens. Thus they are capable both of protecting themselves and of gaining a complete victory.[†]

> *Tu Yu:* Those expert at preparing defenses consider it fundamental to rely on the strength of such obstacles as mountains, rivers and foothills. They make it impossible for the enemy to know where to attack. They secretly conceal themselves as under the nine-layered ground.
>
> Those expert in attack consider it fundamental to rely on the seasons and the advantages of the ground; they use inundations and fire according to the situation. They make it impossible for an enemy to know where to prepare. They release the attack like a lightning bolt from above the nine-layered heavens.

8. To foresee a victory which the ordinary man can foresee is not the acme of skill;

> *Li Ch'üan:* . . . When Han Hsin destroyed Chao State he marched out of the Well Gorge before breakfast. He said: "We will destroy the Chao army and then meet for a meal." The generals were despondent and pretended to agree. Han Hsin drew up his army with the river to its rear. The Chao troops climbed upon their breastworks and, observing this, roared with laughter and taunted him: "The General of Han does not know how to use troops!" Han Hsin then proceeded to defeat the Chao army and after break-fasting beheaded Lord Ch'eng An.
>
> This is an example of what the multitude does not comprehend.[*]

9. To triumph in battle and be universally acclaimed "Expert" is not the acme of skill, for to lift an autumn down requires no great strength; to distinguish between the sun and moon is no test of vision; to hear the thunderclap is no indication of acute hearing.[††]

> *Chang Yü:* By "autumn down" Sun Tzu means rabbits' down, which on the coming of autumn is extremely light.

---

[†]The concept that Heaven and Earth each consist of "layers" or "stages" is an ancient one.

[*]Han Hsin placed his army in "death ground." He burned his boats and smashed his cooking pots. The river was at the rear, the Chao army to the front. Han Hsin had to conquer or drown.

[††]To win a hard-fought battle or to win one by luck is no mark of skill.

10. Anciently those called skilled in war conquered an enemy easily conquered.[†]

11. And therefore the victories won by a master of war gain him neither reputation for wisdom nor merit for valor.

> *Tu Mu*: A victory gained before the situation has crystallized is one the common man does not comprehend. Thus its author gains no reputation for sagacity. Before he has bloodied his blade the enemy state has already submitted.
> *Ho Yen-hsi*: . . . When you subdue your enemy without fighting who will pronounce you valorous?

12. For he wins his victories without erring. "Without erring" means that whatever he does ensures his victory; he conquers an enemy already defeated.

> *Ch'ên Hao*: In planning, never a useless move; in strategy, no step taken in vain.

13. Therefore the skillful commander takes up a position in which he cannot be defeated and misses no opportunity to master his enemy.

14. Thus a victorious army wins its victories before seeking battle; an army destined to defeat fights in the hope of winning.

> *Tu Mu*: . . . Duke Li Ching of Wei said: "Now, the supreme requirements of generalship are a clear perception, the harmony of his host, a profound strategy coupled with far-reaching plans, an understanding of the seasons and an ability to examine the human factors. For a general unable to estimate his capabilities or comprehend the arts of expediency and flexibility when faced with the opportunity to engage the enemy will advance in a stumbling and hesitant manner, looking anxiously first to his right and then to his left, and be unable to produce a plan. Credulous, he will place confidence in unreliable reports, believing at one moment this and at another that. As timorous as a fox in advancing or retiring, his groups will be scattered about. What is the difference between this and driving innocent people into boiling water or fire? Is this not exactly like driving cows and sheep to feed wolves or tigers?"

---

[†]The enemy was conquered easily because the experts previously had created appropriate conditions.

15. Those skilled in war cultivate the *Tao* and preserve the laws and are therefore able to formulate victorious policies.

> *Tu Mu*: The *Tao* is the way of humanity and justice; "laws" are regulations and institutions. Those who excel in war first cultivate their own humanity and justice and maintain their laws and institutions. By these means they make their governments invincible.

16. Now the elements of the art of war are first, measurement of space; second, estimation of quantities; third, calculations; fourth, comparisons; and fifth, chances of victory.

17. Measurements of space are derived from the ground.

18. Quantities derive from measurement, figures from quantities, comparisons from figures, and victory from comparisons.

> *Ho Yen-hsi*:† "Ground" includes both distances and type of terrain; "measurement" is calculation. Before the army is dispatched, calculations are made respecting the degree of difficulty of the enemy's land; the directness and deviousness of its roads; the number of his troops; the quantity of his war equipment and the state of his morale. Calculations are made to see if the enemy can be attacked and only after this is the population mobilized and troops raised.

19. Thus a victorious army is as a hundredweight balanced against a grain; a defeated army as a grain balanced against a hundredweight.

20. It is because of disposition that a victorious general is able to make his people fight with the effect of pent-up waters which, suddenly released, plunge into a bottomless abyss.

> *Chang Yü*: The nature of water is that it avoids heights and hastens to the lowlands. When a dam is broken, the water cascades with irresistible force. Now the shape of an army resembles water. Take advantage of the enemy's unpreparedness; attack him when he does not expect it; avoid his strength and strike his emptiness, and like water, none can oppose you.

---

†This comment appears in the text after V. 18. The factors enumerated are qualities of "shape."

# V

## ENERGY†

SUN TZU said:

1. Generally, management of many is the same as management of few. It is a matter of organization.*

> *Chang Yü:* To manage a host one must first assign responsibilities to the generals and their assistants, and establish the strengths of ranks and files. . . .
>
> One man is a single; two, a pair; three, a trio. A pair and a trio make a five,†† which is a squad; two squads make a section; five sections, a platoon; two platoons, a company; two companies, a battalion; two battalions, a regiment; two regiments, a group; two groups, a brigade; two brigades, an army.** Each is subordinate to the superior and controls the inferior. Each is properly trained. Thus one may manage a host of a million men just as he would a few.

---

†*Shih* (勢), the title of this chapter, means "force," "influence," "authority," "energy." The commentators take it to mean "energy" or "potential" in some contexts and "situation" in others.

*Fen Shu* (分數) is literally "division of [or by] numbers" (or "division and numbering"). Here translated "organization."

††Suggestive that the "pair" and the "trio" carried different weapons.

**A ten-man section; one hundred to the company; two hundred to the battalion; four hundred to the regiment; eight hundred to the group; sixteen hundred to the brigade; thirty-two hundred to the army. This apparently reflects organization at the time Chang Yü was writing. The English terms for the units are arbitrary.

2. And to control many is the same as to control few. This is a matter of formations and signals.

> *Chang Yü:* ... Now when masses of troops are employed, certainly they are widely separated, and ears are not able to hear acutely nor eyes to see clearly. Therefore officers and men are ordered to advance or retreat by observing the flags and banners and to move or stop by signals of bells and drums. Thus the valiant shall not advance alone, nor shall the coward flee.

3. That the army is certain to sustain the enemy's attack without suffering defeat is due to operations of the extraordinary and the normal forces.[†]

> *Li Ch'üan:* The force which confronts the enemy is the normal; that which goes to his flanks the extraordinary. No commander of an army can wrest the advantage from the enemy without extraordinary forces.
>
> *Ho Yen-hsi:* I make the enemy conceive my normal force to be the extraordinary and my extraordinary to be the normal. Moreover, the normal may become the extraordinary and vice versa.

4. Troops thrown against the enemy as a grindstone against eggs is an example of a solid acting upon a void.

> *Ts'ao Ts'ao:* Use the most solid to attack the most empty.

5. Generally, in battle, use the normal force to engage; use the extraordinary to win.

6. Now the resources of those skilled in the use of extraordinary forces are as infinite as the heavens and earth; as inexhaustible as the flow of the great rivers.[*]

7. For they end and recommence; cyclical, as are the movements of the sun and moon. They die away and are reborn; recurrent, as are the passing seasons.

---

[†]The concept expressed by *cheng* (正), "normal" (or "direct") and *ch'i* (奇), "extraordinary" (or "indirect") is of basic importance. The normal (*cheng*) force fixes or distracts the enemy; the extraordinary (*ch'i*) forces act when and where their blows are not anticipated. Should the enemy perceive and respond to a *ch'i* maneuver in such a manner as to neutralize it, the maneuver would automatically become *cheng*.

[*]Sun Tzu uses the characters *chiang* (江) and *ho* (河), which I have rendered "the great rivers."

8. The musical notes are only five in number but their melodies are so numerous that one cannot hear them all.

9. The primary colors are only five in number but their combinations are so infinite that one cannot visualize them all.

10. The flavors are only five in number but their blends are so various that one cannot taste them all.

11. In battle there are only the normal and extraordinary forces, but their combinations are limitless; none can comprehend them all.

12. For these two forces are mutually reproductive; their interaction as endless as that of interlocked rings. Who can determine where one ends and the other begins?

13. When torrential water tosses boulders, it is because of its momentum;

14. When the strike of a hawk breaks the body of its prey, it is because of timing.[†]

> *Tu Yu*: Strike the enemy as swiftly as a falcon strikes its target. It surely breaks the back of its prey for the reason that it awaits the right moment to strike. Its movement is regulated.

15. Thus the momentum of one skilled in war is overwhelming, and his attack precisely regulated.[*]

16. His potential is that of a fully drawn crossbow; his timing, the release of the trigger.[††]

17. In the tumult and uproar the battle seems chaotic, but there is no disorder; the troops appear to be milling about in circles but cannot be defeated.[**]

> *Li Ch'üan*: In battle all appears to be turmoil and confusion. But the flags and banners have prescribed arrangements; the sounds of the cymbals, fixed rules.

[†]Or regulation of its distance from the prey.
[*]Following Tu Mu.
[††]Here again the specific character meaning "crossbow" is used.
[**]Sun Tzu's onomatopoetic terms suggest the noise and confusion of battle.

18. Apparent confusion is a product of good order; apparent cowardice, of courage; apparent weakness, of strength.†

> *Tu Mu*: The verse means that if one wishes to feign disorder to entice an enemy he must himself be well-disciplined. Only then can he feign confusion. One who wishes to simulate cowardice and lie in wait for his enemy must be courageous, for only then is he able to simulate fear. One who wishes to appear to be weak in order to make his enemy arrogant must be extremely strong. Only then can he feign weakness.

19. Order or disorder depends on organization; courage or cowardice on circumstances; strength or weakness on dispositions.

> *Li Ch'üan*: Now when troops gain a favorable situation the coward is brave; if it be lost, the brave become cowards. In the art of war there are no fixed rules. These can only be worked out according to circumstances.

20. Thus, those skilled at making the enemy move do so by creating a situation to which he must conform; they entice him with something he is certain to take, and with lures of ostensible profit they await him in strength.

21. Therefore a skilled commander seeks victory from the situation and does not demand it of his subordinates.

> *Ch'ên Hao*: Experts in war depend especially on opportunity and expediency. They do not place the burden of accomplishment on their men alone.

22. He selects his men and they exploit the situation*

> *Li Ch'üan*: ... Now, the valiant can fight; the cautious defend, and the wise counsel. Thus there is none whose talent is wasted.
> *Tu Mu*: ... Do not demand accomplishment of those who have no talent.
> When Ts'ao Ts'ao attacked Chang Lu in Han Chung, he left Generals Chang Liao, Li Tien, and Lo Chin in command of over one thousand men to defend Ho Fei. Ts'ao Ts'ao sent instructions

---

†Following Tu Mu.
*The text reads: "Thus he is able to select men. ..." That is, men capable of exploiting any situation. A system of selection not based on nepotism or favoritism is the inference.

to the Army Commissioner, Hsieh Ti, and wrote on the edge of the envelope: "Open this only when the rebels arrive." Soon after, Sun Ch'üan of Wu with one hundred thousand men besieged Ho Fei. The generals opened the instructions and read: "If Sun Ch'üan arrives, Generals Chang and Li will go out to fight. General Lo will defend the city. The Army Commissioner shall not participate in the battle.[†] All the other generals should engage the enemy."

Chang Liao said: "Our Lord is campaigning far away, and if we wait for the arrival of reinforcements the rebels will certainly destroy us. Therefore the instructions say that before the enemy is assembled we should immediately attack him in order to blunt his keen edge and to stabilize the morale of our own troops. Then we can defend the city. The opportunity for victory or defeat lies in this one action."

Li Tien and Chang Liao went out to attack and actually defeated Sun Ch'üan, and the morale of the Wu army was rubbed out. They returned and put their defenses in order and the troops felt secure. Sun Ch'üan assaulted the city for ten days but could not take it and withdrew.

The historian Sun Sheng in discussing this observed: "Now war is a matter of deception. As to the defense of Ho Fei, it was hanging in the air, weak and without reinforcements. If one trusts solely to brave generals who love fighting, this will cause trouble. If one relies solely on those who are cautious, their frightened hearts will find it difficult to control the situation."

*Chang Yü*: Now the method of employing men is to use the avaricious and the stupid, the wise and the brave, and to give responsibility to each in situations that suit him. Do not charge people to do what they cannot do. Select them and give them responsibilities commensurate with their abilities.

24. He who relies on the situation uses his men in fighting as one rolls logs or stones. Now the nature of logs and stones is that on stable ground they are static; on unstable ground, they move. If square, they stop; if round, they roll.

25. Thus, the potential of troops skillfully commanded in battle may be compared to that of round boulders which roll down from mountain heights.

---

[†]Ts'ao Ts'ao took care to keep the political officer out of the picture!

*Tu Mu:* . . . Thus one need use but little strength to achieve much.

*Chang Yü:* . . . Li Ching said: "In war there are three kinds of situation:

When the general is contemptuous of his enemy and his officers love to fight, their ambitions soaring as high as the azure clouds and their spirits as fierce as hurricanes, this is situation in respect to morale.

When one man defends a narrow mountain defile which is like sheep's intestines or the door of a dog-house, he can withstand one thousand. This is situation in respect to terrain.

When one takes advantage of the enemy's laxity, his weariness, his hunger and thirst, or strikes when his advanced camps are not settled, or his army is only half-way across a river, this is situation in respect to the enemy."

Therefore when using troops, one must take advantage of the situation exactly as if he were setting a ball in motion on a steep slope. The force applied is minute but the results are enormous."

# VI

## WEAKNESSES AND STRENGTHS

Sun Tzu said:

1. Generally, he who occupies the field of battle first and awaits his enemy is at ease; he who comes later to the scene and rushes into the fight is weary.

2. And therefore those skilled in war bring the enemy to the field of battle and are not brought there by him.

3. One able to make the enemy come of his own accord does so by offering him some advantage. And one able to prevent him from coming does so by hurting him.

> *Tu Yu:* . . . If you are able to hold critical points on his strategic roads the enemy cannot come. Therefore Master Wang said: "When a cat is at the rat hole, ten thousand rats dare not come out; when a tiger guards the ford, ten thousand deer cannot cross."

4. When the enemy is at ease, be able to weary him; when well fed, to starve him; when at rest, to make him move.

5. Appear at places to which he must hasten; move swiftly where he does not expect you.

6. That you may march a thousand *li* without wearying yourself is because you travel where there is no enemy.

> *Ts'ao Ts'ao:* Go into emptiness, strike voids, bypass what he defends, hit him where he does not expect you.

7. To be certain to take what you attack is to attack a place the enemy does not protect. To be certain to hold what you defend is to defend a place the enemy does not attack.

8. Therefore, against those skilled in attack, an enemy does not know where to defend; against the experts in defense, the enemy does not know where to attack.

9. Subtle and insubstantial, the expert leaves no trace; divinely mysterious, he is inaudible. Thus he is master of his enemy's fate.

> *Ho Yen-hsi:* ... I make the enemy see my strengths as weaknesses and my weaknesses as strengths while I cause his strengths to become weaknesses and discover where he is not strong. ... I conceal my tracks so that none can discern them; I keep silence so that none can hear me.

10. He whose advance is irresistible plunges into his enemy's weak positions; he who in withdrawal cannot be pursued moves so swiftly that he cannot be overtaken.

> *Chang Yü:* ... Come like the wind, go like the lightning.

11. When I wish to give battle, my enemy, even though protected by high walls and deep moats, cannot help but engage me, for I attack a position he must succor.

12. When I wish to avoid battle I may defend myself simply by drawing a line on the ground; the enemy will be unable to attack me because I divert him from going where he wishes.

> *Tu Mu:* Chu-ko Liang camped at Yang P'ing and ordered Wei Yen and various generals to combine forces and go down to the east. Chu-ko Liang left only ten thousand men to defend the city while he waited for reports. Ssǔ-ma I said: "Chu-ko Liang is in the city; his troops are few; he is not strong. His generals and officers have lost heart." At this time Chu-ko Liang's spirits were high as usual. He ordered his troops to lay down their banners and silence their drums, and did not allow his men to go out. He opened the four gates and swept and sprinkled the streets.
>
> Ssǔ-ma I suspected an ambush, and led his army in haste to the Northern Mountains.
>
> Chu-ko Liang remarked to his Chief of Staff: "Ssǔ-ma I thought I had prepared an ambush and fled along the mountain

ranges." Ssŭ-ma I later learned of this and was overcome with regrets.[†]

13. If I am able to determine the enemy's dispositions while at the same time I conceal my own then I can concentrate and he must divide. And if I concentrate while he divides, I can use my entire strength to attack a fraction of his.[*] There, I will be numerically superior. Then, if I am able to use many to strike few at the selected point, those I deal with will be in dire straits.[††]

> *Tu Mu*: . . . Sometimes I use light troops and vigorous horsemen to attack where he is unprepared, sometimes strong crossbowmen and bow-stretching archers to snatch key positions, to stir up his left, overrun his right, alarm him to the front, and strike suddenly into his rear.
>
> In broad daylight I deceive him by the use of flags and banners and at night confuse him by beating drums. Then in fear and trembling he will divide his forces to take precautionary measures.

14. The enemy must not know where I intend to give battle. For if he does not know where I intend to give battle he must prepare in a great many places. And when he prepares in a great many places, those I have to fight in any one place will be few.

15. For if he prepares to the front his rear will be weak, and if to the rear, his front will be fragile. If he prepares to the left, his right will be vulnerable and if to the right, there will be few on his left. And when he prepares everywhere he will be weak everywhere.[**]

> *Chang Yü*: He will be unable to fathom where my chariots will actually go out, or where my cavalry will actually come from, or where my infantry will actually follow up, and therefore he will disperse and divide and will have to guard against me everywhere. Consequently his force will be scattered and weakened and his

---

[†]This story provides the plot for a popular Chinese opera. Chu-ko Liang sat in a gate tower and played his lute while the porters swept and sprinkled the streets and Ssŭ-ma I's host hovered on the outskirts. Ssŭ-ma I had been fooled before by Chu-ko Liang and would be fooled again.

[*]Lit. "one part of his."

[††]Karlgren GS 1120m for "dire straits."

[**]Lit. "if there is no place he does not make preparations there is no place he is not vulnerable." The double negative makes the meaning emphatically positive.

strength divided and dissipated, and at the place I engage him I can use a large host against his isolated units.

16. One who has few must prepare against the enemy; one who has many makes the enemy prepare against him.

17. If one knows where and when a battle will be fought his troops can march a thousand *li* and meet on the field. But if one knows neither the battleground nor the day of battle, the left will be unable to aid the right, or the right, the left; the van to support the rear, or the rear, the van. How much more is this so when separated by several tens of *li*, or, indeed, by even a few!

> *Tu Yü:* Now those skilled in war must know where and when a battle will be fought. They measure the roads and fix the date. They divide the army and march in separate columns. Those who are distant start first, those who are near by, later. Thus the meeting of troops from distances of a thousand *li* takes place at the same time. It is like people coming to a city market.†

18. Although I estimate the troops of Yüeh as many, of what benefit is this superiority in respect to the outcome?*

†Tu Mu tells the following interesting story to illustrate the point:

Emperor Wu of the Sung sent Chu Ling-shih to attack Ch'iao Tsung in Shu. The Emperor Wu said: "Last year Liu Ching-hsuan went out of the territory inside the river heading for Huang Wu. He achieved nothing and returned. The rebels now think that I should come from outside the river but surmise that I will take them unaware by coming from inside the river. If this is the case they are certain to defend Fu Ch'eng with heavy troops and guard the interior roads. If I go to Huang Wu, I will fall directly into their trap. Now, I will move the main body outside the river and take Ch'eng Tu, and use distracting troops towards the inside of the river. This is a wonderful plan for controlling the enemy."

Yet he was worried that his plan would be known and that the rebels would learn where he was weak and where strong. So he handed a completely sealed letter to Ling Shih. On the envelope he wrote "Open when you reach Pai Ti." At this time the army did not know how it was to be divided or from where it would march.

When Ling Shih reached Pai Ti, he opened the letter which read: "The main body of the army will march together from outside the river to take Ch'eng Tu. Tsang Hsi and Chu Lin from the central river road will take Kuang Han. Send the weak troops embarked in more than ten high boats from within the river toward Huang Wu."

Chiao Tsung actually used heavy troops to defend within the river and Ling Shh exterminated him.

*These references to Wu and Yüeh are held by some critics to indicate the date of composition of the text.

19. Thus I say that victory can be created. For even if the enemy is numerous, I can prevent him from engaging.

*Chia Lin*: Although the enemy be numerous, if he does not know my military situation, I can always make him urgently attend to his own preparations so that he has no leisure to plan to fight me.

20. Therefore, determine the enemy's plans and you will know which strategy will be successful and which will not;

21. Agitate him and ascertain the pattern of his movement.

22. Determine his dispositions and so ascertain the field of battle.†

23. Probe him and learn where his strength is abundant and where deficient.

24. The ultimate in disposing one's troops is to be without ascertainable shape. Then the most penetrating spies cannot pry in nor can the wise lay plans against you.

25. It is according to the shapes that I lay the plans for victory, but the multitude does not comprehend this. Although everyone can see the outward aspects, none understands the way in which I have created victory.

26. Therefore, when I have won a victory I do not repeat my tactics but respond to circumstances in an infinite variety of ways.

27. Now an army may be likened to water, for just as flowing water avoids the heights and hastens to the lowlands, so an army avoids strength and strikes weakness.

28. And as water shapes its flow in accordance with the ground, so an army manages its victory in accordance with the situation of the enemy.

29. And as water has no constant form, there are in war no constant conditions.

30. Thus, one able to gain the victory by modifying his tactics in accordance with the enemy situation may be said to be divine.

31. Of the five elements, none is always predominant; of the four seasons, none lasts forever; of the days, some are long and some short, and the moon waxes and wanes.

---

†Lit. "the field of life and death."

# VII

## MANEUVER[†]

SUN TZU said:

1. Normally, when the army is employed, the general first receives his commands from the sovereign. He assembles the troops and mobilizes the people. He blends the army into a harmonious entity and encamps it.*

> Li Ch'üan: He receives the sovereign's mandate and in compliance with the victorious deliberations of the temple councils reverently executes the punishments ordained by Heaven.

2. Nothing is more difficult than the art of maneuver. What is difficult about maneuver is to make the devious route the most direct and to turn misfortune to advantage.

3. Thus, march by an indirect route and divert the enemy by enticing him with a bait. So doing, you may set out after he does and arrive before him. One able to do this understands the strategy of the direct and the indirect.

---

†Lit. "struggle" or "contest of the armies" as each strives to gain an advantageous position.

*This verse can be translated as I have, following Li Ch'uan and Chia Lin, or "He encamps the army so that the Gates of Harmony confront one another" following Ts'ao Ts'ao and Tu Mu. After assembling the army, the first task of a commander would be to organize it, or to "harmonize" its diverse elements.

*Ts'ao Ts'ao*: . . . Make it appear that you are far off. You may start after the enemy and arrive before him because you know how to estimate and calculate distances.

*Tu Mu*: He who wishes to snatch an advantage takes a devious and distant route and makes of it the short way. He turns misfortune to his advantage. He deceives and fools the enemy to make him dilatory and lax, and then marches on speedily.[†]

4. Now both advantage and danger are inherent in manuever.[*]

*Ts'ao Ts'ao*: One skilled will profit by it; if he is not, it is dangerous.

5. One who sets the entire army in motion to chase an advantage will not attain it.

6. If he abandons the camp to contend for advantage the stores will be lost.

*Tu Mu*: If one moves with everything the stores will travel slowly and he will not gain the advantage. If he leaves the heavy baggage behind and presses on with the light troops, it is to be feared the baggage would be lost.

7. It follows that when one rolls up the armor and sets out speedily, stopping neither day nor night and marching at double time for a hundred *li,* the three commanders will be captured. For the vigorous troops will arrive first and the feeble straggle along behind, so that if this method is used only one-tenth of the army will arrive.[††]

*Tu Mu*: . . . Normally, an army marches thirty *li* in a day, which is one stage. In a forced march of double distance it covers two stages. You can cover one hundred *li* only if you rest neither day nor night. If the march is conducted in this manner the troops will be taken prisoner. . . . When Sun Tzu says that if this method is

[†]This comment appears under v. 2 in the text.

[*]Giles based his reading on the TT and translated: "Maneuvering with an army is advantageous; with an undisciplined multitude most dangerous." Sun Hsing-yen also thought this was the meaning of the verse. This too literal translation completely misses the point. Ts'ao Ts'ao's interpretation is surely more satisfactory. The verse is a generalization that introduces what follows. A course of action that may appear advantageous usually contains within itself the seeds of disadvantage. The converse is also true.

[††]By "rolling up armor" Sun Tzu undoubtedly meant that heavy individual equipment would be bundled together and left at base.

used only one out of ten will arrive he means that when there is no alternative and you must contend for an advantageous position, you select the most robust man of ten to go first while you order the remainder to follow in the rear. So of ten thousand men you select one thousand who will arrive at dawn. The remainder will arrive continuously, some in late morning and some in mid-afternoon, so that none is exhausted and all arrive in succession to join those who preceded them. The sound of their marching is uninterrupted. In contending for advantage, it must be for a strategically critical point. Then, even one thousand will be sufficient to defend it until those who follow arrive.

8. In a forced march of fifty *li* the commander of the van will fall, and using this method but half the army will arrive. In a forced march of thirty *li*, but two-thirds will arrive.[†]

9. It follows that an army which lacks heavy equipment, fodder, food and stores will be lost.[*]

> *Li Ch'üan*: . . . The protection of metal walls is not as important as grain and food.

10. Those who do not know the conditions of mountains and forests, hazardous defiles, marshes and swamps, cannot conduct the march of an army;

11. Those who do not use local guides are unable to obtain the advantages of the ground.

> *Tu Mu*: The *Kuan Tzu* says: "Generally, the commander must thoroughly acquaint himself beforehand with the maps so that he knows dangerous places for chariots and carts, where the water is too deep for wagons; passes in famous mountains,[††] the principal rivers, the locations of highlands and hills; where rushes, forests, and reeds are luxuriant; the road distances; the size of cities and

---

[†]This may also be rendered as "The general of the Upper Army [as distinguished from the generals commanding the Central and Lower Armies] will be defeated" or "will be checked." Here the Upper Army would refer to the advance guard when the three divisions of the army marched in column. In other words, the advantages and disadvantages of forced marches must be carefully weighed, and the problem of what should be carried and what left in a secure base considered.

[*]The verse that follows this one repeats a previous verse and is a *non sequitur* here. It has been dropped.

[††]"Famous" because of their strategic significance.

towns; well-known cities and abandoned ones, and where there are flourishing orchards. All this must be known, as well as the way boundaries run in and out. All these facts the general must store in his mind; only then will he not lose the advantage of the ground."

Li Ching said: ". . . We should select the bravest officers and those who are most intelligent and keen, and using local guides, secretly traverse mountain and forest noiselessly and concealing our traces. Sometimes we make artificial animals' feet to put on our feet; at others we put artificial birds on our hats and quietly conceal ourselves in luxuriant undergrowth. After this, we listen carefully for distant sounds and screw up our eyes to see clearly. We concentrate our wits so that we may snatch an opportunity. We observe the indications of the atmosphere; look for traces in the water to know if the enemy has waded a stream, and watch for movement of the trees which indicates his approach."

*Ho Yen-hsi*: . . . Now, if having received instructions to launch a campaign, we hasten to unfamiliar land where cultural influence has not penetrated and communications are cut, and rush into its defiles, is it not difficult? If I go with a solitary army the enemy awaits me vigilantly. For the situations of an attacker and a defender are vastly different. How much more so when the enemy concentrates on deception and uses many misleading devices! If we have made no plans we plunge in headlong. By braving the dangers and entering perilous places we face the calamity of being trapped or inundated. Marching as if drunk, we may run into an unexpected fight. When we stop at night we are worried by false alarms; if we hasten along unprepared we fall into ambushes. This is to plunge an army of bears and tigers into the land of death. How can we cope with the rebels' fortifications, or sweep him out of his deceptive dens?

Therefore in the enemy's country, the mountains, rivers, highlands, lowlands, and hills which he can defend as strategic points; the forests, reeds, rushes, and luxuriant grasses in which he can conceal himself; the distances over the roads and paths, the size of cities and towns, the extent of the villages, the fertility or barrenness of the fields, the depth of irrigation works, the amounts of stores, the size of the opposing army, the keenness of weapons—all must be fully known. Then we have the enemy in our sights and he can be easily taken.

12. Now war is based on deception. Move when it is advantageous

and create changes in the situation by dispersal and concentration of forces.[†]

13. When campaigning, be swift as the wind; in leisurely march, majestic as the forest; in raiding and plundering, like fire; in standing, firm as the mountains.[*] As unfathomable as the clouds, move like a thunderbolt.

14. When you plunder the countryside, divide your forces.[††] When you conquer territory, divide the profits.[**]

15. Weigh the situation, then move.

16. He who knows the art of the direct and the indirect approach will be victorious. Such is the art of maneuvering.

17. The Book of Military Administration says: "As the voice cannot be heard in battle, drums and bells are used. As troops cannot see each other clearly in battle, flags and banners are used."[‡]

18. Now gongs and drums, banners and flags are used to focus the attention of the troops. When the troops can be thus united, the brave cannot advance alone, nor can the cowardly withdraw. This is the art of employing a host.

> *Tu Mu*: . . . The Military Law states: "Those who when they should advance do not do so and those who when they should retire do not do so are beheaded."
>
> When Wu Ch'i fought against Ch'in, there was an officer who before battle was joined was unable to control his ardor. He advanced and took a pair of heads and returned. Wu Ch'i ordered him beheaded.
>
> The Army Commissioner admonished him, saying: "This is a talented officer; you should not behead him." Wu Ch'i replied: "I am confident he is an officer of talent, but he is disobedient."
>
> Thereupon he beheaded him.

---

[†]Mao Tse-tung paraphrases this verse several times.

[*]Adopted as his slogan by the Japanese warrior Takeda Shingen.

[††]Yang P'ing-an emends and reads: "Thus wherever your banners point, the enemy is divided." There does not seem to be any justification for this change.

[**]Rather than "divide the profits" Yang P'ing-an reads: "defend it to the best advantage." The text does not substantiate this rendering.

[‡]This verse is interesting because in it Sun Tzu names a work that antedates his own.

19. In night fighting use many torches and drums, in day fighting many banners and flags in order to influence the sight and hearing of our troops.[†]

> *Tu Mu*: . . . Just as large formations include smaller ones, so large camps include smaller ones. The army of the van, rear, right and left has each its own camp. These form a circle round the headquarters of the commander-in-chief in the center. All the camps encompass the headquarters. The several corners are hooked together so that the camp appears like the *Pi Lei* constellation.[*]
>
> The distance between camps is not greater than one hundred paces or less than fifty. The roads and paths join to enable troops to parade. The fortifications face each other so that each can assist the others with bows and crossbows.
>
> At every crossroad a small fort is built; on top firewood is piled; inside there are concealed tunnels. One climbs up to these by ladders; sentries are stationed there. After darkness, if a sentry hears drumbeats on the four sides of the camp he sets off the beacon fire. Therefore if the enemy attacks at night he may get in at the gates, but everywhere there are small camps, each firmly defended, and to the east, west, north or south he does not know which to attack.
>
> In the camp of the commander-in-chief or in the smaller camps, those who first know the enemy has come allow them all to enter; they then beat the drums and all the camps respond. At all the small forts beacon fires are lit, making it as light as day. Whereupon the officers and troops close the gates of the camps and man the fortifications and look down upon the enemy. Strong crossbows and powerful bows shoot in all directions. . . .
>
> Our only worry is that the enemy will not attack at night, for if he does he is certain to be defeated.

20. Now an army may be robbed of its spirit and its commander deprived of his courage.[††]

> *Ho Yen-hsi*: . . . Wu Ch'i said: "The responsibility for a martial host of a million lies in one man. He is the trigger of its spirit."

---

[†]Or "the enemy," it is not clear which. Possibly both. Tu Mu's comment is not particularly relevant to the verse but is included because it indicates a remarkably high degree of skill in the science of castramentation.

[*]Markal? *Pi* is Alpharatz.

[††]Or "of his wits," I am not sure which.

*Mei Yao-ch'en*: ... If an army has been deprived of its morale, its general will also lose his heart.

*Chang Yü*: Heart is that by which the general masters. Now order and confusion, bravery and cowardice, are qualities dominated by the heart. Therefore the expert at controlling his enemy frustrates him and then moves against him. He aggravates him to confuse him and harasses him to make him fearful. Thus he robs his enemy of his heart and of his ability to plan.

21. During the early morning spirits are keen, during the day they flag, and in the evening thoughts turn toward home.[†]

22. And therefore those skilled in war avoid the enemy when his spirit is keen and attack him when it is sluggish and his soldiers homesick. This is control of the moral factor.

23. In good order they await a disorderly enemy; in serenity, a clamorous one. This is control of the mental factor.

*Tu Mu*: In serenity and firmness they are not destroyed by events.

*Ho Yen-hsi*: For the lone general who with subtlety must control a host of a million against an enemy as fierce as tigers, advantages and disadvantages are intermixed. In the face of countless changes he must be wise and flexible; he must bear in mind all possibilities. Unless he is stout of heart and his judgment not confused, how would he be able to respond to circumstances without coming to his wits' end? And how settle affairs without being bewildered? When unexpectedly confronted with grave difficulties, how could he not be alarmed? How could he control the myriad matters without being confused?

24. Close to the field of battle, they await an enemy coming from afar; at rest, an exhausted enemy; with well-fed troops, hungry ones. This is control of the physical factor.

25. They do not engage an enemy advancing with well-ordered banners nor one whose formations are in impressive array. This is control of the factor of changing circumstances.[*]

26. Therefore, the art of employing troops is that when the enemy

---

[†]Mei Yao-ch'en says that "morning," "day," and "evening" represent the phases of a long campaign.

[*]Or the "circumstantial factor." "They" in these verses refers to those skilled in war.

occupies high ground, do not confront him; with his back resting on hills, do no oppose him.

27. When he pretends to flee, do not pursue.

28. Do not attack his *élite* troops.

29. Do not gobble proffered baits.

*Mei Yao-ch'en*: The fish which covets bait is caught; troops who covet bait are defeated.
*Chang Yü*: The "Three Strategies" says: "Under fragrant bait there is certain to be a hooked fish."

30. Do not thwart an enemy returning homewards.

31. To a surrounded enemy you must leave a way of escape.

*Tu Mu*: Show him there is a road to safety, and so create in his mind the idea that there is an alternative to death. Then strike.
*Ho Yen-hsi*: When Ts'ao Ts'ao surrounded Hu Kuan he issued an order: "When the city is taken, the defenders will be buried." For month after month it did not fall. Ts'ao Jen said: "When a city is surrounded it is essential to show the besieged that there is a way to survival. Now, Sir, as you have told them they must fight to the death everyone will fight to save his own skin. The city is strong and has a plentiful supply of food. If we attack them many officers and men will be wounded. If we persevere in this it will take many days. To encamp under the walls of a strong city and attack rebels determined to fight to the death is not a good plan!" Ts'ao Ts'ao followed this advice, and the city submitted.

32. Do not press an enemy at bay.

*Tu Yu*: Prince Fu Ch'ai said: "Wild beasts, when at bay, fight desperately. How much more is this true of men! If they know there is no alternative they will fight to the death."

During the reign of Emperor Hsüan of the Han, Chao Ch'ung-kuo was suppressing a revolt of the Ch'iang tribe. The Ch'iang tribesmen saw his large army, discarded their heavy baggage, and set out to ford the Yellow River. The road was through narrow defiles, and Ch'ung Kuo drove them along in a leisurely manner.

Someone said: "We are in pursuit of great advantage but proceed slowly."

Ch'ung-kuo replied: "They are desperate. I cannot press them. If I do this easily they will go without even looking around. If I press them they will turn on us and fight to the death."

All the generals said: "Wonderful!"

33. This is the method of employing troops.

# VIII

## THE NINE VARIABLES

SUN TZU said:

1. In general, the system of employing troops is that the commander receives his mandate from the sovereign to mobilize the people and assemble the army.[†]

2. You should not encamp in low-lying ground.

3. In communicating ground, unite with your allies.

4. You should not linger in desolate ground.

5. In enclosed ground, resourcefulness is required.

6. In death ground, fight.

7. There are some roads not to follow; some troops not to strike; some cities not to assault; and some ground which should not be contested.

> *Wang Hsi*: In my opinion, troops put out as bait, *élite* troops, and an enemy in well-regulated and imposing formation should not be attacked.

---

[†]As Sun Tzu uses almost identical words to introduce Chapter vii, Yang P'ing-an would drop this. He would also drop v. 2–6 inclusive, as they occur later in discussion of the "Nine Grounds," and replace them with v. 26–32 inclusive from Chapter vii. Where Sun Tzu uses a negative in v. 2–6, it is not the peremptory form he used previously. Hence I do not feel justified in accepting the emendations proposed. The "Nine Variables" are then expressed in v. 2–7 inclusive.

*Tu Mu*: Probably this refers to an enemy in a strategic position behind lofty walls and deep moats with a plentiful store of grain and food, whose purpose is to detain my army. Should I attack the city and take it, there would be no advantage worth mentioning; if I do not take it the assault will certainly grind down the power of my army. Therefore I should not attack it.

8. There are occasions when the commands of the sovereign need not be obeyed.[†]

*Ts'ao Ts'ao*: When it is expedient in operations, the general need not be restricted by the commands of the sovereign.

*Tu Mu*: The *Wei Liao Tzu* says: "Weapons are inauspicious instruments; strife contrary to virtue; the general, the Minister of Death, who is not responsible to the heavens above, to the earth beneath, to the enemy in his front, or to the sovereign in his rear."

*Chang Yü*: Now King Fu Ch'ai said: "When you see the correct course, act; do not wait for orders."

9. A general thoroughly versed in the advantages of the nine variable factors knows how to employ troops.

*Chia Lin*: The general must rely on his ability to control the situation to his advantage as opportunity dictates. He is not bound by established procedures.

10. The general who does not understand the advantages of the nine variable factors will not be able to use the ground to his advantage even though familiar with it.

*Chia Lin*: . . . A general prizes opportune changes in circumstances.

11. In the direction of military operations one who does not understand the tactics suitable to the nine variable situations will be unable to use his troops effectively, even if he understands the "five advantages."[*]

*Chia Lin*: . . . The "five variations" are the following: A road, although it may be the shortest, is not to be followed if one knows it is dangerous and there is the contingency of ambush.

An army, although it may be attacked, is not to be attacked if

---

[†]A catch-all that covers the variable circumstances previously enumerated.

[*]A confusing verse that baffles all the commentators. If Chia Lin is correct, the "five advantages" must be the situations named in v. 2–6 inclusive.

it is in desperate circumstances and there is the possibility that the enemy will fight to the death.

A city, although isolated and susceptible to attack, is not to be attacked if there is the probability that it is well stocked with provisions, defended by crack troops under command of a wise general, that its ministers are loyal and their plans unfathomable.

Ground, although it may be contested, is not to be fought for if one knows that, after getting it, it will be difficult to defend, or that he gains no advantage by obtaining it, but will probably be counter-attacked and suffer casualties.

The orders of a sovereign, although they should be followed, are not to be followed if the general knows they contain the danger of harmful superintendence of affairs from the capital.

These five contingencies must be managed as they arise and as circumstances dictate at the time, for they cannot be settled beforehand.

12. And for this reason, the wise general in his deliberations must consider both favorable and unfavorable factors.[†]

*Ts'ao Ts'ao*: He ponders the dangers inherent in the advantages, and the advantages inherent in the dangers.

13. By taking into account the favorable factors, he makes his plan feasible; by taking into account the unfavorable, he may resolve the difficulties.[*]

*Tu Mu*: . . . If I wish to take advantage of the enemy I must perceive not just the advantage in doing so but must first consider the ways he can harm me if I do.

*Ho Yen-hsi*: Advantage and disadvantage are mutually reproductive. The enlightened deliberate.

14. He who intimidates his neighbours does so by inflicting injury upon them.

*Chia Lin*: Plans and projects for harming the enemy are not confined to any one method. Sometimes entice his wise and virtuous men away so that he has no counselors. Or send treacherous people

---

[†]Sun Tzu says these are "mixed."

[*]Sun Tzu says that by taking account of the favorable factors the plan is made "trustworthy" or "reliable." "Feasible" (or "workable") is as close as I can get it.

to his country to wreck his administration. Sometimes use cunning deceptions to alienate his ministers from the sovereign. Or send skilled craftsmen to encourage his people to exhaust their wealth. Or present him with licentious musicians and dancers to change his customs. Or give him beautiful women to bewilder him.

15. He wearies them by keeping them constantly occupied, and makes them rush about by offering them ostensible advantages.

16. It is a doctrine of war not to assume the enemy will not come, but rather to rely on one's readiness to meet him; not to presume that he will not attack, but rather to make one's self invincible.

*Ho Yen-hsi*: ... The "Strategies of Wu" says: "When the world is at peace, a gentleman keeps his sword by his side."

17. There are five qualities which are dangerous in the character of a general.

18. If reckless, he can be killed;

*Tu Mu*: A general who is stupid and courageous is a calamity. Wu Ch'i said: "When people discuss a general they always pay attention to his courage. As far as a general is concerned, courage is but one quality. Now a valiant general will be certain to enter an engagement recklessly and if he does so he will not appreciate what is advantageous."

19. If cowardly, captured;

*Ho Yen-hsi*: The *Ssu-ma Fa* says: "One who esteems life above all will be overcome with hesitancy. Hesitancy in a general is a great calamity."

20. If quick-tempered you can make a fool of him;

*Tu Yu*: An impulsive man can be provoked to rage and brought to his death. One easily angered is irascible, obstinate, and hasty. He does not consider difficulties.
*Wang Hsi*: What is essential in the temperament of a general is steadiness.

21. If he has too delicate a sense of honor you can calumniate him;

*Mei Yao-ch'en*: One anxious to defend his reputation pays no regard to anything else.

22. If he is of a compassionate nature you can harass him.

*Tu Mu*: He who is humanitarian and compassionate and fears only casualties cannot give up temporary advantage for a long-term gain and is unable to let go this in order to seize that.

23. Now these five traits of character are serious faults in a general and in military operations are calamitous.

24. The ruin of the army and the death of the general are inevitable results of these shortcomings. They must be deeply pondered.

# IX

## MARCHES

Sun Tzu said:

1. Generally when taking up a position and confronting the enemy, having crossed the mountains, stay close to valleys. Encamp on high ground facing the sunny side.[†]

2. Fight downhill; do not ascend to attack.[*]

3. So much for taking position in mountains.

4. After crossing a river you must move some distance away from it.

5. When an advancing enemy crosses water do not meet him at the water's edge. It is advantageous to allow half his force to cross and then strike.

> *Ho Yen-hsi*: During the Spring and Autumn period the Duke of Sung came to Hung to engage the Ch'u army. The Sung army had deployed before the Ch'u troops had completed crossing the river. The Minister of War said: "The enemy is many, we are but few. I request permission to attack before he has completed his crossing." The Duke of Sung replied: "You cannot."
>
> When the Ch'u army had completed the river crossing but had not yet drawn up its formations, the Minister again asked permis-

---

[†]Lit. "Looking in the direction of growth, camp in a high place." The commentators explain that *sheng* (生), "growth," means *yang* (陽), "sunny"—that is, the south.

[*]The TT reading is adopted. Otherwise: "In mountain warfare, do not ascend to attack."

sion to attack and the Duke replied: "Not yet. When they have drawn up their army we will attack."

The Sung army was defeated, the Duke wounded in the thigh, and the officers of the Van annihilated.[†]

6. If you wish to give battle, do not confront your enemy close to the water.[*] Take position on high ground facing the sunlight. Do not take position downstream.

7. This relates to taking up positions near a river.

8. Cross salt marshes speedily. Do not linger in them. If you encounter the enemy in the middle of a salt marsh you must take position close to grass and water with trees to your rear.[††]

9. This has to do with taking up position in salt marshes.

10. In level ground occupy a position which facilitates your action. With heights to your rear and right, the field of battle is to the front and the rear is safe.[**]

11. This is how to take up position in level ground.

12. Generally, these are advantageous for encamping in the four situations named.[‡] By using them the Yellow Emperor conquered four sovereigns.[‡‡]

13. An army prefers high ground to low; esteems sunlight and dislikes shade. Thus, while nourishing its health, the army occupies a firm position. An army that does not suffer from countless diseases is said to be certain of victory.[§]

---

[†]The source of Mao Tse-tung's remark: "We are not like the Duke of Sung."

[*]The commentators say that the purpose of retiring from the banks or shores is to lure the enemy to attempt a crossing.

[††]Possibly salt flats from time to time inundated, as one sees in north and east China, rather than the salt marshes negotiable only by boat, with which we are more familiar.

[**]Sun Tzu says: "To the front, death; to the rear, life." The right flank was the more vulnerable; shields were carried on the left arm.

[‡]That is, the methods described are to be used in encamping the army. Chang Yü takes the verses to relate to encamping but then proceeds to quote Chu-ko Liang on fighting in such places.

[‡‡]Supposed to have reigned 2697–2597 B.C.

[§]Lit. "the one hundred diseases."

14. When near mounds, foothills, dikes or embankments, you must take position on the sunny side and rest your right and rear on them.

15. These methods are all advantageous for the army, and gain the help the ground affords.[†]

16. Where there are precipitous torrents, "Heavenly Wells," "Heavenly Prisons," "Heavenly Nets," "Heavenly Traps," and "Heavenly Cracks," you must march speedily away from them. Do not approach them.

> *Ts'ao Ts'ao*: Raging waters in deep mountains are "precipitous torrents." A place surrounded by heights with low-lying ground in the center is called a "Heavenly Well." When you pass through mountains and the terrain resembles a covered cage it is a "Heavenly Prison." Places where troops can be entrapped and cut off are called "Heavenly Nets." Where the land is sunken, it is a "Heavenly Trap." Where mountain gorges are narrow and where the road is sunken for several tens of feet, this is a "Heavenly Crack."

17. I keep a distance from these and draw the enemy toward them. I face them and cause him to put his back to them.

18. When on the flanks of the army there are dangerous defiles or ponds covered with aquatic grasses where reeds and rushes grow, or forested mountains with dense tangled undergrowth you must carefully search them out, for these are places where ambushes are laid and spies are hidden.

19. When the enemy is near by but lying low he is depending on a favorable position. When he challenges to battle from afar he wishes to lure you to advance, for when he is in easy ground he is in an advantageous position.[*]

20. When the trees are seen to move the enemy is advancing.

21. When many obstacles have been placed in the undergrowth, it is for the purpose of deception.

22. Birds rising in flight is a sign that the enemy is lying in ambush;

---

[†]The verse that immediately follows this in the text reads: "When rain falls in the upper reaches of a river and foaming water descends those who wish to ford must wait until the waters subside." This is obviously out of place here. I suspect it is part of the commentary that has worked its way into the text.

[*]Another version seems to have read: ". . . is offering an ostensible advantage."

when the wild animals are startled and flee he is trying to take you unaware.

23. Dust spurting upward in high straight columns indicates the approach of chariots. When it hangs low and is widespread infantry is approaching.

> *Tu Mu*: When chariots and cavalry travel rapidly they come one after another like fish on a string and therefore the dust rises high in slender columns.
>
> *Chang Yü*: . . . Now when the army marches there should be patrols out to the front to observe. If they see dust raised by the enemy, they must speedily report this to the commanding general.

24. When dust rises in scattered areas the enemy is bringing in firewood; when there are numerous small patches which seem to come and go he is encamping the army.†

25. When the enemy's envoys speak in humble terms, but he continues his preparations, he will advance.

> *Chang Yü*: When T'ien Tan was defending Chi Mo the Yen general Ch'i Che surrounded it. T'ien Tan personally handled the spade and shared in the labor of the troops. He sent his wives and concubines to enroll in the ranks and divided his own food to entertain his officers. He also sent women to the city walls to ask for terms of surrender. The Yen general was very pleased. T'ien Tan also collected twenty-four thousand ounces of gold, and made the rich citizens send a letter to the Yen general which said: "The city is to be surrendered immediately. Our only wish is that you will not make our wives and concubines prisoners." The Yen army became increasingly relaxed and negligent and T'ien Tan sallied out of the city and inflicted a crushing defeat on them.

26. When their language is deceptive but the enemy pretentiously advances, he will retreat.

27. When the envoys speak in apologetic terms, he wishes a respite.*

---

†Li Ch'üan's reading, "bringing in firewood," is adopted. They are dragging bundles of firewood. The comments that interrupt this verse are devoted to discussions of how people collect firewood!

*This verse, out of place in the text, has been moved to the present context.

28. When without a previous understanding the enemy asks for a truce, he is plotting.

> *Ch'ên Hao*: . . . If without reason one begs for a truce it is assuredly because affairs in his country are in a dangerous state and he is worried and wishes to make a plan to gain a respite. Or otherwise he knows that our situation is susceptible to his plots and he wants to forestall our suspicions by asking for a truce. Then he will take advantage of our unpreparedness.

29. When light chariots first go out and take position on the flanks the enemy is forming for battle.

> *Chang Yü*: In the "Fish Scale Formation" chariots are in front, infantry behind them.

30. When his troops march speedily and he parades his battle chariots he is expecting to rendezvous with reinforcements.[†]

31. When half his force advances and half withdraws he is attempting to decoy you.

32. When his troops lean on their weapons, they are famished.

33. When drawers of water drink before carrying it to camp, his troops are suffering from thirst.

34. When the enemy sees an advantage but does not advance to seize it, he is fatigued.[*]

35. When birds gather above his camp sites, they are empty.

> *Ch'ên Hao*: Sun Tzu is describing how to distinguish between the true and the false in the enemy's aspect.

36. When at night the enemy's camp is clamorous, he is fearful.[††]

> *Tu Mu*: His troops are terrified and insecure. They are boisterous to reassure themselves.

37. When his troops are disorderly, the general has no prestige.

---

[†]This is not exactly clear. He expects to rendezvous with reinforcing troops? Or are his dispersed detachments concentrating?

[*]The fact that this series of verses is expressed in elementary terms does not restrain the commentators, who insist on explaining each one at considerable length.

[††]See Plutarch's description in "Alexander" of the Persian camp the night before the battle of Gaugemala.

*Ch'ên Hao*: When the general's orders are not strict and his deportment undignified, the officers will be disorderly.

38. When his flags and banners move about constantly he is in disarray.

*Tu Mu*: Duke Chuang of Lu defeated Ch'i at Ch'ang Sho. Tsao Kuei requested permission to pursue. The Duke asked him why. He replied: "I see that the ruts of their chariots are confused and their flags and banners drooping. Therefore I wish to pursue them."

39. If the officers are short-tempered they are exhausted.

*Ch'ên Hao*: When the general lays on unnecessary projects, everyone is fatigued.
*Chang Yü*: When administration and orders are inconsistent, the men's spirits are low, and the officers exceedingly angry.

40. When the enemy feeds grain to the horses and his men meat and when his troops neither hang up their cooking pots nor return to their shelters, the enemy is desperate.[†]

*Wang Hsi*: The enemy feeds grain to the horses and the men eat meat in order to increase their strength and powers of endurance. If the army has no cooking pots it will not again eat. If the troops do not go back to their shelters they have no thoughts of home and intend to engage in decisive battle.

41. When the troops continually gather in small groups and whisper together the general has lost the confidence of the army.[*]

42. Too frequent rewards indicate that the general is at the end of his resources; too frequent punishments that he is in acute distress.[††]

43. If the officers at first treat the men violently and later are fearful of them, the limit of indiscipline has been reached.[**]

---

[†]Chang Yü says that when an army "burns its boats" and "smashes its cooking pots" it is at bay and will fight to the death.

[*]Comments under this verse are principally devoted to explaining the terms used. Most of the commentators agree that when the men gather together and carry on whispered conversations they are criticizing their officers. Mei Yao-ch'en observes that they are probably planning to desert. The verse that immediately follows is a paraphrase of this one, and is dropped.

[††]Ho Yen-hsi remarks that in the management of his affairs the general should seek a balance of tolerance and severity.

[**]Or "at first to bluster but later to be in fear of the enemy's host"? Ts'ao Ts'ao, Tu Mu, Wang Hsi and Chang Yü all take the *ch'i* (其) here to refer to the enemy,

44. When the enemy troops are in high spirits, and, although facing you, do not join battle for a long time, nor leave, you must thoroughly investigate the situation.

45. In war, numbers alone confer no advantage. Do not advance relying on sheer military power.[†]

46. It is sufficient to estimate the enemy situation correctly and to concentrate your strength to capture him.[*] There is no more to it than this. He who lacks foresight and underestimates his enemy will surely be captured by him.

47. If troops are punished before their loyalty is secured they will be disobedient. If not obedient, it is difficult to employ them. If troops are loyal, but punishments are not enforced, you cannot employ them.

48. Thus, command them with civility and imbue them uniformly with martial ardor and it may be said that victory is certain.

49. If orders which are consistently effective are used in instructing the troops, they will be obedient. If orders which are not consistently effective are used in instructing them, they will be disobedient.

50. When orders are consistently trustworthy and observed, the relationship of a commander with his troops is satisfactory.

but this thought does not follow the preceding verse too well. Tu Yu's interpretation, which I adopt, seems better.

[†]"For it is not by the numbers of the combatants but by their orderly array and their bravery that prowess in war is wont to be measured." Procopius, *History of the Wars*, p. 347.

[*]Ts'ao Ts'ao misinterprets *tsu* (足) here in the phrase *tsu i* (足以) meaning "it is sufficient." His mistake obviously confused the commentators and none cared to take issue with him. Wang Hsi starts off bravely enough by saying: "I think those who are skilled in creating changes in the situation by concentration and dispersion need only gather their forces together and take advantage of a chink in the enemy's defenses to gain the victory," but in the end allows Ts'ao Ts'ao's prestige to overcome his own better judgment.

# X

# TERRAIN†

SUN TZU said:

1. Ground may be classified according to its nature as accessible, entrapping, indecisive, constricted, precipitous, and distant.*

2. Ground which both we and the enemy can traverse with equal ease is called accessible. In such ground, he who first takes high sunny positions convenient to his supply routes can fight advantageously.

3. Ground easy to get out of but difficult to return to is entrapping. The nature of this ground is such that if the enemy is unprepared and you sally out you may defeat him. If the enemy is prepared and you go out and engage, but do not win, it is difficult to return. This is unprofitable.

4. Ground equally disadvantageous for both the enemy and ourselves to enter is indecisive. The nature of this ground is such that although the enemy holds out a bait I do not go forth but entice him by marching off. When I have drawn out half his force, I can strike him advantageously.

---

†"Topography" or "conformation of the ground."

*Mei Yao-ch'en defines "accessible" ground as that in which roads meet and cross; "entrapping" ground as net-like; "indecisive" ground as that in which one gets locked with the enemy; "constricted" ground as that in which a valley runs between two mountains; "precipitous" ground as that in which there are mountains, rivers, foothills, and ridges, and "distant" ground as level. Sun Tzu uses "distant" to indicate that there is a considerable distance between the camps of the two armies.

*Chang Yü*: . . . Li Ching's "Art of War" says: "In ground which offers no advantage to either side we should lure the enemy by feigned departure, wait until half his force has come out, and make an intercepting attack."

5. If I first occupy constricted ground I must block the passes and await the enemy. If the enemy first occupies such ground and blocks the defiles I should not follow him; if he does not block them completely I may do so.

6. In precipitous ground I must take position on the sunny heights and await the enemy.[†] If he first occupies such ground I lure him by marching off; I do not follow him.

*Chang Yü*: If one should be the first to occupy a position in level ground, how much more does this apply to difficult and dangerous places![*] How can such terrain be given to the enemy?

7. When at a distance from an enemy of equal strength it is difficult to provoke battle and unprofitable to engage him in his chosen position.[††]

8. These are the principles relating to six different types of ground. It is the highest responsibility of the general to inquire into them with the utmost care.

*Mei Yao-ch'en*: Now the nature of the ground is the fundamental factor in aiding the army to set up its victory.

9. Now when troops flee, are insubordinate,[**] distressed, collapse in disorder or are routed, it is the fault of the general. None of these disasters can be attributed to natural causes.

10. Other conditions being equal, if a force attacks one ten times its size, the result is flight.

---

[†]Generally I have translated the *Yang* of *Yin-Yang* as "south" or "sunny," and *Yin* as "north" or "shady." In the context of Sun Tzu these terms have no cosmic connotations.

[*]*Hsien* (險) means a "narrow pass," hence "dangerous" and by implication "strategic."

[††]The phrase following "engage" is added to clarify Sun Tzu's meaning.

[**]The character rendered "insubordinate" is *shih* (弛), "to unstring a bow"; hence, "lax," "remiss," "loose." The commentators make it clear that in this context the character means "insubordinate."

*Tu Mu*: When one is to be used to attack ten we should first compare the wisdom and the strategy of the opposing generals, the bravery and cowardice of the troops, the question of weather, of the advantages offered by the ground, whether the troops are well fed or hungry, weary or rested.

11. When troops are strong and officers weak the army is insubordinate.

*Tu Mu*: The verse is speaking of troops and non-commissioned officers[†] who are unruly and overbearing, and generals and commanders who are timid and weak.

In the present dynasty at the beginning of the Ch'ang Ch'ing reign period[*] T'ien Pu was ordered to take command in Wei for the purpose of attacking Wang T'ing-ch'ou. Pu had grown up in Wei and the people there held him in contempt, and several tens of thousands of men all rode donkeys about the camp. Pu was unable to restrain them. He remained in his position for several months and when he wished to give battle, the officers and troops dispersed and scattered in all directions. Pu cut his own throat.

12. When the officers are valiant and the troops ineffective the army is in distress.[††]

13. When senior officers are angry and insubordinate, and on encountering the enemy rush into battle with no understanding of the feasibility of engaging and without awaiting orders from the commander, the army is in a state of collapse.

*Ts'ao Ts'ao*: "Senior officers" means subordinate generals. If . . . in a rage they attack the enemy without measuring the strength of both sides, then the army is assuredly in a state of collapse.

14. When the general is morally weak and his discipline not strict, when his instructions and guidance are not enlightened, when there are no consistent rules to guide the officers and men and when the formations are slovenly the army is in disorder.[**]

---

[†]*Wu* (伍) denotes a file of five men or the leader of such a file; a corporal; a non-commissioned officer.

[*]A.D. 820–825.

[††]Bogged down or sinking, as in a morass. The idea is that if the troops are weak the efforts of the officers are as vain as if the troops were in a bog.

[**]The term rendered "slovenly" is literally "vertically and horizontally."

*Chang Yü*:   . . . Chaos self-induced.

15. When a commander unable to estimate his enemy uses a small force to engage a large one, or weak troops to strike the strong, or when he fails to select shock troops for the van, the result is rout.

> *Ts'ao Ts'ao*: Under these conditions he commands "certain-to-flee" troops.
>
> *Ho Yen-hsi*:   . . . In the Han the "Gallants from the Three Rivers" were "Sword Friends" of unusual talent. In Wu the shock troops were called "Dissolvers of Difficulty"; in Ch'i "Fate Deciders"; in the T'ang "Leapers and Agitators." These were various names applied to shock troops; nothing is more important in the tactics of winning battles than to employ them.[†]
>
> Generally when all the troops are encamped together the general selects from every camp its high-spirited and valiant officers who are distinguished by agility and strength and whose martial accomplishments are above the ordinary. These are grouped to form a special corps. Of ten men, but one is selected; of ten thousand, one thousand.
>
> *Chang Yü*:   . . . Generally in battle it is essential to use *élite* troops as the vanguard sharp point. First, because this strengthens our own determination; second, because they blunt the enemy's edge.

16. When any of these six conditions prevails the army is on the road to defeat. It is the highest responsibility of the general that he examine them carefully.

17. Conformation of the ground is of the greatest assistance in battle. Therefore, to estimate the enemy situation and to calculate distances and the degree of difficulty of the terrain so as to control victory are virtues of the superior general. He who fights with full knowledge of these factors is certain to win; he who does not will surely be defeated.

18. If the situation is one of victory but the sovereign has issued orders not to engage, the general may decide to fight. If the situation is such that he cannot win, but the sovereign has issued orders to engage, he need not do so.

---

[†]Unfortunately the functions of the "Leapers and Agitators" are not explained. Undoubtedly one may have been to arouse the ardor of the troops by wild gyrating and acrobatic sword play for which the Chinese are justly renowned, and possibly at the same time to impress the enemy with their ferocity and skill.

19. And therefore the general who in advancing does not seek personal fame, and in withdrawing is not concerned with avoiding punishment, but whose only purpose is to protect the people and promote the best interests of his sovereign, is the precious jewel of the state.

> *Li Ch'üan:* . . . Such a general has no personal interest.
> *Tu Mu:* . . . Few such are to be had.

20. Because such a general regards his men as infants they will march with him into the deepest valleys. He treats them as his own beloved sons and they will die with him.

> *Li Ch'üan:* If he cherishes his men in this way he will gain their utmost strength. Thus, the Viscount of Ch'u needed but to speak a word and the soldiers felt as if clad in warm silken garments.[†]
> *Tu Mu:* During the Warring States when Wu Ch'i was a general he took the same food and wore the same clothes as the lowliest of his troops. On his bed there was no mat; on the march he did not mount his horse; he himself carried his reserve rations. He shared exhaustion and bitter toil with his troops.
> *Chang Yü:* . . . Therefore the Military Code says: "The general must be the first in the toils and fatigues of the army. In the heat of summer he does not spread his parasol nor in the cold of winter don thick clothing. In dangerous places he must dismount and walk. He waits until the army's wells have been dug and only then drinks; until the army's food is cooked before he eats; until the army's fortifications have been completed, to shelter himself."[*]

21. If a general indulges his troops but is unable to employ them; if he loves them but cannot enforce his commands; if the troops are disorderly and he is unable to control them, they may be compared to spoiled children, and are useless.

> *Chang Yü:* . . . If one uses kindness exclusively the troops become like arrogant children and cannot be employed. This is the reason Ts'ao Ts'ao cut off his own hair and so punished himself.[††] . . . Good commanders are both loved and feared.

---

[†]The Viscount commiserated with those suffering from the cold. His words were enough to comfort the men and raise their flagging spirits.

[*]Military essays and codes were generally entitled *Ping Fa*. Chang Yü does not identify the one from which he quotes.

[††]After having issued orders that his troops were not to damage standing grain,

22. If I know that my troops are capable of striking the enemy, but do not know that he is invulnerable to attack, my chance of victory is but half.

23. If I know that the enemy is vulnerable to attack, but do not know that my troops are incapable of striking him, my chance of victory is but half.

24. If I know that the enemy can be attacked and that my troops are capable of attacking him, but do not realize that because of the conformation of the ground I should not attack, my chance of victory is but half.

25. Therefore when those experienced in war move they make no mistakes; when they act, their resources are limitless.

26. And therefore I say: "Know the enemy, know yourself; your victory will never be endangered. Know the ground, know the weather; your victory will then be total."

Ts'ao Ts'ao carelessly permitted his own grazing horse to trample it. He thereupon ordered himself to be beheaded. His officers tearfully remonstrated, and Ts'ao Ts'ao then inflicted upon himself this symbolic punishment to illustrate that even a commander-in-chief is amenable to military law and discipline.

# XI

# THE NINE VARIETIES OF GROUND[†]

SUN TZU said:

1. In respect to the employment of troops, ground may be classified as dispersive, frontier, key, communicating, focal, serious, difficult, encircled, and death.*

2. When a feudal lord fights in his own territory, he is in dispersive ground.

Ts'ao Ts'ao: Here officers and men long to return to their nearby homes.

3. When he makes but a shallow penetration into enemy territory he is in frontier ground.[††]

4. Ground equally advantageous for the enemy or me to occupy is key ground.**

---

[†]The original arrangement of this chapter leaves much to be desired. Many verses are not in proper context; others are repetitious and may possibly be ancient commentary that has worked its way into the text. I have transposed some verses and eliminated those that appear to be accretions.

*There is some confusion here. The "accessible" ground of the preceding chapter is defined in the same terms as "communicating" ground.

[††]Lit. "light" ground, possibly because it is easy to retire or because the officers and men think lightly of deserting just as the expedition is getting under way.

**This is contestable ground, or, as Tu Mu says, "strategically important."

5. Ground equally accessible to both the enemy and me is communicating.

> *Tu Mu:* This is level and extensive ground in which one may come and go, sufficient in extent for battle and to erect opposing fortifications.

6. When a state is enclosed by three other states its territory is focal. He who first gets control of it will gain the support of All-under-Heaven.[†]

7. When the army has penetrated deep into hostile territory, leaving far behind many enemy cities and towns, it is in serious ground.

> *Ts'ao Ts'ao:* This is ground difficult to return from.

8. When the army traverses mountains, forests, precipitous country, or marches through defiles, marshlands, or swamps, or any place where the going is hard, it is in difficult ground.[*]

9. Ground to which access is constricted, where the way out is tortuous, and where a small enemy force can strike my larger one is called "encircled."[††]

> *Tu Mu:* . . . Here it is easy to lay ambushes and one can be utterly defeated.

10. Ground in which the army survives only if it fights with the courage of desperation is called "death."

> *Li Ch'üan:* Blocked by mountains to the front and rivers to the rear, with provisions exhausted. In this situation it is advantageous to act speedily and dangerous to procrastinate.

11. And therefore, do not fight in dispersive ground; do not stop in the frontier borderlands.

12. Do not attack an enemy who occupies key ground; in communicating ground do not allow your formations to become separated.[**]

---

[†]The Empire is always described as "All-under-Heaven."

[*]The commentators indulge in some discussion respecting the interpretation of the character rendered "difficult." Several want to restrict the meaning to ground susceptible to flooding.

[††]The verb may be translated as "tie down" rather than "strike."

[**]Ts'ao Ts'ao says they must be "closed up."

13. In focal ground, ally with neighbouring states; in deep ground, plunder.†

14. In difficult ground, press on; in encircled ground, devise stratagems; in death ground, fight.

15. In dispersive ground I would unify the determination of the army.*

16. In frontier ground I would keep my forces closely linked.

> *Mei Yao-ch'en*: On the march the several units are connected; at halts the camps and fortified posts are linked together.

17. In key ground I would hasten up my rear elements.

> *Ch'ên Hao*: What the verse means is that if . . . the enemy, relying on superior numbers, comes to contest such ground, I use a large force to hasten into his rear.††
> *Chang Yü*: . . . Someone has said that the phrase means "to set out after the enemy and arrive before him."**

18. In communicating ground I would pay strict attention to my defenses.

19. In focal ground I would strengthen my alliances.

> *Chang Yü*: I reward my prospective allies with valuables and silks and bind them with solemn covenants. I abide firmly by the treaties and then my allies will certainly aid me.

20. In serious ground I would ensure a continuous flow of provisions.

21. In difficult ground I would press on over the roads.

22. In encircled ground I would block the points of access and egress.

> *Tu Mu*: It is military doctrine that an encircling force must leave a gap to show the surrounded troops there is a way out, so that they will not be determined to fight to the death. Then, taking

---

†Li Ch'üan thinks the latter half should read "do not plunder," as the principal object when in enemy territory is to win the affection and support of the people.

*This and the nine verses that immediately follow have been transposed to this context. In the text they come later in the chapter.

††The question is, whose "rear" is Sun Tzu talking about? Ch'ên Hao is reading something into the verse as it stands in present context.

**The "someone" is Mei Yao-ch'en, who takes *hou* (後) to mean "after" in the temporal sense.

advantage of this, strike. Now, if I am in encircled ground, and the enemy opens a road in order to tempt my troops to take it, I close this means of escape so that my officers and men will have a mind to fight to the death.[†]

23. In death ground I could make it evident that there is no chance of survival. For it is the nature of soldiers to resist when surrounded; to fight to the death when there is no alternative, and when desperate to follow commands implicitly.

24. The tactical variations appropriate to the nine types of ground, the advantages of close or extended deployment, and the principles of human nature are matters the general must examine with the greatest care.[*]

25. Anciently, those described as skilled in war made it impossible for the enemy to unite his van and his rear; for his elements both large and small to mutually cooperate; for the good troops to succor the poor and for superiors and subordinates to support each other.[††]

26. When the enemy's forces were dispersed they prevented him from assembling them; when concentrated, they threw him into confusion.

> *Meng:* Lay on many deceptive operations. Be seen in the west and march out of the east; lure him in the north and strike in the south. Drive him crazy and bewilder him so that he disperses his forces in confusion.
>
> *Chang Yü:* Take him unaware by surprise attacks where he is unprepared. Hit him suddenly with shock troops.

27. They concentrated and moved when it was advantageous to do so;[**] when not advantageous, they halted.

28. Should one ask: "How do I cope with a well-ordered enemy host

---

[†]A long story relates that Shen Wu of the Later Wei, when in such a position, blocked the only escape road for his troops with the army's livestock. His forces then fought desperately and defeated an army of two hundred thousand.

[*]This verse is followed by seven short verses that again define terms previously defined in v. 2 to 10 inclusive. This appears to be commentary that has worked its way into the text.

[††]The implication is that even were the enemy able to concentrate, internal dissensions provoked by the skilled general would render him ineffective.

[**]Lit. "They concentrated where it was advantageous to do so and then acted. When it was not advantageous they stood fast." In another commentary Shih Tzu-mei says not to move unless there is advantage in it.

about to attack me?" I reply: "Seize something he cherishes and he will conform to your desires."[†]

29. Speed is the essence of war. Take advantage of the enemy's unpreparedness; travel by unexpected routes and strike him where he has taken no precautions.

> *Tu Mu*: This summarizes the essential nature of war ... and the ultimate in generalship.

> *Chang Yü*: Here Sun Tzu again explains ... that the one thing esteemed is divine swiftness.

30. The general principles applicable to an invading force are that when you have penetrated deeply into hostile territory your army is united, and the defender cannot overcome you.

31. Plunder fertile country to supply the army with plentiful provisions.

32. Pay heed to nourishing the troops; do not unnecessarily fatigue them. Unite them in spirit; conserve their strength. Make unfathomable plans for the movements of the army.

33. Throw the troops into a position from which there is no escape and even when faced with death they will not flee. For if prepared to die, what can they not achieve? Then officers and men together put forth their utmost efforts. In a desperate situation they fear nothing; when there is no way out they stand firm. Deep in a hostile land they are bound together, and there, where there is no alternative, they will engage the enemy in hand-to-hand combat.[*]

34. Thus, such troops need no encouragement to be vigilant. Without extorting their support the general obtains it; without inviting their affection he gains it; without demanding their trust he wins it.[††]

35. My officers have no surplus of wealth but not because they disdain worldly goods; they have no expectation of long life but not because they dislike longevity.

---

[†]Comments between question and answer omitted.

[*]There are several characters in Chinese that basically mean "to fight." That used here implies "close combat."

[††]This refers to the troops of a general who nourishes them, who unites them in spirit, who husbands their strength, and who makes unfathomable plans.

*Wang Hsi*: ... When officers and men care only for worldly riches they will cherish life at all costs.

36. On the day the army is ordered to march the tears of those seated soak their lapels; the tears of those reclining course down their cheeks.

*Tu Mu*: All have made a covenant with death. Before the day of battle the order is issued: "Today's affair depends upon this one stroke. The bodies of those who do not put their lives at stake will fertilize the fields and become carrion for the birds and beasts."

37. But throw them into a situation where there is no escape and they will display the immortal courage of Chuan Chu and Ts'ao Kuei.†

38. Now the troops of those adept in war are used like the "Simultaneously Responding" snake of Mount Ch'ang. When struck on the head its tail attacks; when struck on the tail, its head attacks, when struck in the center both head and tail attack.*

39. Should one ask: "Can troops be made capable of such instantaneous co-ordination?" I reply: "They can." For, although the men of Wu and Yüeh mutually hate one another, if together in a boat tossed by the wind they would cooperate as the right hand does with the left.

40. It is thus not sufficient to place one's reliance on hobbled horses or buried chariot wheels.††

41. To cultivate a uniform level of valor is the object of military administration.** And it is by proper use of the ground that both shock and flexible forces are used to the best advantage.‡

*Chang Yü*: If one gains the advantage of the ground then even weak and soft troops can conquer the enemy. How much more so

---

†The exploits of these heroes are recounted in SC, ch. 68.

*This mountain was anciently known as Mt. Hêng. During the reign of the Emperor Wên (Liu Hêng) of the Han (179–159 B.C.) the name was changed to "Ch'ang" to avoid the taboo. In all existing works "Hêng" was changed to "Ch'ang."

††Such "Maginot Line" expedients are not in themselves sufficient to prevent defending troops from fleeing.

**Lit. "To equalize courage [so that it is that of] one [man] is the right way of administration."

‡Chang Yü makes it clear why terrain should be taken into account when troops are disposed. The difference in quality of troops can be balanced by careful sector assignment. Weak troops can hold strong ground, but might break if posted in a position less strong.

if they are tough and strong! That both may be used effectively is because they are disposed in accordance with the conditions of the ground.

42. It is the business of a general to be serene and inscrutable, impartial and self-controlled.[†]

*Wang Hsi*: If serene he is not vexed; if inscrutable, unfathomable; if upright, not improper; if self-controlled, not confused.

43. He should be capable of keeping his officers and men in ignorance of his plans.

*Ts'ao Ts'ao*: . . . His troops may join him in rejoicing at the accomplishment, but they cannot join him in laying the plans.

44. He prohibits superstitious practices and so rids the army of doubts. Then until the moment of death there can be no troubles.[*]

*Ts'ao Ts'ao*: Prohibit talk of omens and of supernatural portents. Rid plans of doubts and uncertainties.
*Chang Yü*: The *Ssu-ma Fa* says: "Exterminate superstitions."

45. He changes his methods and alters his plans so that people have no knowledge of what he is doing.

*Chang Yü*: Courses of action previously followed and old plans previously executed must be altered.

46. He alters his camp-sites and marches by devious routes, and thus makes it impossible for others to anticipate his purpose.[††]

47. To assemble the army and throw it into a desperate position is the business of the general.

---

[†]Giles translated: "It is the business of a general to be quiet and thus ensure secrecy; upright and just and thus maintain order." The commentators do not agree, but none takes it in this sense, nor does the text support this rendering. I follow Ts'ao Ts'ao and Wang Hsi.

[*]The 之 at the end of this sentence is emended to read 災, which means a natural or "heaven sent" calamity. Part of Ts'ao Ts'ao's comment that is omitted indicates that various texts were circulating in his time.

[††]Or perhaps, "makes it impossible for the enemy to learn *his* plans." But Mei Yao-ch'en thinks the meaning is that the enemy will thus be rendered incapable of laying plans. Giles infers that the general, by altering his camps and marching by devious routes, can prevent the enemy "from anticipating his purpose," which seems the best. The comments do not illuminate the point at issue.

48. He leads the army deep into hostile territory and there releases the trigger.†

49. He burns his boats and smashes his cooking pots; he urges the army on as if driving a flock of sheep, now in one direction, now in another, and none knows where he is going.*

50. He fixes a date for rendezvous and after the troops have met, cuts off their return route just as if he were removing a ladder from beneath them.

51. One ignorant of the plans of neighboring states cannot prepare alliances in good time; if ignorant of the conditions of mountains, forests, dangerous defiles, swamps, and marshes he cannot conduct the march of an army; if he fails to make use of native guides he cannot gain the advantages of the ground. A general ignorant of even one of these three matters is unfit to command the armies of a Hegemonic King.††

> Ts'ao Ts'ao: These three matters have previously been elaborated. The reason Sun Tzu returns to the subject is that he strongly disapproved of those unable to employ troops properly.

52. Now when a Hegemonic King attacks a powerful state he makes it impossible for the enemy to concentrate. He overawes the enemy and prevents his allies from joining him.**

> Mei Yao-ch'en: In attacking a great state, if you can divide your enemy's forces your strength will be more than sufficient.

53. It follows that he does not contend against powerful combinations nor does he foster the power of other states. He relies for the attainment

---

†"Release" of a trigger, or mechanism, is the usual meaning of the expression *fa chi* (發機). The idiom has been translated: "puts into effect his expedient plans." Wang Hsi says that when the trigger is released "there is no return" (of the arrow or bolt). Lit. this verse reads: "He leads the army deep into the territory of the Feudal Lords and there releases the trigger" (or "puts into effect his expedient plans"). Giles translates the phrase in question as "shows his hand," that is, takes irrevocable action.

*Neither his own troops nor the enemy can fathom his ultimate design.

††Emending 四五者—"[these] four or five [matters]"—to read 此三者—"these three [matters]."

**This verse and next present problems. Chang Yü thinks the verse means that if the troops of a Hegemonic King (or a ruler who aspires to such status) attack hastily (or recklessly, or without forethought) *his* allies will not come to *his* aid. The other commentators interpret the verse as I have.

of his aims on his ability to overawe his opponents. And so he can take the enemy's cities and overthrow the enemy's state.[†]

> *Ts'ao Ts'ao*: By "Hegemonic King" is meant one who does not ally with the feudal lords. He breaks up the alliances of All-under-Heaven and snatches the position of authority. He uses prestige and virtue to attain his ends.[*]
>
> *Tu Mu*: The verse says if one neither covenants for the help of neighbors nor develops plans based on expediency but in furtherance of his personal aims relies only on his own military strength to overawe the enemy country then his own cities can be captured and his own state overthrown.[††]

54. Bestow rewards without respect to customary practice; publish orders without respect to precedent.[**] Thus you may employ the entire army as you would one man.

> *Chang Yü*: ... If the code respecting rewards and punishments is clear and speedily applied then you may use the many as you do the few.

55. Set the troops to their tasks without imparting your designs; use them to gain advantage without revealing the dangers involved. Throw them into a perilous situation and they survive; put them in death ground and they will live. For when the army is placed in such a situation it can snatch victory from defeat.

56. Now the crux of military operations lies in the pretense of accommodating one's self to the designs of the enemy.[‡]

---

[†]The commentators differ in their interpretations of this verse. Giles translates: "Hence he does not strive to ally himself with all and sundry nor does he foster the power of other states. He carries out his own secret designs, keeping his antagonists in awe. Thus he is able to capture their cities and overthrow their kingdoms." But I feel that Sun Tzu meant that the "Hegemonic King" need not contend against "powerful combinations" because he isolates his enemies. He does not permit them to form "powerful combinations."

[*]Possibly Giles derived his interpretation from this comment.

[††]Also a justifiable interpretation, which illustrates how radically the commentators frequently differ.

[**]This verse, obviously out of place, emphasizes that the general in the field need not follow prescribed procedures in recognition of meritorious service but should bestow timely rewards. The general need not follow customary law in respect to administration of his army.

[‡]Possibly too free a translation, but the commentators agree that this is the idea Sun Tzu tries to convey. I follow Tu Mu.

57. Concentrate your forces against the enemy and from a distance of a thousand *li* you can kill his general.[†] This is described as the ability to attain one's aim in an artful and ingenious manner.

58. On the day the policy to attack is put into effect, close the passes, rescind the passports,[*] have no further intercourse with the enemy's envoys and exhort the temple council to execute the plans.[††]

59. When the enemy presents an opportunity, speedily take advantage of it.[**] Anticipate him in seizing something he values and move in accordance with a date secretly fixed.

60. The doctrine of war is to follow the enemy situation in order to decide on battle.[‡]

61. Therefore at first be shy as a maiden. When the enemy gives you an opening be swift as a hare and he will be unable to withstand you.

[†]I follow Ts'ao Ts'ao here. A strategist worthy of the name defeats his enemy from a distance of one thousand *li* by anticipating his enemy's plans.

[*]Lit. "break the tallies." These were carried by travelers and were examined by the Wardens of the Passes. Without a proper tally no one could legally enter or leave a country.

[††]The text is confusing. It seems literally to read: "From [the rostrum of] the temple, exhort [the army?] [the people?] to execute the plans." The commentators are no help.

[**]Another difficult verse. Some commentators think it should read: "When the enemy sends spies, immediately let them enter." The difficulty is in the idiom *k'ai ho* (開闔), literally, "to open the leaf of a door," thus, "to present an opportunity [to enter]." Ts'ao Ts'ao says the idiom means "a cleavage," "a gap," or "a space." Then, he goes on, "you must speedily enter." Other commentators say the idiom means "spies" or "secret agents." I follow Ts'ao Ts'ao.

[‡]The commentators again disagree: v. 58–61 are susceptible to varying translations or interpretations.

# XII

## ATTACK BY FIRE

SUN TZU said:

1. There are five methods of attacking with fire. The first is to burn personnel; the second, to burn stores; the third, to burn equipment; the fourth, to burn arsenals; and the fifth, to use incendiary missiles.[†]

2. To use fire, some medium must be relied upon.

> *Ts'ao Ts'ao*: Rely upon traitors among the enemy.[*]
> *Chang Yü*: All fire attacks depend on weather conditions.

3. Equipment for setting fires must always be at hand.

> *Chang Yü*: Implements and combustible materials should be prepared beforehand.

4. There are suitable times and appropriate days on which to raise fires.

5. "Times" means when the weather is scorching hot; "days" means when the moon is in Sagittarius, Alpharatz, *I,* or *Chen* constellations, for these are days of rising winds.[††]

---

[†]There is a mistake in the text here. Tu Yu emends and explains that flame-tipped arrows are fired into the enemy's barracks or camp by strong crossbowmen. Other commentators vary in their interpretations, but Tu Yu's emendation is logical.

[*]"among the enemy" added. Ch'ên Hao remarks that one does not only rely on traitors.

[††]Sun Hsing-yen has emended the original text in accordance with the TT and YL, but the original seems better and I follow it. I cannot place the *I* and *Chen* constellations.

6. Now in fire attacks one must respond to the changing situation.

7. When fire breaks out in the enemy's camp immediately coordinate your action from without. But if his troops remain calm bide your time and do not attack.

8. When the fire reaches its height, follow up if you can. If you cannot do so, wait.

9. If you can raise fires outside the enemy camp, it is not necessary to wait until they are started inside. Set fires at suitable times.[†]

10. When fires are raised up-wind do not attack from down-wind.

11. When the wind blows during the day it will die down at night.[*]

12. Now the army must know the five different fire-attack situations and be constantly vigilant.[††]

13. Those who use fire to assist their attacks are intelligent; those who use inundations are powerful.

14. Water can isolate an enemy but cannot destroy his supplies or equipment.[**]

15. Now to win battles and take your objectives, but to fail to exploit these achievements is ominous and may be described as "wasteful delay."[‡]

16. And therefore it is said that enlightened rulers deliberate upon the plans, and good generals execute them.

17. If not in the interests of the state, do not act. If you cannot succeed, do not use troops. If you are not in danger, do not fight.[‡‡]

18. A sovereign cannot raise an army because he is enraged, nor can a general fight because he is resentful. For while an angered man may

---

[†]A warning not to be cooked in your own fire is to be inferred from the last sentence.

[*]Following Chang Yü.

[††]Following Tu Mu.

[**]Following Ts'ao Ts'ao.

[‡]Mei Yao-ch'en is the only commentator who caught Sun Tzu's meaning: situations must be exploited.

[‡‡]The commentators make it clear that war is to be used only as a last resort.

again be happy, and a resentful man again be pleased, a state that has perished cannot be restored, nor can the dead be brought back to life.

19. Therefore, the enlightened ruler is prudent and the good general is warned against rash action.[†] Thus the state is kept secure and the army preserved.

[†]Last three words added. Rage and resentment lead to rash action.

# XIII

## EMPLOYMENT OF SECRET AGENTS†

SUN TZU said:

1. Now when an army of one hundred thousand is raised and dispatched on a distant campaign the expenses borne by the people together with the disbursements of the treasury will amount to a thousand pieces of gold daily. There will be continuous commotion both at home and abroad, people will be exhausted by the requirements of transport, and the affairs of seven hundred thousand households will be disrupted.*

Ts'ao Ts'ao: Anciently, eight families comprised a community. When one family sent a man to the army, the remaining seven contributed to its support. Thus, when an army of one hundred thousand was raised those unable to attend fully to their own ploughing and sowing amounted to seven hundred thousand households.

2. One who confronts his enemy for many years in order to struggle for victory in a decisive battle yet who, because he begrudges rank, honors and a few hundred pieces of gold, remains ignorant of his ene-

---

†The character used in the title means "the space between" two objects (such as a crack between two doors) and thus "cleavage," "division," or "to divide." It also means "spies," "spying," or "espionage."

*I have translated "to a distance of one thousand *li*" as "on a distant campaign." The figure need not be taken as specific.

my's situation, is completely devoid of humanity. Such a man is no general; no support to his sovereign; no master of victory.

3. Now the reason the enlightened prince and the wise general conquer the enemy whenever they move and their achievements surpass those of ordinary men is foreknowledge.

> *Ho Yen-hsi*: The section in the Rites of Chou entitled "Military Officers" names "The Director of National Espionage." This officer probably directed secret operations in other countries.[†]

4. What is called "foreknowledge" cannot be elicited from spirits, nor from gods, nor by analogy with past events, nor from calculations. It must be obtained from men who know the enemy situation.

5. Now there are five sorts of secret agents to be employed. These are native, inside, doubled, expendable, and living.[*]

6. When these five types of agents are all working simultaneously and none knows their method of operation, they are called "The Divine Skein" and are the treasure of a sovereign.[††]

7. Native agents are those of the enemy's country people whom we employ.

8. Inside agents are enemy officials whom we employ.

> *Tu Mu*: Among the official class there are worthy men who have been deprived of office; others who have committed errors and have been punished. There are sycophants and minions who are covetous of wealth. There are those who wrongly remain long in lowly office; those who have not obtained responsible positions, and those whose sole desire is to take advantage of times of trouble to extend the scope of their own abilities. There are those who are two-faced, changeable, and deceitful, and who are always sitting on the fence. As far as all such are concerned you can secretly inquire after their welfare, reward them liberally with gold and silk, and so tie them to you. Then you may rely on them to seek out the real facts of the situation in their country, and to ascertain its plans

---

[†]Probably an appeal to the authority of tradition to support the legitimacy of espionage and subversion which are contrary to the spirit of Confucian teaching.

[*]I use "expendable" in lieu of "death."

[††]The idea is that information may be gathered in as fish are by pulling on a single cord and so drawing together the various threads of a net.

---

directed against you. They can as well create cleavages between the sovereign and his ministers so that these are not in harmonious accord.

9. Doubled agents are enemy spies whom we employ.

*Li Ch'üan*: When the enemy sends spies to pry into my accomplishments or lack of them, I bribe them lavishly, turn them around, and make them my agents.

10. Expendable agents are those of our own spies who are deliberately given fabricated information.

*Tu Yu*: We leak information which is actually false and allow our own agents to learn it. When these agents operating in enemy territory are taken by him they are certain to report this false information. The enemy will believe it and make preparations accordingly. But our actions will of course not accord with this, and the enemy will put the spies to death.

*Chang Yü*: . . . In our dynasty Chief of Staff Ts'ao once pardoned a condemned man whom he then disguised as a monk, and caused to swallow a ball of wax and enter Tangut. When the false monk arrived he was imprisoned. The monk told his captors about the ball of wax and soon discharged it in a stool. When the ball was opened, the Tanguts read a letter transmitted by Chief of Staff Ts'ao to their Director of Strategic Planning. The chieftain of the barbarians was enraged, put his minister to death, and executed the spy monk. This is the idea. But expendable agents are not confined to only one use. Sometimes I send agents to the enemy to make a covenant of peace and then I attack.

11. Living agents are those who return with information.

*Tu Yu*: We select men who are clever, talented, wise, and able to gain access to those of the enemy who are intimate with the sovereign and members of the nobility. Thus they are able to observe the enemy's movements and to learn of his doings and his plans. Having learned the true state of affairs they return and tell us. Therefore they are called "living" agents.

*Tu Mu*: These are people who can come and go and communicate reports. As living spies we must recruit men who are intelligent but appear to be stupid; who seem to be dull but are strong in heart; men who are agile, vigorous, hardy, and brave; well-versed in lowly matters and able to endure hunger, cold, filth, and humiliation.

12. Of all those in the army close to the commander none is more intimate than the secret agent; of all rewards none more liberal than those given to secret agents; of all matters none is more confidential than those relating to secret operations.

*Mei Yao-ch'en*: Secret agents receive their instructions within the tent of the general, and are intimate and close to him.
*Tu Mu*: These are "mouth to ear" matters.

13. He who is not sage and wise, humane and just, cannot use secret agents. And he who is not delicate and subtle cannot get the truth out of them.

*Tu Mu*: The first essential is to estimate the character of the spy to determine if he is sincere, truthful, and really intelligent. Afterwards, he can be employed. . . . Among agents there are some whose only interest is in acquiring wealth without obtaining the true situation of the enemy, and only meet my requirements with empty words.† In such a case I must be deep and subtle. Then I can assess the truth or falsity of the spy's statements and discriminate between what is substantial and what is not.
*Mei Yao-ch'en*: Take precautions against the spy having been turned around.

14. Delicate indeed! Truly delicate! There is no place where espionage is not used.

15. If plans relating to secret operations are prematurely divulged the agent and all those to whom he spoke of them shall be put to death.*

*Ch'ên Hao*: . . . They may be killed in order to stop their mouths and prevent the enemy hearing.

16. Generally in the case of armies you wish to strike, cities you wish to attack, and people you wish to assassinate, you must know the names of the garrison commander, the staff officers, the ushers, gate keepers, and the bodyguards. You must instruct your agents to inquire into these matters in minute detail.

---

†Such agents are now aptly described as "paper mills."
*Giles translated: "If a secret piece of news is divulged by a spy before the time is ripe. . . ." Sun Tzu is not talking about "news" here but about espionage affairs, or matters or plans relating to espionage.

*Tu Mu*:: If you wish to conduct offensive war you must know the men employed by the enemy. Are they wise or stupid, clever or clumsy? Having assessed their qualities, you prepare appropriate measures. When the King of Han sent Han Hsin, Ts'ao Ts'an, and Kuan Ying to attack Wei Pao he asked: "Who is the commander-in-chief of Wei?" The reply was: "Po Chih." The King said: "His mouth still smells of his mother's milk. He cannot equal Han Hsin. Who is the Cavalry commander?" The reply was: "Feng Ching." The King said: "He is the son of General Feng Wu-che of Ch'in. Although worthy, he is not the equal of Kuan Ying. And who is the infantry commander?" The reply was: "Hsiang T'o." The King said: "He is no match for Ts'ao Ts'an. I have nothing to worry about."

17. It is essential to seek out enemy agents who have come to conduct espionage against you and to bribe them to serve you. Give them instructions and care for them.[†] Thus doubled agents are recruited and used.

18. It is by means of the doubled agent that native and inside agents can be recruited and employed.

*Chang Yü*: This is because the doubled agent knows those of his own countrymen who are covetous as well as those officials who have been remiss in office. These we can tempt into our service.

19. And it is by this means that the expendable agent, armed with false information, can be sent to convey it to the enemy.

*Chang Yü*: It is because doubled agents know in what respects the enemy can be deceived that expendable agents may be sent to convey false information.

20. It is by this means also that living agents can be used at appropriate times.

21. The sovereign must have full knowledge of the activities of the five sorts of agents. This knowledge must come from the doubled agents, and therefore it is mandatory that they be treated with the utmost liberality.

---

[†]These agents, according to Giles' translation, are to be "tempted with bribes, led away and comfortably housed."

22. Of old, the rise of Yin was due to I Chih, who formerly served the Hsia; the Chou came to power through Lu Yu, a servant of the Yin.[†]

*Chang Yü*: I Chih was a minister of Hsia who went over to the Yin. Lu Wang was a minister of Yin who went over to the Chou.

23. And therefore only the enlightened sovereign and the worthy general who are able to use the most intelligent people as agents are certain to achieve great things. Secret operations are essential in war; upon them the army relies to make its every move.

*Chia Lin*: An army without secret agents is exactly like a man without eyes or ears.

[†]Several of the commentators are outraged that these worthies are described by Sun Tzu as "spies" or "agents," but of course they were.

# BIBLIOGRAPHY

## I

### Books in English

Aston, W. G. *The Nihongi*. Transactions and Proceedings of the Japan Society, Supplement I. London, 1896. Kegan Paul.

De Bary, WILLIAM T., and others. *Sources of Chinese Tradition*. New York, 1960. Columbia University Press.

Baynes, Cary F. *The I Ching, or Book of Changes*. The Richard Wilhelm Translation. London, 1951. Routledge & Kegan Paul.

Calthrop, Captain E. F. *The Book of War*. London, 1908. John Murray.

Carlson, Evans F. *Twin Stars of China*. New York, 1940. Dodd, Mead & Co.

Cheng, Lin. *The Art of War*. Shanghai, China, 1946. The World Book Company Ltd.

Dubs, Professor Homer H. (trans.). *History of the Former Han Dynasty* (3 vols.). Baltimore, Md., 1946, 1955. The Waverly Press.

—— *Hsün Tze, The Moulder of Ancient Confucianism*. London, 1927. Arthur Probsthain.

—— *The Works of Hsün Tze*. London, 1928. Arthur Probsthain.

Duyvendak, J. J. L. *Tao Te Ching*. The Book of the Way and Its Virtue. London, 1954. John Murray.

—— *The Book of Lord Shang*. London, 1928. Arthur Probsthain.

Fitzgerald, C. P. *China, A Short Cultural History* (rev. ed.). London, 1950. The Cresset Press Ltd.

Fung, Yu-lan. *A History of Chinese Philosophy* (trans. Bodde). Princeton, 1952. Princeton University Press.

Gale, Esson M. (trans.). *Discourses on Salt and Iron*. Sinica Leidensia, vol. ii. Leiden, 1931. E. J. Brill Ltd.

Giles, Lionel (trans.). *Sun Tzu on the Art of War*. London, 1910. Luzac & Co.

Granet, Marcel. *Chinese Civilization*. London, 1957. Routledge & Kegan Paul Ltd.

Legge, James. *The Chinese Classics*. London, 1861. Trubner & Co.

Liang, Ch'i-ch'ao. *Chinese Political Thought*. London, 1930. Kegan Paul; Trench, Trubner & Co. Ltd.

Liao, W. K. (trans.). *The Complete Works of Han Fei-tzu* (2 vols.). London, 1939 (vol. i); 1959 (vol. ii). Arthur Probsthain.

McCullogh, Helen Craig (trans.). *The Taiheiki. A Chronicle of Medieval Japan*. New York, 1959. Columbia University Press.

Machell-Cox, E. *Principles of War by Sun Tzu*. Colombo, Ceylon. A Royal Air Force Welfare Publication.

Mao Tse-tung. *Selected Works*. London, 1955. Lawrence & Wishart.

—— *Strategic Problems in the Anti-Japanese Guerrilla War*. Peking, 1954. Foreign Language Press.

Mei, Y. P. *Motse, the Neglected Rival of Confucius*. London, 1934. Arthur Probsthain.

—— *The Ethical and Political Works of Motse*. London, 1929. Arthur Probsthain.

Müller, Max F. (ed.). *The Sacred Books of the East* (vol. xv): *The Yi King* (trans. Legge). Oxford, 1882. The Clarendon Press.

Murdoch, James. *A History of Japan* (3rd impression). London, 1949. Routledge & Kegan Paul Ltd.

Payne, Robert. *Mao Tse-tung, Ruler of Red China*. London, 1951. Secker & Warburg.

Ryusaka, Tsunuda, de Bery, and Keene. *Sources of the Japanese Tradition*. New York, 1958. Columbia University Press.

Sadler, Professor A. L. *The Makers of Modern Japan*. London, 1937. George Allen & Unwin Ltd.

—— *Three Military Classics of China*. Sydney, Australia, 1944. Australasian Medical Publishing Co. Ltd.

Sansom, George B. *A History of Japan to 1334* (San II). London, 1958. The Cresset Press.

—— *Japan, A Short Cultural History* (2nd impression, revised) (San I). London, 1952. The Cresset Press Ltd.

Schwartz, Benjamin I. *Chinese Communism and The Rise of Mao* (3rd printing). Cambridge, Mass., 1958. Harvard University Press.

Snow, Edgar. *Red Star over China* (Left Book Club Edition). London, 1937. Victor Gollancz Ltd.

Tjan Tjoe Som (Tseng, Chu-sen). *The Comprehensive Discussions in The White Tiger Hall*. Leiden, 1952. E. J. Brill.

Waley, Arthur. *The Analects of Confucius*. London, 1938. George Allen & Unwin Ltd.

Walker, Richard L. *The Multi-State System of Ancient China*. Hamden, Conn., 1953. The Shoe String Press.

Watson, Burton. *Ssu-ma Ch'ien, Grand Historian of China.* New York, 1958. Columbia University Press.

## II

### Monographs and Articles in English

Bodde, Dirk. *Statesman, Patriot and General in Ancient China.* New Haven, Conn., 1943. A Publication of the American Oriental Society.

Chang, Ch'i-yün. *China's Ancient Military Geography.* Chinese Culture, vii, no. 3. Taipeh, December 1959.

Extracts from China Mainland Magazines. "Fragmentary Notes on the Way Comrade Mao Tse-tung Pursued his Studies in his Early Days." American Consulate General. Hong Kong, 191, 7 December 1959.

Lanciotti, Lionello. *Sword Casting and Related Legends in China, I, II.* East and West, Year VI, N. 2, N. 4. Rome, 1955, 1956.

Needham, J. *The Development of Iron and Steel Technology in China.* London, 1958. The Newcomen Society.

North, Robert C. "The Rise of Mao Tse-tung." *The Far Eastern Quarterly,* vol. xi, no. 2, February 1952.

Rowley, Harold H. *The Chinese Philosopher Mo Ti* (reprint from *Bulletin of the John Rylands Library,* vol. xxxi, no. 2, November 1948). Manchester, 1948. The Manchester University Press.

Selections from China Mainland Magazines. "Comrade Lin Piao in the Period of Liberation War in the Northeast." American Consulate General. Hong Kong, 217, 11 July 1960.

Teng, Ssu-yü. *New Light on the History of the T'aip'ing Rebellion.* Cambridge, Mass., 1950. Harvard University Press.

Van Straelen, H. *Yoshida Shoin.* Monographies du T'oung Pao, vol. ii. Leiden, 1952. E. J. Brill.

## III

### Books, Monographs and Articles in Western Languages
### (other than English)

Amiot, J. J. L. *Mémoires concernant l'histoire, les sciences, les arts les mœurs, les usages, etc. des Chinois.* Chez Nyon l'aîné. Paris, 1782.

Ashiya, Mizuyo. *Der Chinesische Kriegsphilosoph der Vorchristlichen Zeit.* Wissen und Wehr, 1939, 416-27.

Chavannes, Edouard. *Les Mémoires historiques de Se-ma Ts'ien.* Paris. Ernest Leroux.

Cholet, E. *L'Art militaire dans l'antiquité chinoise.* Paris, 1922. Charles-Lavauzelle.

Cotenson, G. de. "L'Art militaire des Chinois, d'après leurs classiques." *Le Nouvelle Revue*. Paris, August 1900.

Gaillois, Brig.-Gen. R. *Lois de la guerre en Chine*. Preuves, 1956.

Konrad, N. I. *Wu Tzu*. Traktat o Voennom Iskusstve. Moscow, 1958. Publishing House of Eastern Literature.

——— *Sun Tzu*. Traktat o Voennom Iskusstve. Moscow, 1950. Publishing House of the Academy of Science USSR.

Maspero, Henri. *La Chine Antique* (Nouvelle éd.). Paris, 1955. Imprimerie Nationale.

Nachin, L. (ed.). *Sun Tse et les anciens Chinois Ou Tse et Se Ma Fa*. Paris, 1948. Editions Berger-Levrault.

Sidorenko, J. I. *Ssun-ds' Traktat über Die Kriegskunst*. Berlin, 1957. Ministerium Für Nationale Verteidigung.

# IV

## Works in Chinese

*Chan Kuo Shih.*

戰國史

Yang K'uan. "A History of the Warring States." People's Press. Shanghai, 1956.

*Chao Chu Sun Tzu Shih San P'ien.*

趙註孫子十三篇

Chao Pen-hsüeh. "Chao (Pen-hsueh's) Commentary on the Thirteen Chapters of Sun Tzu." Peiyang Military Academy Press. Peking, 1905.

*Chin I Hsin P'ien Sun Tzu Ping Fa.*

今譯新編孫子兵法

Kuo Hua-jo. "A Modern Translation of Sun Tzu's Art of War with New Chapter Arrangement." People's Press. Peking, 1957.

*Ch'in Ting Ku Chin T'u Shu Chi Ch'eng.*

欽定古今圖書集成

Chung Hua Shu Chü. Short Title: *T'u Shu*. "Photographic reproduction of the Palace Edition of 1731. Chapter 83 "Military Canon." Shanghai, 1934.

*Chung Kuo Ping Ch'i Shih Kao.*

中國兵器史稿

Chou Wei and San Lien Shu Tien. "A Draft History of Chinese Weapons." Peking, 1957.

*Ku Chin Wei Shu K'ao Pu Cheng.*

古今僞書考補証

Huang Yun-mei. "A Further Inquiry into Apocryphal Books both Ancient and Modern." Shantung People's Press, 1959.

Pei T'ang Shu Ch'ao.

# 北堂書鈔

Yü Shih-nan. "Selected Passages Transcribed in the Northern Hall." (558–638).

Shih Ch'i Hsuan.

# 史記選

Wang Po-hsiang. "Selections from the Historical Records." People's Literary Press. Peking, 1958.

Ssu-ma Fa.

# 司馬法

Chung Hua Shu Chü. "The Art of War of Ssu-ma Jang-chiu." Ssu Pu Pei Yao ed. Shanghai.

Sun Tzu Shih San P'ien Chiao Chien Chi Yao.

# 孫子十三篇校箋舉要

Yang P'ing-an. "Notes on the Collation of Sun Tzu's Thirteen Chapters." Peking University Journal of the Humanities, no. i, 1958.

Sun Tzu Chi Chiao.

# 孫子集校

Yang P'ing-an and Chung Hua Shu Chu. "A Collated Critical Study of Sun Tzu." Shanghai, 1959.

Sun Tzu.

# 孫子

Chung Hua Shu Chü and Sun Hsing-yen. The Sun Tzu with Commentaries. Ssu Pu Pei Yao ed. Shanghai, 1931.

Sun-Wu Ping Fa.

# 孫吳兵法

Ta Chung Shu Chü. "The Arts of War of Sun (Tzu) and Wu (Ch'i)." Shanghai, 1931.

T'ai P'ing Yü Lan.

# 太平御覽

Li Fang, 3rd series. Ssu Pu Tsung K'an, chs. 270–359. Commercial Press. Shanghai, 1935.

T'ung Chih.

# 通志

Cheng Ch'iao. Facsimile Reproduction of Palace ed. of 1859, ch. 68.

T'ung Tien.

# 通典

Tu Yu. Facsimile Reproduction of Palace ed. of 1859, chs. 148–62.

*Wei Shu T'ung K'ao.*

# 僞書通考

Chang Hsin-cheng. "A Comprehensive Study of Apocryphal Books" (rev. ed.). Commercial Press. Shanghai, 1957.

*Wu Ch'i Ping Fa.*

# 吳起兵法

Chung Hua Shu Chü. "The Art of War of Wu Ch'i." *Ssu Pu Pei Yao* ed. Shanghai, 1931.

*Wu Ching Tsung Yao.*

# 武經總要

Tseng Kung-liang. "Essentials of the Martial Classics." *Ssu K'u Ch'uan Shu* ed.

# INDEX

## The Art of Business

# The Art of War